O · U · R
DAILY
TIMES
W · I · T · H
GOD

Discovery House Publishers

Books, music, and videos that feed the soul with the Word of God

Box 3566 Grand Rapids, MI 49501

OUR DAILY TIMES WITH GOD

Favorite Selections From
OUR DAILY BREAD

Our Daily Times With God:
Favorite Selections From Our Daily Bread

© 1988 Radio Bible Class. All rights reserved.

Discovery House Publishers is affiliated with RBC Ministries, Grand Rapids, Michigan 49512

Discovery House books are distributed to the trade exclusively by Barbour Publishing, Inc., Uhrichsville, Ohio 44683

Unless indicated otherwise, Scripture quotations are from The New King James Version. © 1979, 1980, 1982, Thomas Nelson Publishers, Inc.

ISBN 0-929239-01-6

88–203545

Printed in the United States of America

99 00 01 02 / CHG / 15 14 13 12 11 10 9 8

One God, one law, one element,
And one far-off divine event,
To which the whole creation moves.
—Alfred, Lord Tennyson, *In Memoriam*

Contents

A Personal Word

Our greatest challenge as Christians is to maintain fellowship with Jesus Christ at all times. Daily duties, life's battle for bread, and the inviting stimuli of people, places, sights, and sounds all conspire to squeeze time out of our daily quiet time. What's left is a little quiet needed for sleeping.

Adding to this challenge is our tendency to settle for a cursory check-in with God to begin the day. This can quickly solidify into a somewhat lifeless habit of asking Him for the same things, in the same way, every day.

When our devotional time gets locked into a legalistic or dreaded duty, we become victims of the "law" that kills rather than victors in the Spirit who gives life.

God is a Spirit who breathes with life—eternal life! And to stay in touch with Him and His Son requires that our spirit be one with His. Therefore, we must confess our sins when He points them out, repent, and chart a new course of obedience. We need to see our devotional experience as an exciting opportunity to keep ourselves open to surprises from God.

Because God is infinite, He communicates with us in ways as limitless as each new experience of meditating on His Word. We also "hear" His voice through good devotional books such as this one and by exploring His vast and wonderful creation. But every word from Him has its roots in sacred Scripture.

As we listen to God, ponder His Word, and meditate on His commands, testimonies, and precepts, His Spirit will search us with His penetrating light, and we should respond by talking to Him freely anywhere, anytime, about anything.

Before God can work through us, *He must work in us.* That's why we must keep on growing in our relationship with Him. The more we understand the Father's unfailing love for us, the more we will love Him and want to serve Him.

I pray that this volume will help you spend time with Jesus—our Lord and our God—and make that time the highest priority of each day.

—Dennis J. De Haan, Editor
Our Daily Bread

Introduction

Oxford University in England has a chapel with unique stained-glass windows. Mosaic inlays depicting Old Testament stories decorate the exterior windows, and the interior windows show corresponding scenes from the New Testament. When the sun shines through a window, the two scenes blend. People inside the chapel see Abraham preparing to sacrifice Isaac and in the foreground the cross of Calvary. In another case, people see the brazen serpent on the pole and in the foreground Christ hanging on the cross.

This book attempts to do for you what the windows do for visitors to the Oxford chapel; it shows how events from the Old and New Testaments intertwine. It does this in three ways.

First, it explains fifty-two events in relationship to past or future biblical happenings. Old Testament events often culminate in Christ, and the seeds of New Testament events are often sown in the Old Testament.

Second, it suggests a theme for each event, develops the theme, and relates it to other biblical themes and concepts.

Third, it reinforces each theme with seven daily devotionals from both Old and New Testaments to give a broad perspective on God's truth.

The events that are covered range from Creation to the Second Coming and are in Bible-book order. The book includes almost all the major events of the Bible and, in some cases, lesser events with significant themes.

The fifty-two themes include such important topics as power, sin, pride, sovereignty, jealousy, integrity, faith, depression, failure, servanthood, temptation, and hope.

We have arranged this devotional book by events to show God's involvement in the happenings of everyday life. He invented history. In fact, both Testaments emphasize what God and His people have done in real places at specific times.

People in Bible times learned that God met their needs when they remembered what He had done for them in the past. Likewise, by reliving some of these events, we find that God can meet our needs as well.

We hope that your daily use of this book will give you a new appreciation for God's intimate interest in your life, help you to understand Bible events and doctrine, and deepen your love for the One who transcends all time.

Week 1

CREATION

In the beginning God created the heavens and the earth. . . . God saw everything that He had made, and indeed it was very good (Genesis 1:1, 31).

THEME

GOD'S POWER

When asked why he wanted to become president, John F. Kennedy replied, "That's where the power is."

Although people bow before the mighty on Pennsylvania Avenue or in Red Square, absolute power resides at an unknown address—deep in the universe. And were it not for creation, we would never have known such power.

Creation was God's signed original, and He spared no detail in His grand and glorious work of art. Even though sin spoiled God's handiwork and led to one calamity after another, Old Testament writers kept pointing back to creation as proof that God's power was sufficient to rescue people in peril. Thus creation became a focal point for an important truth: God has the power to deliver from danger.

In New Testament times, God became man, died, and resurrected Himself. This grave-robbing act brought creation full circle to its life-giving essence and provided the basis for another eternal principle: God has the power to deliver from death.

Whether we speak of the majesty of the first creation or the miracle of the second, we must declare as new creations, waiting for a new heaven and earth, "Thine is the power."

Sunday

PSALM 8

O LORD, our Lord, how excellent is
Your name in all the earth (Psalm 8:1).

A friend of mine has a good reputation as an upholsterer. He believes in doing every job right. His work is so superior that his name is known far beyond our area. He has upholstered furniture for the state capitol, for top hotels, and for some of the wealthiest people in our state. Because of the quality of his work, he has made a name for himself.

God's excellent name is also known because of His workmanship. In Psalm 8 the psalmist said, in effect, Look to the heavens. See the majesty of God reflected in the planets and the stars. Look at the marvels of the sea and the wonders of the animal world—amazing and wonderful creations from God's hand that live together in awe-inspiring balance and beauty. And look at man—crowned with glory and honor, made a little lower than the angels, and given authority over all creation (vv. 5–6).

Let us praise God, the One who spoke the heavens into being by the word of His power, the One who keeps the stars and planets spinning on their unseen courses. Let us magnify Him, the One who gives us the mysteries of the oceans, the rugged beauty of the mountains, and the intricate marvels of plant and animal life. Let us exalt Him, the One who made us and crowned us with glory and honor.

"O LORD, our Lord, how excellent is Your name in all the earth."
—D.C.E.

The Creator deserves all praise from His creation.

Monday

HEBREWS 11:1–6

**In the beginning God created
the heavens and the earth (Genesis 1:1).**

By faith we know that the earth came into existence through the creative power of God. Columnist Sydney J. Harris makes this observation: "Suppose, in olden days, you said to a medieval monk, 'The universe is made up of millions of galaxies of incredible size. Not only that, but each galaxy is rushing away from all the others, faster and faster. And the farther they get, the faster they go.' The monk would think you were mad." The point Mr. Harris is making is that either viewpoint we take—the "traditional religious viewpoint" or the "dominant scientific viewpoint"—involves faith. He concludes that a person who can accept the idea of a "black hole" in space, should have no difficulty believing in a "pearly gate" in Heaven.

Some scientists may accuse us of being naive because we believe the creation story as recorded in the book of Genesis. Yet they are inconsistent in making such a charge because they also arrive at their position by faith. But their faith is based on their own limited observation and fallible interpretation. And that puts those who reject God at a disadvantage. The basis of their confidence is faulty and unreliable. As Christians, we have a distinct advantage: we accept what the Creator Himself declares in the Bible. Our faith is based on what He has proclaimed. We need never be ashamed to say that we accept His word by faith. It gives us true understanding. —R.W.D.

**Creation is not only more complex than we think it is.
It is more complex than we can think.**

Tuesday

PSALM 19:1–6

**The fool has said in his heart,
"There is no God" (Psalm 14:1).**

An unbelieving lawyer had a plaque on his office wall that read: GOD IS NOWHERE. His small daughter, while waiting for him one day, passed the time by copying that motto over and over on a piece of paper. Unintentionally she spaced the letters in a way that completely changed their meaning. Adding a space between the letters *W* and *H*, she wrote GOD IS NOW HERE.

This story suggests what happens in life. People with an unbelieving frame of mind say that the world is the result of a long, evolutionary process. Because of their prejudiced slant on things, they see no evidence of the Almighty's hand in nature, even though it is found all around them. They feel completely justified in concluding that there is no God. Christians, however, behold the beauty and design in that same creation and conclude that God is everywhere. With the psalmist we say, "The heavens declare the glory of God; and the firmament shows His handiwork" (Psalm 19:1).

The letters on the sign in the attorney's office may be read two different ways, but only one meaning is true. Many people look at God's mighty handiwork in the universe and think that it simply says "wild chance." But others see it as saying "wise Creator." The Bible gives us the right interpretation. Those who see God as NOW HERE instead of NOWHERE are the ones who know how to read the sign.

—R.W.D.

Nature is but a name for an effect whose cause is God.
—Cowper

15

Wednesday

GENESIS 1:9–13

O Lᴏʀᴅ, how manifold are Your works!
In wisdom You have made them all (Psalm 104:24).

While eating a slice of watermelon, William Jennings Bryan thought of a way to use it as an illustration in one of his speeches. After estimating that the melon was about forty pounds, he collected a number of seeds and weighed them. Applying a little mathematics, he was amazed to find that it took nearly five thousand to make up a pound. Then he sat down at his desk and wrote, "Recently someone planted just one of those little seeds in the ground. Under the influence of sunshine and shower, it took off its coat and went to work gathering about two hundred thousand times its own weight. It forced all the material through a tiny stem and built a watermelon. On the outside it had a covering of green; within that, a rind of white; and within that, a core of red. Scattered on the inside were more seeds—each capable of doing the same work all over again. What architect drew the plan? Where did that little watermelon seed get its tremendous strength? Where did it find its flavoring extract and its coloring matter?" Bryan then pointed out that until we can explain a watermelon, we dare not underestimate the power of the Almighty. In supplying us with these wonders, which our finite minds cannot understand, the Lord has shown us His infinite wisdom and power.

Viewing the wonders of God, as witnessed by even a single watermelon, we are amazed at His marvelous handiwork. In humble adoration we exclaim with the psalmist, "In wisdom You have made them all." —H.G.B.

**The signature of wisdom impressed on the works of God
proclaims His glory. —Newton**

Thursday

**"Your father knows the things
you have need of before you ask Him" (Matthew 6:8).**

A group of scientists are directing their thoughts and needs into the heavens, but not to the God of the Bible. They have calculated that as many as fifty million civilizations may exist somewhere in space, and they believe that some of them may have found methods to improve our lives and control the time of death. In November, 1974, these scientists, using special technology, beamed a message to a cluster of stars on the outer edge of our galaxy. But even if that signal were picked up, they estimate that it would take forty-eight thousand years for an answer to come back.

To Christians, these efforts seem ridiculous and destined to failure. Yet those scientists are serious about their efforts, while we, who do have contact with "another world," sometimes act as if our prayers are not heard. Every child of God has the opportunity to get in touch, not with other creatures, but with the Creator Himself! We have immediate access through prayer to the One who stretched out all the galaxies in the heavens. He hears us the instant we pray and answers according to His will. Through the wonderful privilege of prayer, every Christian can come to One who is all-powerful, who listens in heaven, and who can and does change the affairs of people.

In light of our relationship to Him, we can send our messages to heaven with renewed confidence, because we know personally our God-listener. —M.R.D.II

**When we bend our knees to pray,
God bends His ear to listen.**

Friday

PSALM 50:1–6

The Mighty One, God the LORD, has spoken . . .
from the rising of the sun to its going down (Psalm 50:1).

Who has not marveled at the beauty of a sunset? We stand motionless, awestruck, hushed by the flaming sky as the sun moves toward the western horizon. Seeming to hesitate a moment, the glowing orb drops out of sight, leaving the sky ablaze with brilliant shades of pink, orange, and red. The frustrations of the day are silenced by the majestic yet soothing voice of God as we view a glorious sunset.

Because the earth's atmosphere slightly slows and bends the sun's rays, the sun appears oval-shaped rather than round. And dust or smog in the air creates the dazzling array of colors that gives us so much visual pleasure at day's end. And scientists tell us that a sunset can be even more beautiful than most of us have seen. In the *Encyclopedia Science Supplement,* astronomer John B. Irwin wrote, "When conditions are just right, the last diminishing bit of the yellow-orange sun suddenly changes into a brilliant emerald green. This green flash puts an exciting exclamation point to the end of the day."

To Christians, every sunset is an exclamation point given to us by God the Creator to end the day. It's as if the Lord were saying, "Set aside your worries. Rest from your labors. Forget about those disappointments. I am still here, taking care of My universe. I am in control. I have not changed. Look up beyond the sun to Me and be at peace." —D.C.E.

The voice of God in nature assures us of His power.

Saturday

As Charles Simeon, the great nineteenth century English preacher, lay mortally ill in his Cambridge home, he realized that his time on earth was fast slipping away. He turned to those at his bedside and asked, "Do you know what comforts me just now? I find infinite consolation in the fact that in the beginning God created the heaven and the earth." His friends asked how that thought could give solace as he faced death. He answered with the confidence of one about to meet the Lord, "Why, if God can bring all the wonder of the worlds out of nothing, He may still make something out of me!"

To think of the glory that awaits God's children—to have a spirit perfectly pure and a resurrected body that will enable us to enjoy eternity to its fullest—staggers the imagination. The great changes we will experience in glory are beyond our understanding.

Even now God's transforming power is at work in us. At conversion we became children of God and were made "alive together with Christ" (Eph. 2:5). But that is not all. Paul said that in the future God will "show the exceeding riches of His grace in His kindness toward us in Christ Jesus" (Eph. 2:7). No wonder the apostle John exclaimed with astonishment, "It has not yet been revealed what we shall be."

Glorious prospects await those who have trusted Christ for salvation. God is not done with us yet. The best is yet to be. —P.R.V.

**While you prepare a place for us, Lord,
prepare us for that place.**

Week 2

THE FALL

"And I will put enmity between you and the woman, and between your seed and her Seed; He shall bruise your head, and you shall bruise His heel" (Genesis 3:15).

THEME

SIN

In his early years, Ansel Adams, the famous landscape photographer, studied piano. Once, while playing Chopin for a friend, he could not get his hands coordinated. The next day the friend gave him a backhanded critique by telling him, "You never missed a wrong note."

Although no one knows exactly when or where Adam and Eve sounded the first sour note, people have been playing wrong notes perfectly ever since. The tragic Eden error called sin means missing the mark.

The discord that started in God's garden has been heard throughout history. As the *New England Primer* put it, "In Adam's sin, we sinned all." As Adam and Eve experienced guilt, loneliness, and estrangement, so have all of their offspring.

Without the Fall, death could never have sung the blues' dark song, and lying, hatred, and pride would not have become the funeral march of the masses.

The mad sounds of sin would still be humanity's only tune had it not been for God's note of grace—He followed Adam and Eve out of the gate.

Sunday

PROVERBS 6:12–19

You who love the LORD, hate evil
(Psalm 97:10).

God hates sin. In Proverbs 6, the author singled out seven specific transgressions that are an abomination to the Lord. Sin is so horrible that when the Lord Jesus, the perfect Son of God, bore our guilt on the cross, the Father turned His back on His beloved Son. And Christ, in the blackness of that dreadful hour, cried out, "My God, My God, why have You forsaken Me?" (Matt. 27:46). If sin is so terrible in the sight of God, then we must fear it, hate it, and avoid it.

Johann Peter Lange, the nineteenth century German theologian and author, told a story about a religious leader who was viciously hated by the emperor of his day. Some of the ruler's advisors said to the monarch, "Burn him, confiscate his property, put him in irons, or have him killed." But others disagreed. They said, "You will not gain anything by all this; for in exile he would find a home with his God; . . . he kisses his chains, death opens heaven to him. There is only one way to render him unhappy; force him to sin. He fears nothing in the world but sin" (F. B. Proctor, *Treasury of Quotations*).

How many people do we know who fear "nothing in the world but sin"? Unfortunately, we often become so comfortable in sin's presence that we practice it rather than fear it. But remember how God views it. May we therefore, as lovers of Him, be haters of sin. —R.W.D.

**It is not enough for gardeners to love flowers;
they must also hate weeds.**

Monday

ROMANS 1:18–25

**They did not like to retain God in their knowledge
(Romans 1:28).**

When we go the wrong way spiritually, we do so, in one sense, on purpose. Douglas Corrigan became known as "wrong-way Corrigan" in 1938 when he took off in his plane from Brooklyn, New York, on an announced flight to Long Beach, California. A little over twenty-three hours later, he touched down in Dublin, Ireland, and asked officials, "Is this Los Angeles?" For years people laughed at his "miscalculations," but finally in 1963 he admitted that his trip across the Atlantic had really been planned. Unable to get clearance to cross the ocean, he went ahead and made the flight "by mistake" on purpose.

There's a striking parallel between Corrigan's action and much of our own experience as Christians. Romans 1 declares that fallen human nature is self-willed and resents God. Although it describes the unregenerate man, it helps us understand how the sin principle still operates in the believer's life. Even though we are new creatures in Christ, the strong, willful tendency remains in us. Some people might think that a Christian would not intentionally choose to do wrong. But the Bible clearly indicates that every believer experiences a struggle between the flesh and the indwelling Spirit (Gal. 5:16–17). That's why we must determine to submit to Him, for He gives us a desire to follow righteousness. Such deliberate surrender will keep us from going the wrong way "by accident" on purpose. —M.R.D.II

**Those who are fully surrendered to the Lord
will never deliberately surrender to the enemy.**

Tuesday

MATTHEW 18:6–9

*"If your hand or foot causes you to sin,
cut it off and cast it from you" (Matthew 18:8).*

On several occasions when visiting men in jail, I have seen them shake their heads mournfully and say, "I never thought it would come to this." When they began to break minor laws, they fully intended to change their ways before getting into serious trouble. But instead, one thing led to another, and they became more and more involved in a life of crime. Now they languish in jail, facing a long imprisonment.

These men failed to realize that sin always progresses. When we flout God's laws in one facet of life, a kind of mathematical law of addition and multiplication goes into effect. Soon sin affects other areas of our lives. It's foolish to think we can keep just one pet sin. That single sin will grow and spread unless we deal radically with it. That's why Jesus spoke of cutting off the offending hand and plucking out the offending eye (Matt. 18:8–9). By using such a strong figure of speech, He was saying, do whatever is necessary to stop.

We cannot afford to toy with sin. Three times in Romans 1, Paul said of unbelievers that "God gave them up" to their evil ways. In other words, He allows wickedness to run its downhill course until judgment falls and there's no escape.

We can avoid the inevitable arithmetic of sin by trusting Jesus as Savior. His power in our lives can overcome any sin. —H.V.L.

No one becomes wicked all at once.

Wednesday

EZRA 9:1–10:1

Many sorrows shall be to the wicked
(Psalm 32:10).

When Ezra learned that many of the Israelites had married heathen women (a practice strictly forbidden by God), he tore his garments, pulled hair from his head and beard, and sat down appalled. Then he fell to his knees and wept as he prayed. Many people were so moved by this that they wept with him. And well they should. Sin is a terrible thing. It offends the Lord. It grieves spiritually sensitive people. And it brings untold misery to the transgressor. In this instance, the men of Israel had to send their foreign wives and their children back to their homeland, which must have caused great pain. But this drastic step was necessary to keep the nation from spiritual disaster.

One day I responded to eighteen letters written by husbands, wives, parents, and grandparents who were deeply hurt because someone close to them had fallen into a sin that was breaking up a family circle. Answering these people reminded me how much pain disobedience causes, and it impressed on me that sin is the ultimate cause of all the anguish and sorrow in our world. Although suffering is unavoidable because of sin's effect on the human family, many people intensify their miseries by recklessly plunging into immorality.

We need a deeper sense of grief over sin and a greater burden for people caught in its snares. The heartbreak of sin is too devastating to underestimate. —H.V.L.

One of the greatest of all evils
is indifference toward all evil.

Thursday

GALATIANS 6:1–9

**For our transgressions are multiplied
before You, and our sins testify against us (Isaiah 59:12).**

A group of young people from Renaissance High School in Detroit cut classes to attend a rock concert in Hart Plaza. They probably thought they had gotten away with their truancy, but the next day, when the *Detroit News* appeared on the newsstand, it carried a color photo of the concert on the front page. And who was in that picture? That's right—the delinquent students of Renaissance High, easily recognizable to anyone. According to the paper, "Eagle-eyed assistant principal Dr. Elijah Porter spotted the students and had a conversation with them." As for the kids, it went on, "There was nothing they could say."

The Bible teaches that we cannot hide our iniquities. We may be able to cover them up for a while and even get away with them for an extended period of time. But the time will inevitably come when we must face up to them, either in this world or in the next. Paul told the Galatians, "Do not be deceived, God is not mocked; for whatever a man sows, that he will also reap" (Gal. 6:7).

Whenever we have a sin we are hiding, we must confess and forsake it. Or, when we are tempted to pursue something we know is wrong, thinking we won't get caught, we must determine to go no further. Our picture may not appear on the front page, but the Bible says we won't get away with it. —D.C.E.

**The seed of wrongdoing may be sown in secret,
but the harvest cannot be concealed.**

Friday

For I know that in me (that is,
in my flesh) nothing good dwells (Romans 7:18).

Several years ago we had a pet raccoon we called Jason. For hours he would entertain us by wrestling with our dog, MacTavish, a kind and gentle Scottish terrier. Jason, on the other hand, was a kind of schizoid terror. One minute he would snuggle up on your lap like a perfect angel and the next he'd be engaged in the most fiendish antics. If unrestrained, he would breakfast on dove eggs, raid the garbage can, or tear up the flowerbed. Although he was a delightful pet, we became increasingly aware that his destructive actions were governed by his wild instincts. Jason would always have the nature of a raccoon, and we had to watch him closely no matter how tame he seemed to be.

Often when I observed Jason's behavior, I thought of the fallen, sinful nature that we as Christians retain even though we are indwelt by the Holy Spirit. Paul referred to this as the "flesh" in which "nothing good dwells" (Rom. 7:18). It may be repressed and restrained, but it is always there. Unless we are daily controlled by the Lord, our old "self" will demonstrate its destructive, pleasure-seeking capacity in some way or another.

Although we are new creatures in Christ, we still possess a tendency to sin. But we need not be governed by it, for we are united to Christ and indwelt by the Holy Spirit. By obeying God's Word and yielding to the Spirit, we can be victorious over the flesh—the "nature of the beast" within. —M.R.D.II

**The secret of self-control is to give
control of ourselves to God.**

Saturday

**A lying tongue is but for a moment
(Proverbs 12:19).**

A college student in Texas became a local hero when word got around that he had rescued a woman from three attackers. But he gained national attention when it became known that his story was untrue. According to *United Press International,* the embarrassed fellow admitted that he did not (as he had originally claimed) use martial arts skills to defend a woman in distress. He confessed that he had picked up his cuts and bruises while meddling in a private argument.

His short-lived glory illustrates what Solomon said about the life expectancy of a lying tongue. According to his inspired words, lying to avoid embarrassment will eventually result in even greater embarrassment. Lying to escape a painful admission of the truth merely delays the consequences of that lie and hopelessly entangles the liar in a web of deceit. But in time the truth comes out. The reasons for this can be found in Proverbs 12. The most important fact is that God hates lies (v. 22), and He views them as unjust weapons of violence (v. 18). As a result, lies do not hold up very long (v. 19). They are the tools of the trade of those who depend on a temporary cover of darkness (v. 20). They should have no place in the life of someone who is committed to doing what is right.

We can learn from the Word of God and from the experience of the embarrassed student. A lie may seem like the easy way out, but it will prove to be like an exit sign placed over a closet door. It leads nowhere. —M.R.D.II

A lie is a coward's way of getting out of trouble.

Week 3

THE FLOOD

The LORD saw that the wickedness of man was great in the earth, . . . "And behold, I Myself am bringing the flood of waters on the earth, to destroy from under heaven all flesh. . . ." Then God remembered Noah . . . And God said . . . "I set My rainbow in the cloud, and it shall be for the sign of the covenant between Me and the earth" (Genesis 6:5, 17; 8:1; 9:12–13).

THEME

RETRIBUTION

Vanessa Williams, the dethroned Miss America, explained on losing her title, "The past just came up and kicked me."

Like America's former beauty queen, most people understand that the past can kick us to death. In fact, death is God's ultimate judgment on the past.

Disobedience, irreverence, murder, and pride tarnished Adam, Cain, Lamech, and the Babel bunch. Genesis gives few specifics about what evils stained Noah's neighbors, but God chose to make an example of them.

As time melds into eternity, the Flood still stands as a startling symbol of sin's penalty. Except for the eight in Noah's family, God killed a whole generation of people.

We don't like the idea of retribution; floods and crosses leave us in despair. But lest we be hopeless, God sent a rainbow and a resurrection.

Sunday

Every intent of the thoughts of his heart
was only evil continually. . . .
So the LORD said, I will destroy man (Genesis 6:5, 7).

It happened again. A mountain in Mexico that had lain dormant for a very long time suddenly came alive, erupting with so much power that it became the world's largest active volcano. The 7300-foot El Chichon giant had been quiet for hundreds of years before its explosive re-awakening. Like the eruption of Mount St. Helens, which broke its long silence in 1980 and transformed its majestic snow-covered peak and placid Spirit Lake into dust and vapor, the explosion was unexpected. The people near the mountains lived in complacency, never anticipating such drastic changes.

These events symbolize all the unexpected changes in history and nature since Noah's day, when God destroyed the wicked. Like the people living near El Chichon and Mount St. Helens, Noah's neighbors lived in complacency. But corruption made their complacency even more foolish—even more deadly. Preoccupied with the pleasures of sin, they thought their evil ways would never catch up with them. But God stepped in unexpectedly.

Sometimes we act as if we believe God is inactive, and that our security is reinforced with concrete and steel. But that's only the way it seems. Time always catches up with us, as it did in Noah's day. Every sinner will someday face a flood or an exploding mountain. Jesus has promised to come back unexpectedly. We should all make sure we are not living in sin's danger zone when He returns. —M.R.D.II

Judgment may be delayed, but it is sure.

Monday

2 PETER 3:1–14

**Since all these things will be dissolved,
what manner of persons ought you to be? (2 Peter 3:11).**

The Leaning Tower of Pisa in Italy is going to fall. Scientists travel yearly to measure the building's slow descent. They report that the 179-foot tower moves about one-twentieth of an inch a year, and is now seventeen feet out of plumb. They further estimate that by the year 2007 the 810-year-old tower will have leaned too far and will collapse onto the nearby *ristorante,* where scientists now gather to discuss their findings. Quite significantly, the word *pisa* means "marshy land," which gives some clue as to why the tower began to lean even before it was completed.

We know that some things, like the Leaning Tower of Pisa, are destined to collapse. But what about the Golden Gate Bridge, the World Trade Center Towers, the Rock of Gibraltar, and the Rocky Mountains? Like that tower, they too are resting on "soft foundations." They too will fall one day—at a time already determined on God's calendar.

Maybe it doesn't seem pressing because we think we'll pass from this earthly scene long before that great judgment day comes. That's not how Peter responded. The inevitable collapse of all things made him think about the eternal society built on righteousness and truth, a society that would continue, even after Gibraltar is gone. It motivated him to build his life on Christ, the only foundation that will never crumble. —M.R.D.II

**Our main business in this world
is to secure an interest in the next.**

Tuesday

PROVERBS 29:1–6

**It is appointed for men to die once,
but after this the judgment (Hebrews 9:27).**

We were out on the lake and the fish were biting. Suddenly we heard a rumble in the distance. Looking up, we saw a mass of dark clouds in the west. The sound of thunder warned of a coming storm. It was a long way off, I thought, so I didn't heed the suggestion of my fishing partner that we start back to the cottage. I hoped the bad weather would move to the north or south of us. But then it happened! A fresh breeze sprang up, and the clouds mounted quickly overhead. We tried starting the motor—but no response. I cranked while my partner rowed frantically. The waves became whitecaps; the rain came in sheets; and the gale tossed our aluminum boat like an autumn leaf. That experience taught me a valuable lesson. *Never wait when a storm is brewing!*

It also preached a powerful sermon. Judgment is coming! It may seem far off to those who are in good health, but our motor can "conk out" at any time. To heed the foreboding signals of death is true wisdom. Look in the mirror before you go to work and observe some of its warnings. Notice those gray hairs and wrinkles. Remember your stiffening joints, shortness of breath, that dizzy spell—it's all "thunder in the distance." Why not hasten to find shelter in Christ before it is too late? Don't depend on your motor or the oars of self-effort. You will have no excuse, for you have been warned! —M. R. De Haan, M.D.

**We are not truly ready to live
until we are prepared to die.**

Wednesday

MATTHEW 13:36–43

Those who do not obey the gospel . . . shall be punished with everlasting destruction (2 Thessalonians 1:8–9).

During the Franco-German War of 1870–71, a homeowner found two unexploded shells near his house. He cleaned them up and put them on display near his fireplace. A few weeks later he showed them to a visitor. His friend, an expert in munitions, had a horrible thought. "What if they're still loaded?" After examining the shells, he exclaimed, "Get them away from the fire immediately! They're as deadly as the day they were made!" Without realizing it, the homeowner had been living in peril.

Likewise, many people unknowingly live in constant jeopardy of something far worse—a Christless eternity in hell. Failing to recognize the consequences of unbelief, they risk sealing their doom at any moment. We cannot exaggerate the danger of rejecting Christ and living in unbelief, for what we do with Him and His offer of salvation determines where we will spend eternity.

The words of our text are among the most chilling found in the Bible. They emphasize the truth of Hebrews 10:31: that it is "a fearful thing to fall into the hands of the living God." Our Lord describes hell as a terrible place of outer darkness (Matt. 22:13) and eternal hopelessness (Matt. 18:8–9). —H.G.B.

**When it comes to salvation,
he who hesitates may be lost!**

Thursday

ROMANS 1:18–32

**God gave them over to a debased mind
(Romans 1:28).**

People who want nothing to do with God make themselves candidates for His ultimate judgment. They spend their days alienated from Him, and will spend eternity banished from God's presence unless they repent.

Aaron Burr, the third Vice President of the United States, was reared in a godly home and admonished to accept Christ by his grandfather Jonathan Edwards. But he refused to listen. Instead, he declared that he wanted nothing to do with God and said he wished the Lord would leave him alone. He achieved a measure of political success in spite of repeated disappointments. But he was also involved in continuous strife. When he was forty-eight years old, he killed Alexander Hamilton in a duel. He lived for thirty-two more years, but was unhappy and unproductive. During this sad chapter in his life he declared to a group of friends, "Sixty years ago I told God that if He would let me alone, I would let Him alone, and God has not bothered about me since." Aaron Burr got what he wanted. —H.V.L.

**There is a way to *stay* out of hell,
but no way to *get* out.**

Friday

He who sits in the heavens shall laugh;
the LORD shall hold them in derision (Psalm 2:4).

Psalm 2 describes wicked leaders who thought they could successfully oppose God and His Anointed. The psalmist indicated that the Lord will "laugh" at them, which is meant to convey the absurdity of man's attempt to defy God. Those who persist in this invite not only His ridicule but also His judgment.

W. S. Pulmer tells what became of godless men and women who persecuted Christians and sent believers to their deaths. Of thirty such Roman officials, Pulmer says, "one became deranged after some atrocious cruelty, one was slain by his own son, one became blind, one was drowned, one was strangled, one died in a miserable captivity, two committed suicide, five were assassinated by their own people or servants, five others died the most miserable and excruciating deaths, . . . and either were killed in battle or after being taken prisoner. Among these was Julian the apostate. In the days of his prosperity, he is said to have pointed his dagger to heaven, defying the Son of God, whom he commonly called 'the Galilean.' But when he was wounded in battle and saw that all was over for him, he exclaimed, 'Thou hast conquered, O Thou Galilean.'"

God's laughter at sinners is no laughing matter. "Kiss the Son, lest He be angry, and you perish in the way, when His wrath is kindled but a little. Blessed are all those who put their trust in Him" (Ps. 2:12). —R.W.D.

Playing with sin is toying with judgment.

Saturday

"Behold, the Lion of the tribe of Judah . . . and in the midst of the elders, stood a Lamb" (Revelation 5:5–6).

The Lord Jesus still extends His offer of salvation. He came to die for our sins, and He gladly saves everyone who trusts in Him. But one day that offer will be withdrawn. The slain Lamb—sacrificed for sin—will become the Lion, bringing judgment upon all who rejected Him.

In *Discover Yourself in the Psalms,* Warren Wiersbe recalled a story told by an evangelist he heard many years ago: "In a frontier town, a horse bolted and ran away with a wagon that had a little child in it. Seeing the child was in danger, a young man risked his life to catch the horse and stop it. The child who was rescued grew up to become a lawless man, and one day he stood before a judge to be sentenced for a serious crime. The prisoner recognized the judge as the man who, years before, had saved his life, so he pled for mercy on the basis of that experience. But the words from the bench silenced all his pleas: 'Young man, then I was your savior; today I am your judge, and I must sentence you to be hanged.'"

Jesus stands before us today as our Savior, the Lamb slain for our sins. But if we do not turn to Him in faith, He will one day stand before us as our righteous Judge. He will say: "On earth I was your Savior, but you would not believe. Here I am your Judge; depart from Me to everlasting punishment."

Those who believe on the Lamb will not have to face the Lion in judgment. —D.C.E.

**What we do with Christ now
will determine what God will do with us later.**

Week 4

TOWER OF BABEL

"Come, let us build ourselves a city, and a tower whose top is in the heavens; let us make a name for ourselves" (Genesis 11:4).

THEME

PRIDE

Michelangelo once overheard some people talking about his sculpture *Pietà* and mistakenly saying that fellow sculptor Il Gobbo had created it. Deeply hurt, he returned after dark and carved his name on it for all generations.

We all want to make our mark, but the Babel ballyhoo was too much. The Babylonians wanted a great city and name, but they also wanted a tower. And not just another Sears Tower; it was probably a temple for another religion. Such arrogance and defiance invited God's wrath.

Isaiah told the story of the earliest instance of pride (Isa. 14:12–14). Instead of a temple, Satan wanted to build a throne above the stars of God. Satan's scheme and the Babel bigheadedness were both godmaking games—an attempt to make the Creator in the creation's image.

The only cure for pride is to understand the Creator's motives; they are not the same as those of the throne-seekers and tower-builders. God wants all glory, but He deserves it because He always desires the best for us.

In sending His Son to walk among proud people, He knew some would not glorify Him. In giving up our life to Him, we find the true source of pride.

Sunday

GENESIS 11:1–9

**"Come, let us build ourselves a city and a tower . . .
let us make a name for ourselves" (Genesis 11:4).**

A twenty-five-year-old acrobat gained widespread attention when he climbed the steel and glass surface of the world's tallest building. In seven and one-half hours he scaled Chicago's 1454-foot, 110-story Sears Tower. On the way up, he carried fifty pounds of climbing equipment and fought off forty-mile-an-hour winds. By the time he reached the top, he had made a name for himself—but he was also in trouble. Police greeted him and took him in handcuffs to the city jail, where he was charged with disorderly conduct, trespassing, and damage to property.

That incident reminded me of the people who built the historic skyscraper of Babel mentioned in Genesis 11:1–9. The tower represented an undertaking by a community of citizens determined to make a name for themselves. They meant it to be a magnificent structure symbolizing their unity and opposition to God. They said, "Come, let us build ourselves a city, and a tower whose top is in the heavens;. . . lest we be scattered abroad over the face of the whole earth." But God was waiting at the top. He stopped their attempt to achieve recognition by breaking down their communication system and thwarting their self-centered, God-defying objectives.

Even though we are Christians, sometimes we get caught up in making a name for ourselves by climbing business, religious, or social towers that deny God His rightful place. If we do, we will eventually be brought down because God is still at the top. —M.R.D.II

If you would build high you must remain low.

Monday

JAMES 4:1–12

For I say . . . to everyone . . . not to think
of himself more highly than he ought (Romans 12:3).

A man who had just been elected to the British Parliament brought his family to London and was giving them a tour of the city. When they entered Westminster Abbey, his eight-year-old daughter seemed awe-struck by the size and beauty of that magnificent structure. Her proud father, curious about what was going on in her mind, asked, "And what, my child, are you thinking about?" She replied, "Daddy, I was just thinking about how big you are in our house, but how small you look here!"

Pride can creep into our lives without our awareness. From time to time it's good for us to be "cut down to size." We need to be reminded not to think of ourselves more highly than we ought to think. It's easy to become proud when we stay in our own circles of life. But when we are thrust into larger situations, with increased demands, pressures, and competition, we come to the shocking realization that "big fish in small ponds" shrink quickly in a large ocean.

One thing that stands out in the Word of God is that the Lord despises the haughty. Under inspiration the psalmist said, "One who has a haughty look and a proud heart, him I will not endure" (Psalm 101:5). And James said, "God resists the proud, but gives grace to the humble" (4:6).

If we ask the Holy Spirit to help us see ourselves as we really are, He will enable us to control our foolish pride. —R.W.D.

**Those who know God will be humble;
those who know themselves cannot be proud.**

Tuesday

PROVERBS 16:16–22

**Pride goes before destruction,
and a haughty spirit before a fall (Proverbs 16:18).**

Theodore Roosevelt and a friend engaged in a nighttime ritual to keep themselves humble. Author Leslie B. Flynn tells about it: "After an evening of conversation they would go outside on a clear night and search the skies until one or the other found a faint speck of light-mist in a certain spot in the sky. Then he would recite, 'That is the Spiral Galaxy in Andromeda. That speck is as large as our Milky Way. It is one of a hundred million galaxies. It consists of a hundred billion suns, each larger than our sun.' Then he would conclude, 'Now that we have our perspective, let's call it a day!'"

Pride is the constant enemy of the Christian. From deep within come subtle reminders of "how important" we are, how "great" are our achievements, or how much "better" we are than others. We need to keep alert to the sin of pride so that we can immediately reject these suggestions. Through prayer, reliance on the Holy Spirit, and continual study of the Scriptures, we will gain heaven's perspective, which will help us maintain a realistic opinion of ourselves.

Believers who strive to walk in Christian maturity will avoid dwelling on thoughts of great accomplishments and spiritual superiority. Paul, a man who had more reason than any of us to be proud, reminded us not to think of ourselves more highly than we ought. Roosevelt's example is a good one to follow. The "Andromeda perspective" will help us win the battle against pride. —D.C.E.

**We see our true selves when we
stand in the shadow of Christ.**

Wednesday

PROVERBS 25:14–16, 27–28

**It is not good to eat much honey;
so to seek one's own glory is not glory (Proverbs 25:27).**

Researchers at Montana State University have challenged the idea that a high-sugar snack generates quick energy. They tested long-distance runners on stationary exercise bicycles and found that athletes who had a sugar-free drink before the workout were able to pedal twenty-five percent longer than those who had a sugar-laden drink. The study concluded that "athletes may be well-advised to abstain from sugar snacks before exercise."

The Bible concurs that too many sweets can affect well-being. King Solomon used the illustration of eating too much honey to point up something more serious—the danger of overindulging in the sweet taste of self-glory. In Proverbs 25, the wise king gave two warnings about the danger of too much self-congratulations and boasting (vv. 14, 27). Looking for attention and bragging about our accomplishments might be sweet to the taste in the short run. But in the long run, bragging does to the personality what eating five pounds of chocolate-covered cherries does to the waistline.

Nothing makes us weaker than a constant diet of self-centeredness and pride. All our energy is used up on ourselves. How much better to deny ourselves the sweet taste of self-glory by exercising discipline and faith. That's how we can become strong enough to meet the challenges we face. —M.R.D.II

Faith steps in when pride steps out.

Thursday

**For if anyone thinks himself to be something,
when he is nothing, he deceives himself (Galatians 6:3).**

Disaster always results when we try to build ourselves up by minimizing the worth of others. That's the message of a fable about a little frog who was startled when he looked up and saw an ox drinking out of the pond. He had never seen such a huge creature. Immediately he hopped away to tell his grandfather. Determined that no one should seem larger in the eyes of his grandson than he, the old bullfrog began to puff himself up as he asked, "Was he bigger than this?" "Oh, yes, Grandfather," answered the little frog, "much larger." Grandfather frog inflated himself more. "Bigger than this?" he queried. "Lots bigger!" replied the grandson. The old frog continued to puff until he exploded.

A good self-image is healthy, but there is a big difference between a sense of our God-given worth as His handiwork and an ego inflated by pride. That's why we must be quick to acknowledge that what we accomplish is done solely by God's grace. Only then can we see how foolish it is to promote our selfish interests. Furthermore, humility will enable us to show appreciation for the achievement and position of others.

The apostle Paul put it clearly, "For I say . . . to everyone who is among you, not to think of himself more highly than he ought to think, but to think soberly, as God has dealt to each one a measure of faith" (Rom. 12:3). If we puff ourselves up, we always get blown out of proportion. —P.R.V.

**God wants people great enough
to be small enough to be used.**

Friday

Before destruction the heart of a man is
haughty, and before honor is humility (Proverbs 18:12).

The poem "Invictus" says, in part, "I am the master of my fate: I am the captain of my soul." This may make good poetry, but it is dangerous theology. If we try to control our own lives, they will end in disaster.

A boy who became a sailor while very young rose rapidly in the profession and was soon made captain of a ship. At the end of one voyage, he was approaching land when a passenger who was familiar with maritime procedures asked if he intended to anchor the ship and call for some help in entering the harbor. "Anchor? Not I! I expect to be in dock with the morning tide." The passenger persisted, urging him to signal for a pilot. "I am my own pilot," came the abrupt reply. Determined to reach port by morning, he took a narrow channel to shorten the distance. His crew of weathered seamen just shook their heads. Passengers said that they were in no hurry and hoped he would take the wider course. He laughed at all of them and repeated his prediction to be on land by daybreak. Indeed, he *was* on land before daybreak. But his vessel was wrecked, and his own life was lost because of his willful pride.

Our voyage through time and into eternity is too treacherous to attempt without God's help. Unless the Lord Jesus is our Captain, we will never make it safely to the heavenly shore. —P.R.V.

Those who guide themselves have a fool for a follower.

Saturday

PHILIPPIANS 2:1–8

**Let nothing be done through
selfish ambition or conceit (Philippians 2:3).**

The aquatic creature called the blowfish has no particular value to the one who catches it—except that it may help to develop the angler's patience because it often seizes bait intended for better fish. The blowfish is unattractive; it has a large mouth and a wrinkled body that looks like worn-out leather. When you turn it over and tickle it, the flabby fish puffs up until it is swollen like a globe.

People can be like that. A little flattery, a little tickling of their vanity and they swell up, giving the semblance of greatness. Pride inflates them, and they puff up like the blowfish. But there's nothing substantial about them; they are all air.

This condition takes other forms with more serious consequences. For example, the Christians to whom Paul wrote in 1 Corinthians 5 were tolerating immorality. Instead of being grieved over sin in their midst, they were actually "puffed up" (1 Cor. 5:2). Here was a sure sign of carnality and immaturity—they were proud when they should have been mourning. God desires that we be "built up" in Christ—never "puffed up" with pride.

The continual attitude of God's children should be the one Paul recommended to the Philippians. He said, "Let nothing be done through selfish ambition or conceit, but in lowliness of mind let each esteem others better than himself" (Phil. 2:3). If we take this seriously, we won't have the characteristics of the puffed-up blowfish. —P.R.V.

The smaller we become, the more room God has to work.

Week 5

ISAAC'S BIRTH

Sarah conceived and bore Abraham a son in his old age (Genesis 21:2).

GOD'S TRUSTWORTHINESS

In John Bunyan's *Pilgrim's Progress*, Giant Despair captured Christian and Hopeful and held them as prisoners in Doubting Castle. They escaped when Christian remembered he had the key called Promise.

Like Christian, we forget God's guarantees. We can't imagine a world without wordmongers who write worthless warranties and politicians who separate promise and performance.

God made promises in the garden and after the Flood, but his words to senior citizens Abraham and Sarah make up the opening chapter of God's promise book to Israel. God assured them that they would be proud parents and that from their lone child a great nation would be born.

Isaac and the nation of Israel escaped the womb a long time ago, and it might be easy to dismiss a God who announces his intentions only to those very old and hard of hearing. We might accuse Him of empty promises except for another child of promise—Jesus Christ.

The long-awaited Bethlehem Baby was the official heir to God's kingdom, and He unselfishly passed on the key called Promise.

Sunday

"Look now toward heaven, and count the stars"
(Genesis 15:5).

Nature can nurture faith. God told Abraham to look at the heavens and contemplate the infinite number of stars. Then He said, "So shall your descendants be." God was saying to Abraham that if He could create and maintain all those stars, He'd have no trouble keeping His promise that Abraham would have a son. The patriarch understood, for we read that "he believed in the LORD " (Gen. 15:6).

An *Our Daily Bread* reader, Mr. T. C. Roddy, Jr., from Rusk, Texas, wrote, "In my front yard are six huge oak trees that must be over 100 years old. . . . I ponder as I look at them and realize that the leaves must have barrels of fresh water each day to stay green. As a retired engineer, I know that no pump ever devised or designed by man could force that amount of water through the dense wooden trunk of these trees. Yet God causes their roots to gather all the water these trees need. . . . To do this, these roots must exert a working pressure of more than 3,000 pounds per square foot just to move the water up to the leaves—not considering the resistance of the wood in the tree trunk. That is just another of God's 'miracles' that occur every day unnoticed."

When we have trouble believing God for the solution to some pressing problem, we can enter the classroom of creation and observe the wonders of nature. Doing so strengthens our faith in the promises found in our textbook, the Bible. —D.J.D.

All I have seen teaches me to trust the Creator
for all I have not seen. —Ralph Waldo Emerson

Monday

GENESIS 17:1–8, 15–22

**Then Abraham fell on his face and laughed
(Genesis 17:17).**

Who wouldn't laugh—a century-old man being told he will become a father, and that his ninety-year-old wife will bear a child? The whole idea must have seemed ridiculous to Abraham. Yet he received the news with great delight. Bowing before God, he expressed his surprise, wonder, and gladness—with no hint of unbelief. In Genesis 18, however, Sarah laughed and God rebuked her. Sarah laughed in unbelief. Abraham laughed in faith.

In a lecture, C. H. Spurgeon said that many Scriptures remain clouded until some trying experience interprets them for us. He told of riding home after a heavy day's work feeling weary and down-hearted. Suddenly 2 Corinthians 12:9 came to his mind, "My grace is sufficient for you." Spurgeon said, "I reached home and looked it up in the original, and at last it came to me in this way. 'My grace is sufficient for YOU.' Said I, 'I should think it is,' and I burst out laughing. I never understood what the holy laughter of Abraham was until then. It seemed to make unbelief so absurd. . . . O brethren, be great believers! Little faith will bring your souls to heaven, but great faith will bring heaven to your souls."

Our faith grows as we grow in our awareness of God's faithfulness. Old promises become joyful surprises with fresh meaning. We see that the all-powerful, all-sufficient God keeps His Word. Then we, too, can laugh the holy laughter of a faith that considers unbelief absurd.

—D.J.D.

Faith expects from God what is beyond all human expectation.

Tuesday

HEBREWS 10:19–25

**Let us hold fast the confession of our hope . . .
for He who promised is faithful (Hebrews 10:23).**

Suppose a wealthy man were to give you a note saying, "Sometime in the future, a time I've decided upon, you will receive fifty thousand dollars that I have set aside for you." Although you might become impatient as you wait for the money, you would confidently expect to get it. But if that same man were to say, "If everything works out, I might give you fifty thousand dollars" you'd expect the money only if he didn't go bankrupt, change his mind, forget his promise, or die. The first situation carries the greatest certainty.

That's the way it is in God's economy. His promises are dated in heaven. And since we know only "in part" (1 Cor. 13:12), we don't always know when they will be fulfilled. But that doesn't matter, for we do have the confidence that God will keep them. Nor does this diminish the value of God's promises, for He backs them all with the infinite riches of His character. He never changes. He never forgets His Word. He never dies. God may seem to delay the fulfillment of a promise, but we can be encouraged that every promise is as good as His word.

Most of us have come to the end of our resources. And there we have discovered that God, at the right time and in the right way, imparted His strength. He was neither slow nor tardy. So we need not be discouraged. We can keep on claiming the promises. God is the faithful promiser. —P.R.V.

Our prospects are as bright as the promises of God.

Wednesday

1 KINGS 8:54–61

"Blessed be the Lord. . . . There has not failed one word of all His good promise" (1 Kings 8:56).

A man who lived in northern Michigan went for a walk in a dense forest so immense that a person could easily get lost. When darkness began to settle in, he decided it was time to head home. He was used to being in the woods and had a keen sense of direction, so he didn't bother to look at his compass. After walking for a long time, however, he decided he'd better check to make sure he was going in the right direction. He was surprised when the compass indicated he was going west—not east as he had thought. But the man was so sure of his own sense of direction that he thought there must be something wrong with the compass. He was about to throw it away in disgust when the thought came to him: My compass has never lied to me yet—maybe I should believe it. The man eventually found his way out of the woods and arrived home safely because he trusted his compass and didn't rely on himself.

Solomon told the congregation of Israel that not "one word of all His good promise" had failed. That assurance still stands. What God promises, He performs. His instructions are always trustworthy. He will never lead us astray. If we think so highly of our own judgment that we refuse to rely on God's sure word, we are asking for trouble and will only become more confused. His words have never failed, and they never will. —R.W.D.

The Bible always points the believer in the right direction.

Thursday

GENESIS 18:1–14

"Is anything too hard for the LORD?"
(Genesis 18:14).

The Lord is able to meet all our needs, whatever they may be. Nothing is too difficult for Him. Sarah needed to learn this truth. God's promise to give Abraham a son named Isaac is recorded in Genesis 17:21. In the next chapter that assurance was repeated to the patriarch as he talked outside his tent with three men sent from God. This time Sarah overheard the conversation. To her, having a child at her advanced age was an impossibility, so she "laughed within herself" (v. 12). The Lord then said to Abraham, "Why did Sarah laugh, saying, 'Shall I surely bear a child, since I am old?' Is anything too hard for the LORD?" (vv. 13–14). God was asking Abraham a rhetorical question to which the obvious answer was no.

As Christians, we have the same assurance. Abraham's God is our God, and He is omnipotent. He's the Creator of the universe. Nothing exceeds His power. No problem intimidates Him. No obstacle is too big for Him. Everything is possible with Him. Our heavenly Father is in control of every situation. What comfort we can find in this truth! What confidence it gives us!

The all-knowing, everywhere-present, all-powerful Creator and sovereign God can do anything. When we present our petitions to our heavenly Father in prayer, making sure we ask according to His will, He assures us that nothing is too hard for Him. —R.W.D.

**We do not prove the resources of God
until we trust Him for the impossible.**

Friday

PSALM 89:30–37

My covenant I will not break, nor alter the word
that has gone out of My lips (Psalm 89:34).

When a couple left for vacation, their newly married son and daughter-in-law promised to watch the house, take in the mail, and keep the lawn mowed. The couple hadn't been gone very long before they began to worry. What if the young people were careless about locking the doors, and all their possessions were stolen? What if they didn't pick up the mail, and some checks were stolen? And what if the lawn weren't mowed? What would the neighbors think? The couple nearly ruined their vacation with worry, and they even cut it short by a couple days. When they returned, however, they found the lawn mowed, the mail taken care of, and the house in perfect order. They realized how foolish they had been. Their children had kept their word.

So it is with God. He keeps His word. Isaiah declared that "the word of our God stands forever" (40:8). This brings us great comfort and can free us from worry because it means that God will keep every promise. Here are just a few: "Many are the afflictions of the righteous, but the LORD delivers him out of them all" (Ps. 34:19). "No weapon formed against you shall prosper" (Isa. 54:17). "I will strengthen you, yes, I will help you" (Isa. 41:10). "No good thing will He withhold from those who walk uprightly" (Ps. 84:11).

Those who tend to fret or doubt unnecessarily, can lay hold of a promise and remind themselves that God always keeps His word.
—D.C.E.

**When we worry, we believe more in our problems
than in God's promises.**

Saturday

LORD, who may abide in Your tabernacle? He who swears to his own hurt and does not change (Psalm 15:1, 4).

I wish I could say I have always done what I said I would do. I'd like to be able to claim that even if I have done nothing else in life, I have at least kept all my promises. But I can't.

I also wish I could say that what I have not done affects only me. But again, that would be untrue. Not only have I hurt those who have depended on me, but I have also displeased the Lord in the process.

What I say I will do matters to God. Psalm 15 leaves no doubt about that. It says that the person with whom God shares His presence is one who walks with integrity and speaks the truth in his heart. It says that such a person does not misrepresent others. It says that when he makes a promise, he does what he said he would do, even if it requires personal sacrifice and pain.

The Lord, who has lovingly and mercifully forgiven me, has a record that is different from mine. He adheres flawlessly to the highest standards of integrity. Time and distraction have never kept Him from doing what He said He would do. Even to the point of sacrificing His own Son, He has kept His commitment to punish sin while remaining merciful to all who place their trust in Him.

Because He is true, I as His child and follower should be too. Only as my faith in Him translates into honest living will I become fit for the presence of the One who has so mercifully given Himself to me.

—M.R.D.II

There is one thing Christians give
and still must keep—their word.

Week 6

ABRAHAM OFFERS ISAAC

God tested Abraham, and said to him, . . . "Take now your son, your only son Isaac, whom you love, and go to the land of Moriah, and offer him there as a burnt offering" (Genesis 22:1–2).

THEME

GOD'S PROVISION

In Charles Dickens's *David Copperfield,* the character Traddles lent his good name to Mr. Micawber's money-making scheme. After Copperfield expressed concern, Traddles reassured himself and Copperfield by saying, "He told me, only the other day, that it was provided for. That was Mr. Micawber's expression, 'Provided for.'"

Like Traddles, we want assurance that we have been provided for. We even rely on slogans like "You're in good hands with Allstate." Somehow these deceive us into believing that someone will provide for us. Our need for reassurance reveals our uncertainty about whether God can truly meet all our needs.

By providing a ram for the sacrifice, God taught Abraham and future generations that he could provide when life itself was on the line. If God was concerned about one person's lifeblood, then He must take notice of all humanity's lifebeat.

The people of Christ's day missed the point of Isaac on the altar; they could only strengthen their faith when their sacrifice preceded God's provision. They certainly were not going to offer themselves; they wanted the glory and power of an earthly kingdom, not another gruesome sacrifice. But God gave them what they needed, not what they wanted. He put an end to their kingmaking passions by sacrificing the King.

We can be certain that God will freely give His children all good things—in His unexplainable, unexpected, but all-wise way.

Sunday

GENESIS 22:1–14

And Abraham said, "My son, God will provide
for Himself the lamb for a burnt offering" (Genesis 22:8).

Imagine Abraham's feelings when the Lord told him to offer Isaac as a sacrifice. Think of what went through his mind when they climbed Mount Moriah and Isaac asked, "Where is the lamb?" Yet Abraham had faith that God would provide, and he assured Isaac of his confidence. He was right. God pointed out a ram in the thicket. As a result, Abraham called the place Jehovah-Jireh, which means "the Lord will provide."

In the centuries that have followed, God has continued to demonstrate that He provides for His own. Dr. Robert Schindler and his wife, Marian, founded a mission hospital associated with radio station ELWA in Monrovia, Liberia. In their book *Mission Possible* they wrote, "For us, it was a continued exercise of faith that we would have the right drugs and supplies at the right time. We recall how much we counted on our X-ray machine, something we take for granted [at home]. We even had the opportunity to get an extra one when a friend of ours, a doctor with the U.S. Embassy, asked if we could use a portable X-ray machine. . . . But then as the months dragged out, we knew it must be lost at sea. Then one day our big X-ray machine stopped working. . . . We found it was a major problem which would take several months to fix. . . . But that very afternoon, the ELWA truck pulled up to the hospital with a huge crate from port. You guessed it—it was the portable X-ray machine! We plugged it in, and it worked! We didn't lose a day for X-rays."

Lord, thank You for being our Provider. —D.C.E.

God's provisions are always greater than our problems.

Monday

**"I will come in to him and dine with him,
and he with Me" (Revelation 3:20).**

An elderly couple had no means of support except a weekly gift of money from a man in their church. One Sunday the church scheduled a special meeting in the afternoon. The couple's benefactor, who lived quite far away, wanted to remain in the area for the afternoon service. So he said to the couple, "Would you mind if I joined you for dinner after the morning service?" Immediately the couple thought of the half loaf of stale bread, a bit of butter, and some cheese that was the entire contents of their cupboard. How could this friend dine with them, they wondered. But the man interrupted their worries by adding, "I have brought a basket of things with me and there will be plenty for the three of us." When he arrived at the couple's cottage, he unpacked the basket. Soon the three of them were gathered around a table spread with fried chicken, sliced ham, homemade bread, country butter, and apple pie. The man had not only come to dine with them, but he had also brought all that was needed for the feast.

This pictures Jesus' relationship with us. He desires to fellowship with us, and He provides all we need for the feast. When we open the door of our heart and the Lord Jesus comes in, we have the privilege of "dining" with Him. We have nothing to offer, but into our spiritual poverty He brings all the riches of His grace. What blessed fellowship is ours as He spreads His bounteous table and invites us to dine with Him. —P.R.V.

Grace is God's everything for people who deserve nothing.

Tuesday

GENESIS 22:1–18

**Abraham called the name of the place,
The-Lord-Will-Provide (Genesis 22:14).**

A number of times in the Old Testament, the name "Jehovah" is joined to other names that reveal some of God's distinct characteristics. Abraham said that the place where God supplied a ram should be called "The-Lord-Will-Provide." This name, which is sometimes rendered "Jehovah-Jireh," indicates that God sees beforehand what our needs are, and He provides for them.

A young newlywed planned to entertain some friends. Lacking some necessary items, she went to a neighbor to borrow them. After giving the items to her, the friend asked, "Is that all you want?" "Yes, I think so," the young bride answered. Then her neighbor, an experienced hostess, handed her some other items, explaining that she would need them as well. Later the young woman remarked, "I was so thankful I went to someone who knew exactly what I needed and was willing to supply it."

How well that describes God. Through the sacrifice of His Son, He has given us salvation. But that's not all. He also provides power through the Holy Spirit so that we can do His will. "He who did not spare His own Son, but delivered Him up for us all, how shall He not with Him also freely give us all things?" (Rom. 8:32). Jehovah-Jireh. The Lord will provide. —P.R.V.

Where God guides, He provides.

Wednesday

PHILIPPIANS 4:10–19

And my God shall supply all your need according
to His riches in glory by Christ Jesus (Philippians 4:19).

Philippians 4:19 is familiar to most Christians. We quote it, write it, and underline it in our Bibles. But do we really believe it? Many of our doubts and nagging worries would disappear if we would draw on the truth these words express.

A tragedy in the family of American pastor Wilbur Chapman made it necessary for him to travel to the West Coast. A banker who attended his church visited him just before he was to leave. As the two men talked, the banker took a piece of paper from his pocket and slipped it into his pastor's hand. When Chapman looked at it, he saw that it was a blank check made out to him and signed by the banker. Stunned, he asked, "Do you mean you are giving me a signed check to fill out as I please?" "Yes," said the banker. "I did not know how much you might require, and I want you to draw any amount that will meet your need." Chapman gratefully accepted the check, but he didn't need to use it on his trip. Later he commented, "It gave me a comfortable, happy feeling to know that I had a vast sum at my disposal."

Man's resources cannot be compared with God's unlimited provisions. But this story helps us appreciate the abundant supply we have in Jesus. We can look at Philippians 4:19 as a check made out to the obedient believer, guaranteeing that the deposit of "riches in glory" will never fail. We can count on God's supply, because the check is signed by God Himself. —P.R.V.

Divine resources are never exhausted.

Thursday

"For in Him we live and move and have our being"
(Acts 17:28).

When life gets heavy, humor lightens the load. I have heard, for example, that in Russia peasant farmers enjoy telling this story: A commissar came to a farmer one day and inquired about the year's potato crop. "Oh, it was wonderful," replied the farmer. "Good, good," said the official. "Just how big was it?" "Oh, it was so big it reached up to the very foot of God." The commissar's countenance changed. With a scowl, he said, "But comrade, this is a communist state and we are atheists. You must not forget, there is no God!" "That's right, commissar, that's what I mean. No God—no potatoes."

A deep truth lies hidden in this humorous tale. God is the source of all things—whether we admit it or not. The apostle Paul went so far as to tell his pagan audience, "For in Him we live and move and have our being" (Acts 17:28). And he focused the great creating and sustaining work of God in the person of His Son, Jesus Christ (Col. 1:16–18). Without Him, we could not draw a single breath, our bodies could not function, and we would have no provision for our daily sustenance.

Atheists may have convinced themselves that God does not exist. Yet we who are His children through faith in His Son know otherwise. But do we show it by the way we live? That is the key question. Each day we must depend on Him, so that we recognize every blessing as coming from His gracious hand. —D.J.D.

However long the chain of secondary causes,
the first link is always in God's hand.

Friday

LUKE 12:22-34

Delight yourself also in the LORD, and He shall give you the desires of your heart (Psalm 37:4).

God promises to provide the necessities of life, such as food and clothing. Once we have accepted this, we have laid the foundation for genuine contentment.

"As World War II was drawing to a close, the Allied armies gathered up many hungry orphans. They were placed in camps where they were well-fed. Despite excellent care, they slept poorly. They seemed nervous and afraid. Finally, a psychologist came up with the solution. Each child was given a piece of bread to hold after he was put to bed. . . . This particular piece of bread was just to be held—not eaten. The piece of bread produced wonderful results. The children went to bed knowing instinctively they would have food to eat the next day. That guarantee gave the children a restful and contented sleep" (Charles L. Allen, *God's Psychiatry*).

For most of us, the refrigerator and the cupboard contain enough food for tomorrow's meals. Yet, like those children, we still feel a gnawing anxiety. Why is this? Either we do not trust God or we think we need more than we have. We have substituted desire for need and need for desire. Even Psalm 37:4, "Delight yourself also in the LORD, and He shall give you the desires of your heart," is not an unconditional promise that God will give us whatever we want. We must first delight ourselves in Him. Then our desires will be in line with what He desires to give us—and that will bring us true contentment. —D.J.D.

Contentment comes not from greater wealth but from fewer wants.

Saturday

MATTHEW 6:25–34

"For your heavenly Father knows that you need all these things" (Matthew 6:32).

If we could look behind the unexpected events in our lives, we would be amazed to see God wonderfully providing for our needs. The insignificant turns in the road, the seemingly unimportant events, the often unexplained happenings—all are part of God's loving care.

His gracious providence is also evident in our tangible provisions. In Bristol, England, George Müller operated an orphanage for two thousand children. One evening, knowing they had no food for breakfast the next morning, Müller called his workers together and explained the situation. After two or three prayed, Muller said, "That is sufficient. Let us rise and praise God for prayer answered." The next morning they could not push open the great front door. To see what was holding it closed, they went out the back door and around the building. Stacked up against the front door were boxes filled with food. One of the workers later remarked, "We know Who sent the baskets, but we do not know who brought them!"

God uses many messengers and means to deliver His gifts, whether they are material or spiritual provisions. We may not always recognize that His hand is working behind the scenes, but it is. Sometimes we get down to the last of our resources, but we can rest assured that the Father knows exactly what we need. And this brings contentment to our hearts. Knowing the Source, we can leave to Him the method of His supply. —P.R.V.

God often sends His help by way of human hands.

Week 7

JOSEPH IN EGYPT

Joseph said to them, "Do not be afraid, for am I in the place of God? But as for you, you meant evil against me; but God meant it for good, in order to bring it about as it is this day, to save many people alive" (Genesis 50:19–20).

THEME

GOD'S SOVEREIGNTY

Writing of humanity's limited view of God's sovereignty, John Newton jested: "If you think you see the ark of the Lord falling, you can be sure it is due to a swimming in your head."

In contrast to our finite focus, God sees and knows the when, why, and how of life. And sovereignty means that God controls it all. He certainly did for Joseph. Thrown into a deep, dark pit and then sold to traders by his jealous brothers, Joseph may have questioned God's sovereign plan. But God saw Joseph even in the shadows. And when the camel caravan arrived in Egypt, God was there to meet him.

On the cross, Jesus cried out, "My God, why have You forsaken Me?" Yet three days after Joseph of Arimathea sealed Jesus in a pitch black tomb, God was there to meet Him. The glorious ending of the Joseph story shed a small shaft of light on God's sovereignty, but a brighter and wider beam filled the darkness when an angel said of the seemingly forsaken Christ, "He is not here; for He is risen."

If Jesus struggled with God's plan and then entrusted Himself to the sovereign Ruler of the universe, we can confidently follow Him out of the tomb into the sunshine.

Sunday

GENESIS 45:1–8

"You meant evil against me;
but God meant it for good" (Genesis 50:20).

I am thankful and reassured that God is so wise and so powerful that nothing, absolutely nothing, can cause His purposes to fail. In fact, He is able to take even those things meant for evil and make them work for good.

Joseph's brothers hated him so much that they plotted his murder. Instead, they sold him as a slave to some Ishmaelite traders. In Egypt he gained the favor of Pharaoh, who gave him a position of responsibility second only to that of the king. During a famine, his brothers came to him for food, not realizing who he was. When Joseph finally identified himself, he spoke this assuring word to them: "Do not therefore be grieved or angry with yourselves because you sold me here; for God sent me before you to preserve life" (Gen. 45:5). Later he said to his brothers, "But as for you, you meant evil against me; but God meant it for good, in order to bring it about, as it is this day, to save many people alive" (Gen. 50:20).

To me, that's both exciting and encouraging. I am reassured to realize that no matter what someone might do to harm me, the Lord is able to turn it into my benefit and His glory.

When we are discouraged because of distressing circumstances, we can rejoice in God's wisdom, power, and sovereignty. Romans 8:28 is still true. God is working all things for our good. —R.W.D.

Setbacks pave the way for comebacks.

Monday

"He knows the way that I take; when He has tested me, I shall come forth as gold" (Job 23:10).

William Cowper beautifully expressed the unexplainable workings of an all-wise and all-powerful God in one of his familiar hymns. He wrote: "God moves in a mysterious way His wonders to perform; He plants His footsteps in the sea, and rides upon the storm." Because God works mysteriously, we are sometimes perplexed. From our limited point of view, it often appears that everything is out of control. The heavenly Father, however, wants His children to trust Him even when they cannot understand Him.

While Michelangelo was working on St. Peter's Cathedral, other men working on the building criticized him. They didn't like what they saw and told him so. The great artist responded, "Even if I were able to make my plans and ideas clear to you—which I am not—I am not obliged to do so. I must ask you to do your best to help me, and when the work is complete the conception will be better understood." History has confirmed that he was right. Those who found fault with his work did so out of ignorance. Unable to understand what was in the mind of the artist, they couldn't see the whole picture.

Those who go through the deep waters of trial, affliction, or adversity often cannot understand what God is doing. But God knows, and we must trust Him for the outcome. And someday we'll rejoice in God's wise plan. —R.W.D.

**When God is going to do something wonderful,
He often begins with difficulty.**

Tuesday

JOHN 18:33–37

**"For this cause I was born, and for
this cause I have come into the world" (John 18:37).**

God has a plan for our lives that is complete in every detail. The Sovereign of the universe cannot allow any of His plans to be executed haphazardly. He leaves nothing to happenstance. The life of Jesus is a prime example. His coming as a Babe in Bethlehem, His earthly ministry, His death, and His resurrection all took place according to God's purpose. To show that Jesus was determined to do His father's will, Luke wrote, "He steadfastly set His face to go to Jerusalem" (Luke 9:51). Jesus' death was no turn of fate—it was a fulfillment of God's plan. He had come to give His life a ransom for the sins of the world.

It is also true that the life of every Christian has been designed by the heavenly Father to fulfill a specific purpose. C. H. Spurgeon said, "There is not a spider hanging on the king's wall but has its errand; there is not a nettle that grows in the corner of the churchyard but has its purpose. . . . And I will never have it that God created any man, especially any Christian man, to be a blank, and to be a nothing. He made you for an end. Find out what that end is; find out your niche and fill it."

We must learn to view the events of our life from the divine perspective. God has a plan for our lives. Knowing this will cause us to look for ways to serve Him and glorify Him in everything we do. We have a sense of destiny because we know that God has placed us where we are for a purpose. —P.R.V.

Duties belong to us; results belong to God.

Wednesday

PSALM 76:7–12

Surely the wrath of man shall praise You; with the remainder of wrath You shall gird Yourself (Psalm 76:10).

God is in full control of His universe. Much of the world fails to recognize this truth, for few people understand His power. They do not realize that behind human affairs is an unseen hand—the providential hand of Almighty God—shaping the destinies of nations.

Two incidents from history illustrate God's sovereignty particularly well. Domitian, an anti-Christian Roman ruler, thought he was slowing the expansion of the gospel when he banished the apostle John to Patmos. But God was in control, for on that island He gave John the vision that John wrote as the book of Revelation. And Augustus, an earlier ruler, called for a census of his empire, making it possible for Jesus to be born in Bethlehem rather than in Nazareth. Again, God directed the decision, and prophecy was fulfilled.

James Russell Lowell sensed God's supervision when he wrote: "Truth forever on the scaffold, / Wrong forever on the throne. / Yet that scaffold sways the future, / And, behind the dim unknown / Standeth God within the shadow, / Keeping watch above His own."

English clergyman John Nelson Darby echoed that trust when he wrote: "God's ways are behind the scenes; but He moves all the scenes which He is behind. We have to learn this, and let Him work."

God has a plan for the ages—a plan He will accomplish. Although current events often seem to favor the evil one, God will have the last word. He is in control. —P.R.V.

**God's timetable moves slowly,
but it always moves surely.**

Thursday

ROMANS 8:18–28

**We know that all things work together
for good to those who love God (Romans 8:28).**

A man in China raised horses for a living. When one of his prized stallions ran away, his friends gathered at his home to mourn his great loss. After they had expressed their concern, the man raised this question: "How do I know whether what happened is bad or good?" A couple days later the runaway horse returned with several strays following close behind. The same acquaintances again came to his house—this time to celebrate his good fortune. "But how do I know whether it's good or bad?" the old gentleman asked them. That very afternoon the horse kicked the owner's son and broke the young man's leg. Once more the crowd assembled—now to express their sorrow over the incident. "But how do I know if this is bad or good?" the father asked again. A few days later, war broke out. The man's son was exempted from military service because of his broken leg. Again the friends gathered—

From our limited human perspective, we cannot know with certainty how to interpret life's experiences. For the trusting child of God, however, it's altogether different. We can be assured that God is working for our benefit through everything that happens. We do not need to ask, as did the old Chinese gentleman, "How do I know whether it's good or bad?" According to Romans 8:28, we know that it's always for good. —R.W.D.

**What the unbeliever calls good luck
the believer knows to be God's love.**

Friday

How thankful we can be that we serve a God who is sovereign, loving, all-wise, and all-powerful. Nothing frustrates Him. Nothing stops Him. Nothing escapes His attention. He can take all things—both good and bad—and work them together for the benefit of His children. This truth not only gives us great confidence, joy, and peace, but it also enables us to give thanks "in everything" (1 Thess. 5:18).

"God's plan leaves nothing out. All things . . . work together for good—all things, even trials, at which we murmur and complain. The storms which threaten to uproot the trees really root them more firmly and deeply in the soil. The blows that one might think would make the cast-iron brittle really cause it to undergo a sort of [tempering] and increase its strength and tenacity. The enforced rest of sorrow and pain, sickness and disappointment, John Ruskin compares to the rest in which there is no music, but the making of music; not the end of the tune, but a pause in the choral hymn of our lives, during which the Divine Musician beats the time with unvarying count, catching up the next note as if no breaking-place had come between" (A. T. Pierson, *Vital Union with Christ*).

When we love the Lord and pass through deep waters, we can give thanks because we know that all things, even the bad, are working together for our good. —R.W.D.

**God causes many a tight place
to open into the right place.**

Saturday

PSALM 119:73–80

**I know, O LORD, . . . that in faithfulness
You have afflicted me (Psalm 119:75).**

The writer of Psalm 119 learned valuable lessons in the school of affliction, and he filled his words with testimony about the wisdom of God's direction and the faithfulness of His dealings. He discovered that no matter what the secondary causes were, God permitted every difficulty that came his way.

A small girl had been promised she could climb to a nearby hilltop where her brother enjoyed playing. But when she came within sight of the steep, rough path, she drew back. "There isn't a smooth spot anywhere. It's all bumpy and stony!" she exclaimed. "Yes," said her more experienced older brother, "but how would we ever climb to the top if it wasn't? The stones and bumps are what we step on to get there." So too, God allows affliction; He even puts in our path what some might consider to be stumbling blocks. For the believer, however, obstacles can become steppingstones to the higher ground of Christian victory and blessing.

The Lord knows what He's doing, and we can trust Him implicitly. Everything that comes into our lives is either sent by God or permitted. He has designed it for our discipline or for our comfort. No circumstance lies outside His sovereign love. So we can have faith in His calming words, "This thing is from Me" (1 Kings 12:24). —H.G.B.

**Through suffering God teaches us lessons
we would not or could not learn any other way.**

Week 8

THE BURNING BUSH

The bush burned with fire, but the bush was not consumed. . . . God called to him from the midst of the bush and said, "Moses, Moses!. . . Do not draw near this place. Take your sandals off your feet, for the place where you stand is holy ground" (Exodus 3:2, 4–5).

THEME

GOD'S HOLINESS

The great baseball player Stan Musial once hit a single, a triple, and a home run in his first three times at bat. The pitcher Bobo Newsom, however, didn't think Musial was a perfect hitter. He quipped, "He can't hit doubles."

Neither in baseball nor in any other activity can we mortals attain perfection. We are flawed and marred, tainted and defaced, until God transforms us in eternity.

Nor can contaminated humanity comprehend God's holiness. Holiness means to be set apart, and God is separate in His perfection from all His creation.

The beauty of the burning bush was not just its fearsome portrayal of a holy God but its awesome revelation of the flawless Father's concern for His captive children. Speaking from a common bush, He told Moses His plan for rescuing them.

Some of Christ's disciples saw Him in His transcendent glory at the Mount of Transfiguration, but they also watched Him hunger, weep, and die. In His holy humanity, He called us all to burn with His holiness.

Sunday

And Moses hid his face, for he was afraid to look upon God (Exodus 3:6).

According to a doctor at Johns Hopkins University, man is constituted "in nerve and tissue and brain cell and soul" to function best on faith. In other words, God made us so that we realize our greatest potential when we are free from the devastating effects of fear. Yet all of us have fears. Those who deny this are being dishonest with themselves. We are afraid of others, ourselves, the future, the past, unemployment, public opinion—the list is endless!

The Bible mentions no less than two dozen words relating to fear. They range in meaning from terror to timidity, and most carry a negative connotation. But one kind of fear—the fear of the Lord—is positive and health-producing. Scripture tells us that it is the "beginning of knowledge" (Prov. 1:7), that it is "clean" (Ps. 19:9), that it gives "strong confidence" (Prov. 14:26), and that it is "a fountain of life" (Prov. 14:27). But most significantly, we can choose to be controlled by this fear (Prov. 1:29).

Moses expressed this kind of fear when God confronted him from a burning bush that was not consumed. Moses "hid his face, for he was afraid to look upon God" (Exod. 3:6).

The fear of God is reverent trust. We stand in awe of God, His power, and His holiness. We believe His warnings, His commands, His promises. We hold His character in such high respect that we choose "to hate evil" (Prov. 8:13), knowing that all His commands are for our good. By fearing Him we express our devotion to Him. It is the one fear that overcomes all others. —D.J.D.

Only the fear of God can banish the fear of men.

Monday

COLOSSIANS 3:18–25

**Servants, obey. . . , fearing God (Colossians 3:22).
Perfect love casts out fear (1 John 4:18).**

Jesus commands us to love God (Matt. 22:37), yet Paul enjoins us to fear Him (Col. 3:22). But if we love God, shouldn't we be free from fear? Doesn't perfect love cast out fear? My own experience can help answer this question. I love the Lord, but I still have some fear when I think of the day I will stand before Him. I'm not afraid He will send me to hell; I know that Jesus paid the price for my sins. Yet the thought of standing in the presence of a holy God awes me. This element of fear helps me to try to please God. The kind of fear that is cast out by love, though, is a cringing dread of eternal punishment. God has delivered me from that.

The Wind in the Willows, a children's allegory by Kenneth Grahame, illustrates the love-fear relationship. Two animals, Mole and Rat, meet Friend and Helper, who personifies God. Mole shakes as he whispers, "Rat, are you afraid?" "Afraid," murmurs Rat, his eyes brimming with unutterable love—"Afraid! Of him? Oh, never, never! And yet—and yet—oh, Mole, I am afraid!"

Daniel the prophet must have experienced that same feeling. His love for God was great, yet when he met the Lord in a vision he collapsed in fear (Dan. 8:15–27). One glimpse of God's holiness overwhelmed him with a sense of his own sinfulness.

We must love God, but we must also stand in awe of Him. The combination of love and fear is the key to holy living. —H.V.L.

He who doesn't fear God should fear everything else.

Tuesday

PSALM 89:5–17

**For who in the heavens can be
compared to the LORD? (Psalm 89:6).**

Just east of Atlanta is Stone Mountain, the largest outcropping of exposed granite in the world. On the side of the 1700-foot mountain are carvings of Stonewall Jackson, Jefferson Davis, and Robert E. Lee. To demonstrate the immensity of these figures, workmen once set a table and chairs on the scaffolding over Lee's shoulder. Then several people ate lunch on that huge projection of carved granite. Although this monument is enormous, it doesn't appear as impressive from a distance as it does when seen up close. Its greatness overwhelms close observers.

The words of Ethan in Psalm 89 suggest a similar truth about getting to know God. The psalmist's inspired song is filled with praise to the Lord. The writer magnifies His greatness, His mercy, and His faithfulness. The psalmist could say these things because he enjoyed a close personal relationship with God. Such a vision of the Almighty comes only to one who draws near to the Lord and is overwhelmed by His greatness.

The same is true for us. We come to appreciate the greatness of our God more and more as we come into closer fellowship with Him and experience His presence. Ethan could sing of Jehovah, "You have a mighty arm" (v. 13). But that knowledge translates into blessing for those "who know the joyful sound" (v. 15) and walk in the light of the Lord's countenance.

The nearer we come to Him the greater He becomes to us. —P.R.V.

**God can take the place of anything,
but nothing can take the place of God.**

Wednesday

EXODUS 19:1–19

Serve the LORD with fear,
and rejoice with trembling (Psalm 2:11).

My father was a stickler for showing reverence to God. He became indignant when someone quoted a Bible verse in a humorous vein or referred to God lightly. He insisted that all his children sit up straight when he read the Bible at the table, which he did at every meal. He addressed the Lord in a manner that demonstrated his wonder that we as sinful creatures could communicate with the holy Maker of all things. Thus, he instilled in all eight of his sons a healthy fear of God—an attitude that led to sincere worship and grateful obedience.

The Almighty God wants us to call Him "Father," and He invites us to come boldly into His presence. Yet hundreds of Bible passages in both the Old and the New Testaments make it clear that we must never lose an attitude of reverential awe. Exodus 19 records a unique combination of awesome events that gave the Israelites a proper sense of reverence. God caused a huge fire to rise from the top of the mountain. He produced deafening roars of rolling thunder and blinding flashes of fierce lightning. He made the mountain quake. He generated a trumpet sound that grew louder and louder. And the sound of His voice when He spoke to Moses filled the people with profound respect and reverential fear.

How great and holy is our God. How small and weak are we humans. A continual awareness of this contrast will cause us to "serve the LORD with fear, and rejoice with trembling." —H.V.L.

True worship acknowledges the true worth-ship of God.

Thursday

JOB 42:1–6

He who is coming after me is mightier than I, whose sandals I am not worthy to carry (Matthew 3:11).

As we become more like the Savior, we become more deeply aware of our own sinfulness. This paradox is not the result of morbid introspection nor evidence of a warped self-image. It's an honest recognition of who we are, who Christ is, and how much we long to be like Him.

The caretaker of the home where Beethoven spent his final years led a group of tourists to the room that housed a stately old piano. Lifting the cover with an air of reverence, he said, "This was Beethoven's piano!" A young woman stepped forward, sat down on the music stool, and began playing one of Beethoven's sonatas. Concluding, she spun around and said to the shocked caretaker, "I suppose many people who visit here like to play Beethoven's piano." "Well, Miss," he replied, "last summer the world famous Paderewski was here, and some of his friends wanted him to play, but he said, 'No, I am not worthy.'"

After a glimpse of God's holiness, Isaiah cried out, "Woe is me!" (Isa. 6:5). At the end of his suffering, Job humbly confessed, "Therefore I abhor myself, and repent in dust and ashes" (Job 42:6). And John the Baptist said of the Messiah, "He who is coming after me is mightier than I, whose sandals I am not worthy to carry." A healthy sense of our unworthiness before God makes us rely more than ever on the worthiness of Jesus. That's the secret of becoming like Him. —D.J.D.

**It is only when men begin to worship
that they begin to grow.**

Friday

"Holy, holy, holy, is the LORD of hosts;
the whole earth is full of His glory" (Isaiah 6:3).

God can do nothing that conflicts with His holy character. What He is determines what He does. Since He is holy by nature, all His attributes share in that perfection. Consider the following:

1. As a holy God, He is perfect in His righteousness. We can fully surrender to His will, because we are confident that He will always do with us what is right. The answer to Abraham's question in Genesis 18:25, "Shall not the Judge of all the earth do right?" is an unmistakable yes.

2. As a holy God, He is perfect in His justice. We can know that His judgment will be unquestionably fair. The believer will be judged "according to what he has done" (2 Cor. 5:10). And at the Great White Throne, the wicked will be judged "according to his works" (Rev. 20:13).

3. As a holy God, He is perfect in His truthfulness. We can take Him at His Word. Numbers 23:19 says, "God is not a man, that He should lie. . . . Has He said, and will He not do? Or has He spoken, and will He not make it good?"

4. As a holy God, He is perfect in His faithfulness. We can depend on Him. He will never let us down. We read, "Through the LORD's mercies we are not consumed, because His compassions fail not. They are new every morning; great is Your faithfulness" (Lam. 3:22–23).

We can have absolute confidence in our righteous, just, truthful, and faithful God. He is holy. —R.W.D.

**The holiness of God that convicts the sinner
comforts the saint.**

Saturday

**Those who worship Him must worship Him
in spirit and in truth (John 4:24).**

God, the infinitely holy One, is worthy of our worship. He is our Creator, Sustainer, and Savior. Without His loving care and guidance we would have no hope. We must therefore take the time and put forth the effort to worship Him in a way that brings honor and glory to His name.

When Jesus spoke to the Samaritan woman, He said, "God is Spirit; and those who worship Him must worship in spirit and truth." In the devotional classic *The Practice of the Presence of God,* Brother Lawrence explains what this means. "To worship God in truth is to recognize . . . that God is what He is; that is to say, infinitely perfect, infinitely to be adored, infinitely removed from evil, and thus with every attribute divine." Brother Lawrence then added, "What man shall there be, however small the reason he may have, who will not use all his strength to render to this great God his reverence and worship?"

We need to ask ourselves if this is the way we worship the One who made us? Do we reverence and adore Him from the deepest part of our minds and souls—from the heart? Are we totally honest before Him about what we are? Do we acknowledge who He is? To give Almighty God the honor of which He is worthy, we must approach Him "in spirit and truth." —D.C.E.

Christ is not valued at all until He is valued above all.

Week 9

THE EXODUS

As the LORD commanded Moses and Aaron, so they did. And it came to pass, on that very same day, that the LORD brought the children of Israel out of the land of Egypt (Exodus 12:51).

THEME

FREEDOM

Samuel Bowles, the nineteenth-century American journalist, speaking of slavery, pinpointed the origin of all personal emancipation when he said, "The cause of freedom is the cause of God."

Freedom has its source in the very essence of God, who is totally free to do whatever He wishes. In contrast, we humans are rarely free to do what we desire, and pursuing our desires leads only to more bondage.

Human bondage has been people's plight since God evicted earth's first couple from Eden. The irony of the story is that Adam and Eve started down slavery street by exercising their free will. Although they were the first to plod the prison path, their sons and daughters followed their footsteps.

The Egyptian bondage stands out because God's chosen nation was held captive by pagan rulers. Their bondage was physical, but the issues were spiritual: They worshiped heathen gods and doubted God's promises. Egyptian and Israelite souls were in chains.

In the Exodus and its Passover prelude, God set Jewish bodies and hearts free. But their freedom was short-lived; Assyrian, Babylonian, and Roman domination followed.

The New Testament Jews expected Jesus to set them free from Roman rule; instead a kangaroo court tried and killed Him. What He taught them in life, He demonstrated in death: a life lost is a life gained, and a life found is a life freed.

Sunday

EXODUS 5:1–14, 22, 23

Whoever walks wisely will be delivered (Proverbs 28:26).

The local TV weatherman pointed to his map and said, "Well, friends, I'm afraid that before things get better, they're going to get worse." His forecast could have applied to Israel as God prepared to rescue His people from their slave-camp conditions. The barometer of events was falling rapidly; and the dark, threatening skies would soon turn into a churning, flashing storm of oppression. Earlier the people had talked excitedly about deliverance. Everything looked promising. But something seemed to go wrong. Moses, the designer of the great escape, became Moses, the source of unneeded pain. All of his talk of freedom had only angered the Egyptians, compounding Israel's predicament. As far as Pharaoh was concerned, slaves that had time to dream of freedom had too much time. So he multiplied their production quotas and took away their resources. The situation went from bad to worse. Personally humiliated, Moses bitterly cried out to the Lord for an explanation.

Time, however, showed that the plans of the Lord were not being frustrated. The great "people's express" was getting ready to leave Egypt. All was on schedule. The Lord was deliberately testing His children by allowing their suffering to get worse before it got better.

We can find courage in this. When the world closes in, we know that our condition is not determined by the authorities of this world but by the Lord who is above the world. —M.R.D.II

The darkest hour lies nearest the dawn.

Monday

JOHN 8:31–45

For he who is called in the Lord while a slave is the Lord's freedman (1 Corinthians 7:22).

The image of a duck flying through the air with an arrow embedded in her body is still fresh in my memory. A local newspaper carried the story and picture of a mallard duck that had eluded rescuers who wanted to remove the foreign object. A couple of months later a Canada goose flew into Wisconsin with the same problem. A young bow hunter had hit his mark, but his arrow hadn't stopped the bird. She had evaded game wardens, avoided tranquilizer-laced grain, and even dodged cannon-fired nets. After about a month, apparently exhausted from her injury, the goose was caught with a fishing net. Soon after surgery, veterinarians returned her to freedom. If geese could think, she probably wondered why she had tried so hard and for so long to elude her captors.

The experience of these reluctant captives reminds me of the men Christ spoke to in John 8. They too were slow to realize the seriousness of their condition. They didn't understand Christ's motives. To them, He looked like a captor. He wanted them to surrender their lives to Him. He asked them to become His disciples. He implored them to become spiritual bond-slaves. They were unable to comprehend that by surrendering they could "be made free" (v. 33).

Is it possible we have forgotten that real freedom is found only in being secure in Christ? This relates not only to our ultimate salvation but also to our daily walk with the Lord.

As servants of Christ, we are bound to be free. —M.R.D.II

**Salvation produces a change within
that releases the chains of sin.**

Tuesday

ISAIAH 1:1–20

"Come now, and let us reason together,"
says the LORD (Isaiah 1:18).

The Grand Rapids Press reported an ironic turn of events that happened to a group of motorcyclists traveling to the state capital to protest Michigan's motorcycle helmet law. The group was scheduled to meet at the capitol building to make some speeches and symbolically burn their helmets. But on the way to the protest, one of the bikers lost control of his machine and slammed into a construction warning sign. He suffered head and facial injuries that most likely would have been avoided if he had been wearing a helmet.

Sometimes we are like those cyclists. We look at the ways of the Lord as unnecessarily restrictive. Yet we ask for and expect His protection and blessing while we resist, rebel, and misunderstand His loving guidelines.

But our efforts to be free from restraint have not brought more happiness, freedom, peace, or satisfaction. Instead, we have lost honor, purpose, and security. Those who insist on doing things their way see an increase in disease, divorce, abuse, and violence. No society has ever profited by disobeying the Lord.

We don't like having our style cramped by laws. But when we read the first chapter of Isaiah and consider the alternative, we realize that one principle stands behind every restriction our Lord gives us: It's always for our good. —M.R.D.II

Don't blame the rule if you don't measure up.

Wednesday

Having begun in the Spirit, are you now
being made perfect by the flesh? (Galatians 3:3).

An article in our local newspaper told about an inmate in a penitentiary who had lived all but sixteen months of his thirty-nine years in various penal institutions. Born in a women's reformatory of a convict mother, he spent the first fourteen years of his life in prison as a ward of the court. When he was released, he committed a succession of crimes. He explained his behavior by saying, "I don't know how to live on the outside. My home is inside, and I want to stay here for the rest of my life." This unfortunate man found security in his bondage.

Likewise, adhering to external religious restraints can be easier than serving God in the liberty of the Spirit. This is why some first-century believers in Galatia wanted to live under the Mosaic law, even though in Christ they were no longer bound by it. Apparently they discovered that "freedom" can be frightening.

Many Christians follow a similar pattern. They look for security by placing themselves under a legalistic system that calls for no more than good external behavior. In many instances, the do's and don'ts are merely cultural, not biblical. Although their outward conduct may be honorable, they are actually escaping into a subtle kind of bondage. Obedience to accepted standards has value only when our actions reflect a changed heart and express gratitude to God for His salvation.

We must not hide behind the walls of legalism to avoid the freedom of life on the outside. —M.R.D.II

Only those who are bound to Christ are truly free.

Thursday

JAMES 1:1–12

The testing of your faith produces patience
(James 1:3).

One of the delights of my carefree days of childhood was flying a kite. What happy, peaceful hours I enjoyed with that soaring paper bird tugging on the string anchored to my finger! But if that kite could have talked, it might have said, "Look how high I'm flying and how gracefully I'm floating through the sky. And I'm doing all this in spite of that aggravating boy down there hanging onto the end of the string. I don't need that. Look, I have a tail and broad wings, but that pesky kid is hanging onto that cord as if he expects me to lift him into the wind. Why, if I didn't have the handicap of this string he is holding, I could fly up and reach the moon. If only I were not tied down in this irritating way."

Sometimes when flying my kite I would be distracted and I'd let go of the string. The kite would go wobbling down and become tangled in the branches of a tree. What might that proud paper bird have said then? If it had been an honest kite, it would have admitted, "The very thing I thought was tying me down was holding me up."

Likewise, much of our Christian growth and spiritual progress can be credited to our trials and testings, which so often make us fret. If God were to remove the restrictions that go with these difficult experiences, our lives would be wobbly and weak like that wandering kite. "The testing of your faith produces patience," James said. These testings are the rewarding restraints of One who desires to see His children soar to spiritual heights. —P.R.V.

**Adversity is only sand on your track
to prevent you from skidding.**

Friday

ROMANS 5:12–21

Through one Man's righteous act the free gift came to all men, resulting in justification of life (Romans 5:18).

At noon on January 1, 1863, Abraham Lincoln received the final draft of the Emancipation Proclamation. Twice the president picked up his pen to sign it, and twice he laid it down. Turning to Secretary of State William Seward, he said, "I have been shaking hands since 9:00 this morning, and my right arm is almost paralyzed. If my name ever goes into history, it will be for this act, and my whole soul is in it. If my hand trembles when I sign the proclamation, all who examine the document hereafter will say, 'He hesitated.'" The president then took up the pen again and slowly but firmly wrote, "Abraham Lincoln." That historic act endeared Lincoln to the world as the Great Emancipator.

One greater than Lincoln and with even surer resolve brought freedom to the human race. Jesus signed our liberty with His own blood by dying on the cross to release us from the awful slavery of sin. Oswald Chambers wrote, "Never tolerate the idea of martyrdom about the cross of Jesus Christ. The cross was a superb triumph in which the foundations of hell were shaken. [Jesus Christ] . . . made the redemption the basis of human life, that is, He made a way for every son of man to get into communion with God."

Having trusted the Savior, we are free from sin's condemnation. By His Spirit we have the power to turn from sin and live for Him. And doing so is the only way to honor Christ—our Great Emancipator.

—D.J.D.

The empty tomb assures a full salvation.

Saturday

PROVERBS 16:16–33

He is caught in the cords of his sin
(Proverbs 5:22).

Everybody longs for freedom. But for many people its pursuit leads to bondage. Beloved Bible teacher Henrietta Mears knew the secret of true freedom, and she wanted her students to know it too. With young people in mind, she said, "A bird is free in the air. Place a bird in the water and he has lost his liberty. A fish is free in the water, but leave him on the sand and he perishes. He is out of his realm. So, young people, the Christian is free when he does the will of God and is obedient to God's command. This is as natural a realm for God's child as the water is for the fish, or the air for the bird."

Wise King Solomon urged his son to understand that true freedom is possible only within the sphere of God-centered living, for which He created us. By contrast, bondage predictably and inescapably comes to anyone who ignores God's truth. Proverbs 16 describes the liberty and satisfaction that come from practicing humility, trust, careful conversation, and self-control. But it also warns about the inevitable bondage that comes into the lives of people governed by willful rebellion, pride, arrogance, strife, and malicious trouble-making.

The New Testament introduces us to Jesus—the ultimate source of our freedom. He, our Creator and Redeemer, said, "If you abide in My word, you are My disciples indeed. And you shall know the truth, and the truth shall make you free" (John 8:31–32). —M.R.D.II

**True freedom is not having our own way,
but yielding to God's way.**

Week 10

TEN COMMANDMENTS

And Moses said to the people, "Do not fear; for God has come to test you, and that His fear may be before You, so that you may not sin" (Exodus 20:20).

THEME

LAW

Alexander Solzhenitsyn told the 1978 graduates of Harvard, "I have spent all my life under a Communist regime, and I will tell you that a society without any objective legal scale is a terrible one indeed. But a society with no other scale but the legal one is not quite worthy of man either."

More than three thousand years ago God gave Moses an objective legal document to guide Israel. The Ten Commandments provided moral guidance, and the other laws gave Israel civil, legal, personal, religious, and social instructions.

In the brutal and cruel ancient world, Israel's legal code was a model of wisdom and justice. As a gift from God, it gave every Jew the basis for receiving God's blessing, though no one could live up to its high standards.

The law revealed God's character and each person's sin. In these ways it pointed people to a holy life, but it could not produce right living.

What the law could not do, Jesus did. With His life and death, He replaced the old scale with a perfect new model: Love. Simple, complex love. The Jews couldn't get the old model out of their heads, and Gentile believers couldn't figure out how to use the new one. But for the first time, God gave His people a moral system that fully revealed His character and was worthy of His creation.

Sunday

ROMANS 7:1–6

You who make your boast in the law, do you
dishonor God through breaking the law? (Romans 2:23).

A twenty-five year veteran of the Internal Revenue Service was convicted of income tax evasion. The IRS auditor was caught trying to
exploit what he thought was a flaw in the system. About the time that
story made headlines, the *Detroit News* ran a feature article on the
growing problem of the unethical and immoral conduct of some criminal court judges. The article raised the question, "Who's going to
judge the judges?"

The lawlessness of people familiar with the law is not confined to
courtrooms and the IRS. There is one law that we all have broken—
God's law. Worse than that, some religious people take pride in their
relationship to that law. Without fail, these people are exposed by the
very law they love. The law of God reveals all self-professed lawkeepers
to be lawbreakers.

Writing to the Romans, Paul made it clear that the law of God should
never be used as a basis for self-righteous pride. Instead, it should be
used to show how much we all need God's mercy. The law is a school-
master or tutor to bring us to Christ so that we can be justified by faith
(Gal. 3:24). Only when we rely on God's mercy rather than on our
record of keeping the law will we bring honor to the Lord. And only then
can we be "delivered from the law" (Rom. 7:6). —M.R.D.II

In Christ, we can all live above the law.

Monday

ROMANS 8:1–11

For the law of the Spirit of life in Christ Jesus
has made me free from the law of sin and death (Romans 8:2).

Laws seem to encourage lawbreaking. Issue a strong prohibition, and before long somebody breaks it. Tell a little boy he must stay out of the cookie jar, leave him alone in the kitchen, and what happens? The command creates in him an irresistible desire for one of the forbidden treats. He looks longingly; he yields. Had the order not been issued, the youngster may not have become an offender.

We respond in much the same way to God's holy law. It seems to incite us to do the very thing it is intended to prevent. This is because another law, "the law of sin and death" (Rom. 8:2), also operates within us. Paul said he would not have known covetousness, "unless the law had said, You shall not covet" (Rom. 7:7). That prohibition, when brought in contact with Paul's heart, stirred up within him "all manner of evil desire" (Rom. 7:8). Although the law is good, it has no power to make us obedient.

How then can we fulfill God's law if all it does is condemn us? We must learn to live by "the law of the Spirit of life in Christ Jesus" (Rom. 8:2), which gives us a marvelous freedom and power. It's like flying in an airplane. On the ground the aircraft is subject to gravity. But as it races down the runway, it reaches a point where the laws of aerodynamics displace the law of gravity. So, too, when we yield to what we know is right, God's Spirit takes over, superseding the "law of sin and death," and then we find delight in keeping God's commands (Ps. 119:143). —D.J.D.

Law keeps us limping in the dark;
grace sets us walking in the light.

Tuesday

**Therefore, the law was our tutor
to bring us to Christ (Galatians 3:24).**

The law has never saved anyone, and it never will. God did not give it to redeem us from sin but to show us our need of salvation. That's why the apostle Paul called it "our tutor."

In an unforgettable sermon, evangelist Fred Brown used three images to describe the purpose of the law. First, he likened it to the small mirror dentists use. With the mirror they can detect cavities. But they can't drill with it or use it to pull teeth. The mirror reveals the decayed area or other abnormality, but it can't fix the problem.

Brown then drew another analogy. He said that the law is also like a flashlight. If the lights go out at night, you use it to guide you down the darkened basement stairs to the electrical box. When you point it toward the fuses, it helps you see the one that is burned out. But after you've removed the bad fuse, you don't insert the flashlight in its place. You put in a new fuse to restore the electricity.

In his third image, Brown likened the law to a plumbline. Builders check their work by using a weighted string. If this plumbline reveals that the work is not true to the vertical, the plumbline cannot correct it. The builder must get out a hammer and saw.

Like the mirror, flashlight, and plumbline, the law points out the problem—sin, but it doesn't provide a solution. The only way to salvation is through Jesus Christ, who fulfilled the law. Only He can save. —D.C.E.

The law shows us a need that only grace can fill.

Wednesday

2 CORINTHIANS 5:10–15

**For the love of Christ constrains us
(2 Corinthians 5:14).**

The Lord loves us first, and we in turn love Him. Because we do, we should serve Him out of devotion—not duty. This is the law of love.

A husband and wife didn't really love each other. The man was very demanding, so much so that he prepared a list of rules and regulations for his wife to follow. He insisted that she read them every day and obey them to the letter. Among other things, his "do's and don'ts" indicated such details as what time she had to get up in the morning, when his breakfast should be served, and how the housework should be done.

A few years after the husband died, the woman fell in love with another man, one who dearly loved her, and they were married. This husband did everything he could to make his new wife happy, continually showering her with tokens of his appreciation. One day as she was cleaning house, she found tucked away in a drawer the list of commands her first husband had written for her. As she looked it over, she realized that even though her new husband hadn't given her any kind of list, she was doing everything her first husband's list required. She was so devoted to this man that her deepest desire was to please him out of love, not obligation. Doing things for him was her greatest joy.

So it should be with us in our relationship to Christ. Because He loves us, we love Him and want to serve Him. That's the law of love.
—R.W.D.

**Serving Christ under law is duty;
under love it's delight.**

Thursday

ROMANS 8:29–39

Who shall bring a charge against God's elect?
It is God who justifies (Romans 8:33).

A cat burglar in Northville, Michigan, knows from experience what it is like to live above the law. The story began with a missing diamond ring. Although authorities located the robber, they made no arrest. With tongue-in-cheek, a state trooper described the thief as "small of stature, fleet of foot, and moving with a great deal of stealth." He also explained that because of the suspect's age and first-offender status, no charges could be filed. The real reason for letting the culprit go was that he was not subject to the law. The burglar was the complainant's 7-month-old kitten. The pet was implicated by a metal detector that beeped when waved over the animal. X-rays later confirmed their suspicions. The kitten, of course, was not booked; cats live above the law.

This amusing story reminds us of the Christian's position in relation to God's law. In Romans 8, Paul tells of those who will never be accused and tried by the court of heaven. And in Romans 4:8, the apostle said, "Blessed is the man to whom the LORD shall not impute sin." Of such a person he asks, "Who shall bring a charge against God's elect? It is God who justifies." Believers live above the law because the cross of Christ protects them from eternal condemnation.

If we become careless about sin, we will suffer pain and loss and be disciplined. But, praise God, we will not be sentenced to hell. Christ has delivered us from the curse of the law. —M.R.D.II

When I'm justified through Christ's merits,
God looks at me "just as if I'd" never sinned.

Friday

The letter kills, but the Spirit gives life (2 Corinthians 3:6).

A group of ministers attending an evangelistic conference gave testimonies as to how they came to know Christ. Most spoke of dramatic conversions. One pastor, however, had been born into a Christian home and had grown up in the church. "It seems from my earliest years I have always known and loved the Lord," he said. The other clergymen couldn't identify with this, since most of them remembered a definite time and place when they trusted in Jesus. The first minister quickly added, "But I do remember when 'have to' became 'want to.'"

Yes, that's the key to knowing that our faith is real. The Holy Spirit fills us with a love for God that creates a desire to keep His commands for Christian living, not from force but from the impulse of a renewed heart. That's what Paul meant when he said that "the letter kills, but the Spirit gives life."

If our service for the Lord is all "have to" but no "want to," we have probably become legalistic, having substituted adherence to man-made rules for loving obedience to God's commands. We need to ponder again the great price Jesus paid for our redemption. God exposed His heart of love for us. He inflicted on His beloved Son the punishment we deserve so that we could be forgiven. As we confess our sins and ask the Holy Spirit to fill us, we'll experience afresh His marvelous love. And this will bring us back to the place where "want to" replaces "have to." —D.J.D.

**Legalism weighs us down;
love lifts us up.**

Saturday

But beware lest somehow this liberty of yours become a stumbling block to those who are weak (1 Corinthians 8:9).

Many states in the U.S. allow motorists to make a right turn when the traffic signal is red—if the way is clear. This gives drivers liberty and keeps traffic moving. At some intersections, however, signs say, "No turn on red." These corners are exceptions because they are potential danger spots. By turning on red there, a motorist could cause a serious accident.

In 1 Corinthians 8, we have a similar situation concerning Christian liberty. Paul had perfect freedom to eat meat offered to idols. He knew that there was only one true God and that idols were nothing. Eating meat offered to them was neither right nor wrong. But not all believers felt that way. A person who had a weak conscience believed that the meat was defiled by the idol, and therefore it was off limits. Paul recognized the need to take special care lest by eating he would influence such a person to eat, thus violating his conscience. Concern for weaker believers kept him from exercising his liberty.

As Christians, we are free in Christ—free to engage in social practices and customs not specifically forbidden by biblical commands. Yet the Holy Spirit may prompt us to refrain from some legitimate practices. Then the principle of love must take precedence over the principle of liberty. A mature Christian will heed the "no turn on red" sign to keep from causing a weaker believer "to have a serious accident." —D.J.D.

**None of us has a right to do as we please,
unless we please to do right.**

Week 11

DAY OF ATONEMENT

"This shall be an everlasting statute for you, to make atonement for the children of Israel, for all their sins, once a year" (Leviticus 16:34).

THEME

ATONEMENT

On Easter Sunday in 1908, William Grenfell, a missionary doctor in Labrador, started a sixty-mile journey with his sled dog team to help a desperately ill person. To shorten the trip, he decided to cross a frozen bay, though he knew the ice had begun melting.

The ice broke and Grenfell and his dogs fell into the frigid water. The doctor and three dogs crawled onto a floating piece of ice. To keep himself from freezing to death, he eventually killed his three dogs and covered himself with their bloody skins.

Grenfell struggled for physical survival and found it in a bloody covering. So in a way did ancient Israel. God's people fought both nature and themselves, and their internal battle with sin produced never-ending guilt. In the various tabernacle offerings, God provided a way for people to relieve their guilt through bloody sacrifices. The word *atone* may mean "to cover." Thus in atonement the blood of a slain animal hid a person's sin, bringing forgiveness and access to God.

Because the people could never stop sinning, the need for animals was never ending. The priest was as much butcher as confessor. At best, he had a grisly task.

No less nauseating was Golgotha. No less unfathomable is the mystery of blood—shed to cover the sins of the whole world.

Sunday

ACTS 20:17–27

**"Nor do I count my life dear to myself,
so that I may finish my race with joy" (Acts 20:24).**

In religious art, the pelican has long been a symbol of self-sacrifice. Having observed these strange birds while fishing in gulf coast waters off Florida, I have a difficult time thinking of them as "self-denying saints." They seem more like lazy freeloaders. With pitiful stares that mask hearts full of envy, they look lustfully at every fish I catch. Once in a while, they even try to intercept one before I can reel it in.

Their behavior, however, is not the reason they have become symbols of self-sacrifice. The reason is their appearance. The tip of a pelican's huge beak appears to have been dipped in red dye. According to legend, when a mother pelican cannot find food for her young, she thrusts her beak into her breast and nourishes her little ones with her own blood. The early church saw in this tale a beautiful picture of what Christ did for us and what we in turn should do for one another.

The legend of the pelican, then, not only speaks of the Savior, but also of us, God's blood-bought children. As fallen humans, we are more generally known by our greed than by our self-sacrifice. But that can change. Through faith in Christ's atoning death, we are forgiven and transformed. Therefore, we should no longer be characterized by selfishness. As new creatures, we can, like Christ, practice the art of self-sacrificing love. —M.R.D.II

Nothing satisfies God but the voluntary sacrifice of love.

Monday

1 JOHN 4:7–11

Behold what manner of love
the Father has bestowed on us! (1 John 3:1).

On the chapel wall at Eagle Village, a residential treatment center for boys near Hersey, Michigan, hang the portraits of two twelve-year-old boys—Rick and Rosy. The pictures bring to mind a tragedy that happened several years ago. Boys from Eagle Village were on a canoe expedition on Lake Superior when they pulled ashore to make camp. Rosy spotted something floating in the water, so he pushed off in a canoe to retrieve it. Strong winds quickly blew him offshore. The staff recognized his peril and started off in two canoes to rescue him. When Rick saw that his best friend was in danger, he insisted on going along. The wind tossed all three canoes until finally they capsized. The staff members all made it to shore. But Rick and Rosy were both lost in the depths of Lake Superior. A plaque between the pictures is inscribed: *Rick, who loved enough to give his life for another. Rosy, who was loved enough to have another pay that price.*

This story calls to mind "what manner of love the Father has bestowed on us." He loved us enough to give His Son to die as payment for our sin. And we were loved enough that He would willingly make that sacrifice. Our salvation is the best demonstration of the power of love. —D.C.E.

The true measure of God's love
is that He loves without measure.

Tuesday

HEBREWS 9:11–28

In whom we have redemption through His blood, the forgiveness of sins (Colossians 1:14).

Having trusted Christ as our Savior, we should never cease to glory in His sacrifice for us on the cross. The reality of being identified with Christ in His death, burial, and resurrection should fill us with gratitude in the morning, give us refuge throughout the day, and be a pillow at night upon which to rest.

A small detachment of British troops, surprised by an overwhelming enemy force, fell back under heavy fire. Their wounded lay in a perilous position, facing certain death. They all realized they had to come immediately under the protection of a Red Cross flag if they wanted to survive. All they had was a piece of white cloth, but no red paint. So they used the blood from their wounds to make a large cross on that white cloth. Their attackers respected that grim flag as it was held aloft, and the British wounded were brought to safety (Sir Arthur Conan Doyle, *The Great Boer War*).

Our enemy not only must respect the blood of Christ shed on Calvary's cross, he also is helpless against it. Christ's blood represents the sacrifice of One whose death removed the guilt and condemnation of our sin and broke its hold over us. It is absolute protection against the accusation of Satan, the defeating remembrances of past sins, and the downpull of our Adamic nature. No wonder we glory in the cross.

—D.J.D.

Calvary stands for Satan's fall.

Wednesday

1 CORINTHIANS 1:18–25

For Jews request a sign, and Greeks seek after wisdom; but we preach Christ crucified (1 Corinthians 1:22–23).

When the Lord Jesus came to live on the earth, He came at the Word of the Father (John 1). Everything He said and did was in obedience to God's will and therefore was a true expression of His Father's loving heart. Yet it was not by Christ's great teaching nor through His astounding miracles that He best represented the eternal purposes of God. Rather, He proclaimed the Father's love most eloquently by His sacrificial death on the cross.

A furniture maker trying to explain the theory of his designs to a blind yeoman said that he believed he could express himself best through his craft. "Artists," he said, "express themselves in colors, in words, in stone; well, I don't see why a man can't express himself in wood." The yeoman, with unusual spiritual insight, responded, "In wood? It has been done, sir; yes, the mightiest expression of a man ever the world knew has been in wood!" "What, yeoman?" asked the craftsman. "Sir," the yeoman replied, "the cross of Christ!" (Arthur Hutchinson, *One Increasing Purpose*).

The sacrificial death of the Lord Jesus was the supreme expression of a loving God. That death, that sacrifice, that proclamation of unending love, was for you and for me. —D.C.E.

**Christ took the guilt of our sin
that we might have the gift of His salvation.**

Thursday

2 CORINTHIANS 5:17–21

**For He made Him who knew no sin
to be sin for us (2 Corinthians 5:21).**

Words cannot fully express the worth of Christ's work for us on the cross. To think that He endured separation from the Father because of our sins staggers our finite minds. Elizabeth Barrett Browning tried to capture the deep theological significance of this in these poetic words: "Deserted! God could separate from His own essence rather; / And Adam's sins have swept between the righteous Son and Father. / Yes, once Immanuel's orphaned cry His universe hath shaken; / It went up single, echoless, 'My God, I am forsaken!'"

A girl in Gary, Indiana, terribly burned in a flash fire, lingered between life and death. A delicate and extensive skin graft offered the only hope for her restoration. When the hospital issued a call for volunteer skin donors, a young boy responded. During the surgery, complications set in and the boy died. But through his sacrifice he made it possible for that young girl to be completely restored.

Nothing in our Lord's life called for His death. He was free from sin's fatal infection. Yet He willingly offered Himself to die in our place. A poet wrote: "He suffered in our stead, / He saved His people thus; / The curse that fell upon His head / Was due by right to us."

Having been restored to God's favor by the sacrifice of His Son, we should lift our hearts to our sinless Substitute. —P.R.V.

**Christ was delivered for sins
that we might be delivered from sin.**

Friday

JOHN 20:26–31

Thomas answered and said to Him,
"My Lord and my God" (John 20:28).

The English preacher Alexander Maclaren once asked, "Why is it that one Person, and one Person only, triumphs over space and time and is the same close Friend with whom millions of hearts are in loving touch, as He was to those that gathered around Him upon the earth?" That is a valid question. The following story, attributed to the British statesman Benjamin Disraeli, will help to answer it.

A young scholar approached Disraeli one day. He had developed a new religion and written a book to explain its doctrines. The young man claimed that his newly devised creed surpassed in beauty the message of Christ and His sacrificial crucifixion on Calvary. Disraeli asked the young man about the success of the book's sales, only to hear him complain that he couldn't get anyone to buy it or to believe in his religion. The old statesman placed his hand on the young man's shoulder and said, "No, my boy, you will never get anyone to read your book and believe in your religion until you too have been crucified on a cross and risen from a tomb."

Only the spotless Son of God, the perfect substitute for sinful man, can provide salvation. Only a dying Savior who validates His sacrifice by bodily resurrection can lift the burden of sin's guilt. Because Jesus loved us and gave Himself for us, we should give Him our love. If we have placed our faith in Him, we can exclaim like Thomas in love and adoration, "My Lord and my God." The Savior deserves our heartfelt worship. —P.R.V.

**When we recognize Jesus' lordship,
we'll give Him our worship.**

Saturday

A young woman went to a Scottish preacher and asked how she could resolve her problem with desires that contradicted the will of God. The minister wrote two words on a slip of paper. Then he asked the woman to ponder the words for ten minutes, cross out one of them, and bring the slip back to him. The woman looked at the two words on the slip: "No" and "Lord." It did not take her long to realize that if she said no, she could not say Lord, and if she wanted to call Christ Lord, she could not say no.

Herein lies the secret of discerning God's will for our lives. We cannot know God's choice concerning the limitless options before us until we put ourselves unconditionally at His disposal. We must turn over all our rights. Presenting our bodies as a living sacrifice is another way of saying "Yes, Lord" to any command. Once we settle the question of our yieldedness, we can take the second step, which is to bring our behavior in line with the renewing of our minds. Renewing occurs only when we pattern our thinking after the principles of God's Word, not the prevailing ideas of the world around us.

If you are trying to discover God's plan for your life, you must first make a complete sacrifice of your body. —D.J.D.

**God gives His very best to those
who leave the choice with Him.**

Week 12

WILDERNESS WANDERINGS

And the LORD went before them by day in a pillar of cloud to lead the way, and by night in a pillar of fire to give them light, so as to go by day and night. He did not take away the pillar of cloud by day or the pillar of fire by night from before the people (Exodus 13:21–22).

THEME

GUIDANCE

In Ruth Ainsworth's retelling of *The Pied Piper of Hamelin,* "he put his pipe to his lips . . . and from every door the children ran. Boys and girls, big and little, all followed the piper . . . to live in a land where everything was better and brighter. . . . The fruit would be sweeter, the flowers would be gayer, and even the sparrows would be as bright as peacocks."

Although Israel followed a cloud by day and a fire by night on their journey to a land flowing with milk and honey, their story is no fairy tale; it is an account of real people and a loving God who guided them through four decades of desert wanderings.

The forty-year pilgrimage began when God paved a high and dry freeway through the Red Sea and then closed it up again before His enemies could use it. Israel packed no picnic lunches; God provided first-class dining daily.

But He not only gave His children fine food, He taught them how to live and worship. Unfortunately, they spurned His loving leadership. Rejecting His good guidance, most of them died in the barren land—over one million of them.

But God is not driving the lead car in a funeral procession; He points the way to life.

Sunday

JOSHUA 1:1–9

I will instruct you and teach you in the way you should go (Psalm 32:8).

An old sailor repeatedly got lost at sea, so his friends gave him a compass and urged him to use it. The next time he went out in his boat, he followed their advice and took the compass with him. But as usual he became hopelessly confused and couldn't find land. "Why didn't you use that compass we gave you?" his friends asked after rescuing him again. "You could have saved us a lot of trouble!" The sailor responded, "I didn't dare to! I wanted to go north, but as hard as I tried to make the needle aim in that direction, it just kept on pointing southeast." That old sailor was so certain he knew which way was north that he stubbornly tried to force his own personal persuasion on his compass. Unable to do so, he tossed it aside as worthless and failed to benefit from its guidance.

The Israelites did much the same thing after God engineered their release from Egyptian captivity. Because they foolishly refused to believe God, they spent forty years making a journey that should have taken a few days.

The psalmist promised that God would instruct us and teach us in the way we should go. He will spare those who follow His instructions and warnings from the waste of foolish wandering and the heartache of shipwreck and ruin. When we ask God to point the way, we must be sure to trust the compass of His Word. —R.W.D.

When you pray for God's guidance, don't complain when it is different from your preferred direction.

Monday

He makes me to lie down in green pastures;
He leads me beside the still waters (Psalm 23:2).

A humble Christian, when beset by a tremendous trial, misquoted Scripture but found great comfort in it. He said, "I'm so glad the Bible tells us, 'It came to pass' and not 'It came to stay.'" Those particular words do not speak of the temporal nature of difficulties, but in other places the Bible clearly teaches that God will see us through our trials. Life is not all hardship. If it were, discouragement would overwhelm us and we would give up.

In Exodus 15 we read that the children of Israel tasted the bitter waters of Marah. But then God led them to Elim where they enjoyed wells of sweet water and the coolness of sheltering palms. The people knew that both stops were by God's direction. His "glory cloud" hovered over them to point the way. When it moved, the Israelites moved; when it stopped, they stopped. That cloud clearly marked both Marah and Elim.

Whenever God leads us to a campsite at Marah, where we experience bitterness, sorrow, or disappointment, we must keep in mind that we will one day drink the sweet water of Elim's wells and feel the refreshing shade of its palms. God's comfort will surely come—both on earth and in heaven. And when we are enjoying the encouragement of Elim, we should rejoice, knowing that God is strengthening us for the rest of the journey. —P.R.V.

**In every desert of calamity,
God has an oasis of comfort.**

Tuesday

PSALM 119:105–112

**Your word is a lamp to my feet,
and a light to my path (Psalm 119:105).**

If you have ever carried a lantern on a dark road at night, you know that you cannot see more than one step ahead of you. But as you take that one step, the lamp moves forward, making the next step plain. You reach your destination safely without once walking in darkness. You have light the entire way, even though it is only enough for one step at a time.

Many Christians who have walked with the Lord for a long time say that this is the way He has led them, and they are assured of reaching their destination. But some travelers become upset when the dark curtain of the unknown veils their pathway. The prospect of lurking dangers, possible pitfalls, and tragic missteps causes them to lose the peace and confidence that the Lord intends for them to enjoy.

The writer of Proverbs said, "Trust in the Lord with all your heart. . . . In all your ways acknowledge Him, and He shall direct your paths" (3:5–6). And David recorded this promise, "I will instruct you and teach you in the way you should go; I will guide you with My eye" (Ps. 32:8).

As we refuse to worry about the "tomorrows" and begin to trust God for the "todays," we can find grace and guidance for each step of the way. We don't need to see beyond what God shows us today. When we follow His leading, we have enough light for each step of the way. It is wonderful to be directed by Him. —R.W.D.

**Hold firm the lantern of truth
and it will guide you aright.**

Wednesday

**In all your ways acknowledge Him,
and He shall direct your paths (Proverbs 3:6).**

Many Christians equate God's leading with an overriding feeling or an inner impression. These strong inclinations, however, are not necessarily proof of God's direction. John Hibben, former president of Princeton University, once invited a guest to dinner. Mr. Buchman, an eccentric believer in divine guidance, arrived late and brought along three uninvited guests. When Buchman shook hands with Mrs. Hibben, he said, "The Lord told me to bring these three other men to dinner, too." Mrs. Hibben, not expecting added company, replied, "Oh, I don't think the Lord had anything to do with it." "Why not?" retorted Buchman. "Because," responded Mrs. Hibben, "God is a gentleman." Mrs. Hibben knew something about God and His ways that Buchman had overlooked.

This exchange raises an important question about the primary source for divine guidance. Strong impressions will come to us, but we must always test them to be sure they are in line with God's revealed will. They must never run contrary to what is true and right. Studying Scripture passages in their context gives us discernment, and meditating on them helps us to evaluate our feelings honestly. In his book *Knowing God,* J. I. Packer cautions, "Feelings with an ego-boosting, or escapist, or self-indulging, or self-aggrandizing base must be detected and discredited, not mistaken for guidance."

That's good counsel—especially since we have a lamp for our feet, and a light for our path. —D.J.D.

Feelings are no substitute for facts and faith.

Thursday

HEBREWS 11:32–12:2

Let us run with endurance the race that is set before us, looking unto Jesus (Hebrews 12:1–2).

In *The Complete Disciple,* Paul W. Powell describes a picture of a rugged wagon train painted by a famous artist of the American West. It is night, and the wagons have been drawn into a circle for protection. The men are gathered around the campfire, and the wagonmaster has a map spread out before him. On the map a heavy black line traces the zigzag course they have followed. They had swung north a little, then south, but always toward the west. An argument seems to have erupted about which way to go next. But the leader, with weary determination, has placed one finger on the end of the black line. With his other arm he is pointing toward the shadowy mountains. He seems to be saying, "We may have to go south around a mountain, or north across a river, but our direction will always be west."

Every Christian should have a similar resolve. Running the Christian race is not always easy. High mountains may stand in our way as we continue on the course God has marked out. Difficult circumstances and temptations may cause us to veer in one direction or another. But if we keep our eyes on the goal by "looking unto Jesus," we will not stray from the path He has outlined. As we stay true to the Lord, we will keep heading toward our goal.

And whenever distractions or temptations cause us to stray off course and lose our way, we can look again to Jesus, confess our sin, and He will help us to keep our eyes on the goal. —D.C.E.

**An obstacle cannot stop us
if we keep our eyes on the goal.**

Friday

ECCLESIASTES 1:1–9

**That which has been is what will be
(Ecclesiastes 1:9).**

All of us are bound to repeat ourselves as we go about our daily routines. We eat, sleep, work, and clean up. Then we do the same things again. When the cycle seems endless, we ask, what's the point of it all?

God, however, would have us view this another way. Repetition holds an important secret for the Christian. Part of God's plan for us is that we yield to His guidance in ordinary recurring events.

The world is like a stage on which the drama of eternity is unfolding. Like a great curtain, the sun rises and falls for every performance. And we, the actors, make a decision every time we "repeat our lines." Either we respond impatiently to the repetitious cues—just to get our part over with—or we use our role as an opportunity to get to know the mind and purpose of the Director. Sure, the circumstances are routine and we often feel that "we've been through it all before." But glad participation in redundant activities forms character, strengthens faith, increases hope, and develops endurance. Through the normal course of events, God says to us, "There is more to your earthly existence than the meaningless round of duties."

Repeatedly trusting the Lord is the surest way to make life routinely fresh. —M.R.D.II

If life is a grind, use it to sharpen your character.

Saturday

Your hand shall lead me, and Your
right hand shall hold me (Psalm 139:10).

In a brief Christmas address to the people of the British Empire in 1939, King George VI spoke of his faith in God's leading. World War II had begun, and Great Britain faced the onslaughts of Hitler's reckless military barrage. As the King spoke to the people on that Christmas day, he concluded his remarks with lines written by Minnie Louise Haskins some thirty years earlier: "And I said to the man who stood at the gate of the year: 'Give me a light that I may tread safely into the unknown.' And he replied: 'Go out into the darkness and put your hand into the Hand of God. That shall be to you better than light and safer than a known way.'"

Like Great Britain back in 1939, each of us faces a future whose trademark is change, overlaid, perhaps, with foreboding circumstances. But we need not fear. We have Someone to guide us even in the darkest night. That's why the psalmist could say, "Your hand shall lead me, and Your right hand shall hold me." God's presence enables the Christian to face tomorrow with complete confidence.

Life holds no surprises for God. No path is unknown to Him—no circumstance unsettling. Because the future is perfectly clear to our Father, Christians have the full assurance that we can follow where God leads, whether the way is marked by calm or storm.

We can confidently put our hand in God's, for He forgives the past, controls the present, and holds the future. —P.R.V.

Those who see God's hand in everything
can best leave everything in God's hand.

Week 13

ENTERING PROMISED LAND

So Joshua took the whole land, according to all that the LORD had said to Moses; and Joshua gave it as an inheritance to Israel (Joshua 11:23).

THEME

INHERITANCE

Writing to a new generation after World War 1, Winston Churchill challenged, "You have not an hour to lose. . . . Don't be content with things as they are. 'The earth is yours and the fullness thereof.' Enter your inheritance; accept your responsibility."

God gave Israel the land of Palestine as their inheritance. He first promised it to Abraham, and He reconfirmed His pledge to others throughout Old Testament times.

In addition to whatever land he owned, the Jewish man would pass on his possessions to his children. Only the priests and Levites owned neither land nor possessions; their inheritance was the Lord.

In the Old Testament, a person had rights to an inheritance only through the death of a parent or relative. Under Roman law of New Testament times, a person became an heir at birth, though he might not receive a full inheritance until a family member died.

In Jesus Christ, the truths about inheritance from both testaments reached their pinnacle: He died that we might enter our inheritance; and He gave us a second birth that we might accept our responsibility.

Sunday

When I was a boy, the flame of adventure burned brightly in my soul, filling my life with anticipation. I loved to read stories about pioneers who ventured into the unknown, and I still remember these words of Rudyard Kipling: "There is no sense in going further—it's the edge of civilization, / So they said, and I believed it— / Till a voice, as bad as conscience, rang interminable changes / On one everlasting whisper day and night repeated—Something hidden. Go and find it. Go and look behind the Ranges— / Something lost behind the Ranges. Lost and waiting for you. Go!"

Although I still like to try new things, I have lost some of my adventurous spirit as I've grown older, and I find myself feeling a bit uneasy as I draw closer to retirement, old age, and death. It's natural, I believe, to feel a mixture of fear and anticipation as we face the unknown. But as I trust God and keep walking with Him, I find that fear diminishes and my longing for heaven grows stronger.

The Israelites undoubtedly felt both uneasiness and eagerness as they prepared to enter the Promised Land. Knowing this, Joshua told them to follow the ark, the symbol of God's presence. The people leading the column were to stay far enough behind the ark so that those in the rear could see it. By trusting God and obeying Him, their fear dissolved and their sense of anticipation grew stronger. And it still works that way today. —H.V.L.

**Faith keeps the sails of life
filled with the breath of heaven.**

Monday

PSALM 37:27–40

Wait on the LORD, and keep His way,
and He shall exalt you to inherit the land (Psalm 37:34).

As a rule, it is wrong to take from one person and give to another. Yet when the proper authority takes from a criminal to give to an orphan, it's a different story. Such was the case when the wife of Peruvian President Alan Garcia ordered that a mansion confiscated from a cocaine dealer be converted into an orphanage. According to the Lima press, Mrs. Garcia told lawyers to arrange for the transfer of the house known as "Villa Coca." A hideout for drug smugglers became a haven for homeless children.

God did something like this when He guided the children of Israel to Canaan, the Promised Land. The Lord used the Israelites to judge the idol-worshiping residents of Canaan by driving them out of their land. God gave His people cities and homes they hadn't built, wells they hadn't dug, and vineyards they hadn't planted. He took from His enemies to give to His own people, just as He had promised (Deut. 6:10–11).

As the real owner of heaven and earth, and as the final court of appeal, the Lord assures us that He has the authority and the power to take from the proud and to give to the humble. It's true, the Lord may seem blind to the actions of those who have gained great wealth by vice and violence. But according to Psalm 37, time and eternity will show the wisdom of those who wait on the Lord. They will see the great reverse. —M.R.D.II

At the end of life, we'll find that the only
things we've lost were those we tried to keep.

Tuesday

1 PETER 1:1–9

The LORD knows the days of the upright,
and their inheritance shall be forever (Psalm 37:18).

Columnist L. M. Boyd described the amazing good fortune of a man named Jack Wurm. In 1949, broke and out of a job, he was walking along a San Francisco beach when he came across a bottle with a piece of paper in it. The note inside was the last will and testament of Daisy Singer Alexander, heir to the Singer sewing machine fortune. The note read, "To avoid confusion, I leave my entire estate to the lucky person who finds this bottle and to my attorney, Barry Cohen, share and share alike." According to Boyd, the courts accepted the theory that the heiress had written the note twelve years earlier and had thrown the bottle in the Thames River in London. From there it had drifted across the oceans to the feet of penniless and jobless Jack Wurm. His chance discovery netted him over six million dollars in cash and Singer stock.

But Jack Wurm's inheritance cannot compare with the one belonging to those of us who have trusted Christ as our Savior. We are heirs with Christ. Our eternal future is secure. In one hundred years, Jack Wurm's money will have no value to him, but we will be just beginning to enjoy eternal life, eternal happiness, eternal gratitude, eternal peace, and eternal profit. The psalmist said this "inheritance shall be forever." —M.R.D.II

**If you want to feel rich, just count
all the things you have that money can't buy.**

Wednesday

MATTHEW 5:1–12

"Ask, and it will be given to you; seek, and you will find;
knock, and it will be opened to you" (Matthew 7:7–8).

"For more than 40 years, Ace Pawn Shop had been a fixture on West
Main Street in my hometown. Now it was closing. Fred and Lydia
Fischer had run the shop as a 'mom and pop' operation, and when
Fred died, Lydia found that she couldn't go on alone. Rather than sell
the business, she decided to close shop and move south. As a final
gesture of appreciation to the customers who had made life so good
for them, Lydia sent a card to everyone who had an item in pawn and
offered it back free of charge. The sign in the window told the story:
'Pawn Shop Closing: Claim What Is Yours'" (David Grubbs, *Claim
What Is Yours*).

God has invited all believers in Christ to claim what is ours, and the
Sermon on the Mount lists a number of these wonderful gifts: the
kingdom of heaven (salvation), comfort in mourning, the prospect of
inheriting the earth, spiritual fulfillment, mercy, fellowship with God,
adoption into God's family, and an eternal home in heaven.

When we begin to feel spiritually poor, it's time to ask, seek, and
knock. Before another day passes, we can, by faith, "claim what is
ours." —D.C.E.

He possesses all who knows the Creator of all.

Thursday

HEBREWS 9:16–18, 22–28

For where there is a testament, there must also
of necessity be the death of the testator (Hebrews 9:16).

Robby Flockheart, a street evangelist in Edinburgh, often told two
stories to stress the importance of two truths—that Jesus died but
also lives. In the first story, Robby told about becoming friends with a
man who was later condemned to die. The prisoner called for Robby
and in his presence made out his will, leaving Robby what little money
he had. But on the day of the man's scheduled execution, he was
pardoned. Recounting the circumstances, Robby said, "He lived, but I
lost my legacy. A testament is not in force while the testator lives." In
the second story, Robby told of another person who left him a small
legacy. But Robby never got any of that inheritance either because, as
he told it, "some rogue of a lawyer came along and I never saw a penny
of it. I used to say, 'If the man who left the will had been alive, he
would have made sure his old friend Robby got his money.' But being
dead, he had no power to see his will carried out."

Jesus, the great testator of the new covenant, did die; there is no
question about that. Therefore, the will, certified by His precious
blood, is valid. He has secured eternal redemption for us through His
atoning death. But the Savior did not remain in the grave. After three
days He arose, and today He lives to make sure that His will is fully
carried out. His life ensures that every blessing promised by the New
Testament will be given to everyone who trusts the Savior.

Christ died, making His will valid; and He lives, guaranteeing our
priceless inheritance. —P.R.V.

Only a living Savior could rescue a dying world.

Friday

REVELATION 21:1–8

"He who overcomes shall inherit all things"
(Revelation 21:7).

Fiske planetarium, on the campus of the University of Colorado, needed money, so its director dreamed up a gimmick. He printed brochures offering 1,000-acre lots on the planet Mars for only twenty dollars. Located in the Olympus Mons region, the land is a huge, extinct volcano more than twice as high as Mount Everest. The flyers read: "This land features pink skies, unlimited rock gardens, and not one but two moons. So peaceful, quiet, and romantic—even the natives are friendly. At one-sixth the gravity of Earth, your golf game will improve immensely—drives will be six times longer. Mars will provide a world of adventure for the entire family." The gag was surprisingly successful. People from across the country sent in twenty dollars for a deed, space flight insurance, and a simulated sample of red Martian soil.

But better than any offer for property on Mars is God's promise of heavenly real estate. God is preparing it for Christians, not to make money, but to express His love for all who trust Jesus as their Savior. "New World II" is a real place where the Lord Himself will live with His people. The additional features are beyond description. There will be no tears, pain, or death, and the occupants will rejoice forever in God's everlasting goodness.

How reassuring to know that God's free offer of a home in the heavens is not just some promotional gimmick! It may sound too good to be true, but it isn't. It's too good to pass up. —M.R.D.II

Heaven is a prepared place for a prepared people.

Saturday

**For our citizenship is in heaven
(Philippians 3:20).**

As believers in the Lord Jesus, we are citizens of heaven. Here on earth we are only pilgrims journeying toward our eternal home. Yet all too often we act as if this world is our permanent residence.

Many years ago, a man visited his longtime friend, a British military officer stationed in an African jungle. One day when the friend entered the officer's hut, he was startled to see him dressed in formal attire and seated at a table beautifully set with silverware and fine china. The visitor, thinking his friend might have lost his mind, asked why he was all dressed up and seated at a table so sumptuously arrayed out in the middle of nowhere. The officer explained, "Once a week I follow this routine to remind myself of who I am—a British citizen. I want to maintain the customs of my real home and live according to the codes of British conduct, no matter how those around me live. I want to avoid substituting a foreign culture for that of my homeland."

Christians should have a similar concern. Our true citizenship is in heaven, so we must beware of substituting the foreign culture of this world for that of our real homeland (see Rom. 12:2). We are not to take on its sinful ways or adopt its values. We need to live in such a way that others will see that we are different.

And we need to remember that we are strangers in this world and citizens of heaven. —R.W.D.

**The Christian who lives above the world
draws closer to heaven.**

Week 14

JUDGES RULE ISRAEL

Then the children of Israel did evil in the sight of the LORD, . . . and they forsook the LORD God of their fathers. . . . Then the LORD raised up judges who delivered them out of the hand of those who plundered them (Judges 2:11–12, 16).

THEME

FAILURE

C. T. Studd, the great missionary to China, India, and Africa, ended his life as a morphine addict. Despite all of his success, his last days were dark ones. His mission board dismissed him; he died a few weeks later.

Israel showed power and promise in escaping from Egypt. The people, however, unlike Studd, displayed their selfish addictions early. Trouble erupted only a few miles from Egypt. The faithless people, grumbling and carousing, played out a drama of disaster and death for forty years in the desert.

Joshua's leadership brought new hope to the nation when the people finally entered the Promised Land, but his successors, the judges, gave Israel a topsy-turvy season of success and failure.

Some judges ruled wisely and in peace, but others did not. And the people were mostly wicked during the whole period.

The failure of the judges led the people to demand an earthly king. Saul, David, and Solomon gave Israel some success, but many of the mad monarchs that followed wrote their stories of failure in blood.

For many, the last pretender to the throne was the greatest failure. He too wrote His story in blood—His own. But as King of kings, He turned failure into victory.

Sunday

JUDGES 14

Samson said to his father, "Get her for me, for she pleases me well" (Judges 14:3).

Failure to exercise self-discipline can ruin a person's health and happiness. A girl I know will probably die young if she doesn't control her eating habits. And I'm acquainted with a young man who is destroying himself because he never learned self-discipline. He grew up in a wealthy family and inherited a position that pays a high salary, but he is on the brink of financial disaster because of his drinking and gambling.

Lack of self-discipline caused Samson to make the mistakes that led to his capture by the Philistines, who put out his eyes and forced him to work like an animal. His downfall began when he wanted to marry a heathen girl and wouldn't listen to the objections of his parents. His demand, "Get her for me, for she pleases me well," set the pattern of self-indulgence that ruined his life.

Without self-control, we can squander great talents and waste wonderful opportunities. Our appetites for food, our sexual desires, our enjoyment of recreation, and our drive to succeed can become all-consuming if we fail to hold them in check. People who excel in their sport for many years do so because they eat properly, exercise, and practice regularly. Likewise, people who consistently walk with God discipline themselves to read the Bible, pray, and obey Him.

Self-indulgence guarantees failure; self-discipline assures victory.
—H.V.L.

Discipline yourself so others won't have to.

Monday

JUDGES 16:1–21

"Whoever commits sin is a slave of sin"
(John 8:34).

When we repeatedly give in to a particular sin, we become a slave to it. A man dying of AIDS admitted that he had felt guilty about his homosexual way of life. But he couldn't carry out his resolve to give up his immoral lifestyle. Another young man admitted that his wife left him because of his preoccupation with pornographic literature. He's unhappy, but he can't stay away from smut shops. Similarly, many people who take cocaine know they are ruining their lives, but they feel powerless to give up the habit.

Samson too had become a slave to sin. He continued an affair with Delilah even though he knew she was bent on betraying him to his enemies. Samson was not stupid, but he was a slave to his lust. Like the homosexual, the pornography addict, and the drug user, he could not do what he knew he should.

Once we start down the wrong path, turning back is difficult. Jesus said that whoever keeps on sinning will become a slave to sin (John 8:34). Some of the most dangerous practices bring temporary pleasure. That's why they are so ensnaring. Freedom, however, is found in becoming a slave of Jesus Christ.

When we are in the grip of an evil practice that is ruining our life, we can acknowledge our sin and helplessness to the Lord, submit fully to Him, and be assured that He will deliver us. —H.V.L.

**The pleasures of sin are for a season,
but its wages are for eternity.**

Tuesday

PHILIPPIANS 2:12–17

God . . . works in you both to will and
to do for His good pleasure (Philippians 2:13).

The great inventor Charles Kettering suggests that we learn to fail intelligently. He said, "Once you've failed, analyze the problem and find out why, because each failure is one more step leading up to the cathedral of success. The only time you don't want to fail is the last time you try." Here are three suggestions for turning failure into success: (1) Honestly face defeat; never fake success. (2) Exploit the failure; don't waste it. Learn all you can from it; every bitter experience can teach you something. (3) Never use failure as an excuse for not trying again. We may not be able to reclaim the loss, undo the damage, or reverse the consequences, but we can make a new start.

God does not shield us from the consequences of our actions just because we are His children. But for us, failure is never final because the Holy Spirit is constantly working in us to accomplish His purposes. He may let us fail, but He urges us to view defeat as a steppingstone to maturity. God is working for our good in every situation, and we must act on that good in order to grow.

Knowing how to benefit from failure is the key to success—especially when we trust God to work in us, both to will and to do His good pleasure. —D.J.D.

Success is failure turned inside out.

Wednesday

ISAIAH 54:1–10

"Do not fear, . . . For you will forget the shame of your youth"
(Isaiah 54:4).

Two men walking down a country road decided to take a shortcut home. They passed through a field where a number of cattle were grazing. Deeply engrossed in conversation when they reached the other side of the pasture, they forgot to shut the gate behind them. A few minutes later one of them noticed the oversight and ran back to close the gate. As he did, he remembered the last words of an old friend who summoned all his children to his bedside and gave them this wise counsel: "As you travel down life's pathway, remember to close the gates behind you."

The man knew that problems, difficult situations, heartbreaks, and failures were inevitable, but he wanted his children to know that they didn't have to allow those things to follow them through life.

This is especially true for believers. Once we have confessed a sin and have done what we can to right the wrong, we must put the incident behind us.

The apostle Paul told us to forget the things of the past that will hinder us and to reach forward to those things which are ahead. Then we will be better able to "press toward the goal for the prize of the upward call of God in Christ Jesus" (Phil. 3:14).

When it comes to the failures of the past, we can always close the gate behind us. —R.W.D.

We invite defeat when we remember
what we should forget.

Thursday

ACTS 15:36–41

But Paul insisted that they should not take [him] (Acts 15:38).
Get Mark, . . . for he is useful to me (2 Timothy 4:11).

Although we can never undo a failure, we can learn from the experience and profit by it. A baseball pitcher who loses a game because he throws a fastball right where the batter wants it may come back four days later and hurl a shutout. He'll never erase the lost game from his record, but his failure can teach him valuable lessons that will help him to chalk up more wins than losses.

In Acts we read that John Mark accompanied Paul and Barnabas when they started their first missionary journey (Acts 13:5), but he soon departed from them (Acts 13:13). While he was at home, he apparently regretted what he had done, so he asked to be included the next time his older friends set out. Barnabas wanted to give him another chance, but Paul didn't, so they parted company and formed two teams—Barnabas taking Mark, and Paul taking Silas. Young Mark couldn't erase his first failure, but he must have learned from it because he became a respected Christian leader of his day. Furthermore, God used him to write one of the four gospels; and Paul, in his second prison epistle to Timothy, asked for Mark, saying, "He is useful to me for ministry."

It doesn't do any good to brood about what went wrong. Wishing we could do something over is an exercise in futility. Each day is new. With God's help we can succeed, if we learn from yesterday's failure. Christians live in "the land of beginning again." —H.V.L.

**Failure doesn't mean you'll never succeed;
it will just take longer.**

Friday

PSALM 37:18–24

**Though he fall, he shall not be utterly cast down;
for the LORD upholds him with His hand (Psalm 37:24).**

When the deplorable practice of slavery still existed in the United States, a plantation owner went duck hunting one day with his slave. The master was an atheist, but the slave was a deeply spiritual Christian. On the way, the carriage wheel lost a rim, and the master ordered the slave to hammer it back on. In doing so, he accidentally hit his finger. Instantly some bad words passed from his lips, but just as quickly he was on his knees asking forgiveness.

"Sam," said the master, "you're a Christian. Tell me, why do you struggle and flutter so to live it? Here I am an infidel, and I don't have any problem like that. Certainly infidelity is more peaceful than Christianity." Sam had no answer, but just then some ducks flew overhead. The master raised his gun and fired two shots. "Go after that wounded one, Sam, not the dead one." Spotting the fluttering bird, Sam exclaimed, "I've got an answer for you, Boss. You said Christianity is no good because I have to struggle. Well, I am the duck with the broken wing, and the devil's after me. I'm alive and struggling to get away from him. But Boss, you are the dead duck!"

In learning to live a consistent, Christ-honoring life, we sometimes despair over our failings. Even though we know we can experience victory, we are weak and we often fall. But Christ's restoring grace enables us to get up and go on. Our struggle is a sign of life. —D.J.D.

**To rejoice in righteousness and grieve over wickedness
is proof of a genuine Christian.**

Saturday

PHILIPPIANS 1:8–18

The things which happened to me have actually turned out
for the furtherance of the gospel (Philippians 1:12)

A young pitcher who entered the major leagues had such a blazing fastball that he didn't think he needed to work on his control, his changeup, or his curve. Consequently, he failed to make the grade and was sent back to the minor leagues. Though disappointed, he worked on these pitches, and in time became a superstar.

Winston Churchill failed twice to win an elected office during the early 1920s and had little political influence all through the 1930s. But he kept developing his talents, and in 1940 he became the Prime Minister of England. Today he is acclaimed as a great hero.

The apostle Paul planned to go to Rome to preach the gospel as a free man, but he was taken there as a prisoner instead. It looked as if he had failed to achieve his noble ambition. In his place of confinement, however, he witnessed to the guards with such persuasion that most of them were converted, and from his prison he wrote some of his outstanding epistles. That's why he could write to the Christians in Philippi that everything had turned out for the advancement of the gospel.

When our carefully laid plans fizzle, it's time to analyze our failure and take appropriate action. If we discover that we blundered, we can correct our mistakes. If we trace our seeming lack of success to circumstances beyond our control, we can ask God to teach us what He wants us to learn and trust Him to bring good out of our disappointments. A failure then becomes a steppingstone to success. —H.V.L.

Most successes follow many failures.

Week 15

BOAZ CLAIMS RUTH

And Boaz said to the elders and all the people, "You are witnesses this day that I have bought all that was Elimelech's, and all that was Chilion's and Mahlon's, from the hand of Naomi. Moreover, Ruth, the Moabitess, the wife of Mahlon, I have acquired as my wife" (Ruth 4:9–10).

THEME

REDEMPTION

During the American Revolution, the British Crown offered General Joseph Reed a bribe. He replied at an August 11, 1778, meeting of the Continental Congress by saying, "I am not worth purchasing, but such as I am, the King of Great Britain is not rich enough to do it."

Boaz was rich enough to take Ruth as his wife. As a close relative of Naomi, Ruth's mother-in-law, Boaz paid the price out of duty, but apparently he also loved Ruth.

The Old Testament redeemer had to be a near relative, be willing, and be able to pay the price. Although love for the redeemed was not a requirement, it sometimes motivated the redeemer. More important, God Himself redeemed Israel because He loved the people.

Roman law added an obligation to the rules of redemption: The redeemed had to repay the ransom price. Redeemed people were in debt to their redeemer until they cleared the liability.

Like Joseph Reed, we were not worthy of being purchased, but God loved us so deeply that He bought us with His Son's life. And we can only repay the Redeemer by offering our own lives in return.

Sunday

EPHESIANS 2:1–10

**It is the gift of God, not of works,
lest anyone should boast (Ephesians 2:8–9).**

After hearing the gospel explained, people often say, "You mean there's nothing I can do to deserve it? That's too easy." People object to the idea that God gives unmerited favor so freely to unworthy sinners. Many find it difficult to trust a God who offers salvation as a free gift.

Bible teacher G. Campbell Morgan told of a coalminer who came to him and said, "I would give anything to believe that God would forgive my sins, but I cannot believe that He will forgive them if I just ask Him. It is too cheap." Morgan said, "My dear friend, have you been working today?" "Yes, I was down in the mine." "How did you get out of the pit? Did you pay?" "Of course not. I just got into the cage and was pulled to the top." "Were you not afraid to entrust yourself to that cage? Was it not too cheap?" Morgan asked. "Oh, no," said the miner, "it was cheap for me, but it cost the company a lot of money to sink the shaft." Suddenly, the truth struck him. What cost him nothing—salvation—had not come cheap to God. This miner had never thought of the great price God paid to send His Son so He could rescue fallen humanity. Now he realized that all anyone had to do was to "get into the cage" by faith.

Because of God's grace, salvation is a free gift. But to receive it, we must stop trying to pay for it and start trusting what Christ has done on the cross. It's free, but it's not cheap. —P.R.V.

**Salvation is free to us,
but it cost God an enormous price.**

Monday

PHILIPPIANS 3:7–14

That I may know Him and the power of His resurrection (Philippians 3:10).

Salvation is knowing a Person. We are not saved by anything we do; we experience redemption only through faith in the Lord Jesus Christ. By His perfect life and sacrificial death on the cross of Calvary, He provided it for us. No wonder the longing of the apostle Paul's heart was that he might "know Him."

The *Youth's Living Ideals* magazine related the following story: "An old Christian woman whose age began to tell on her had once known much of the Bible by heart. Eventually only one precious bit stayed with her, 'I know whom I have believed and am persuaded that He is able to keep that which I have committed unto Him against that day' (2 Tim. 1:12). By and by part of that slipped its hold, and she would quietly repeat, 'That which I have committed unto him.' At last, as she hovered on the [borderline] between this world and heaven, her loved ones noticed her lips moving. They bent down to see if she needed anything. She was repeating over and over again to herself the one word of the text, 'Him, Him, Him.' She had lost the whole Bible but one word. But she had the whole Bible in that one word."

Though her memory had failed, that dying saint of God never lost the One she loved so well. Her salvation was based on a living relationship to Jesus Christ. He satisfied her heart's need even in death. The only way of salvation, is through knowing the Savior. —R.W.D.

**Knowing the Scriptures is one thing;
knowing the Savior is another.**

Tuesday

JOHN 3:14–21

But as many as received Him, to them He gave
the right to become the children of God (John 1:12).

"While Andrew Jackson was President of the United States, a man was given a court trial and condemned to die. President Jackson offered to pardon him but the condemned man refused the pardon. Prison authorities, the Attorney General of the United States, and others earnestly endeavored to convince the man to accept the pardon. They tried to impress upon him that it would not only spare his life, but that if he did not accept the pardon it would be an insult to the President. The man persisted. . . . The Attorney General consulted the Supreme Court, asking whether legal authorities could not force the man to receive the pardon. The court ruled that the pardon was merely a printed statement until the man accepted it. If he rejected the pardon, it remained printed matter" (William McCarrell, *My Favorite Illustration*).

It is much the same with God's salvation. Even though the Lord Jesus has provided redemption for everyone, only those who accept His pardon actually benefit from His offer. Until we personally trust Christ as Savior, we will never be free from the judgment of God upon sin. "He who believes in Him is not condemned; but he who does not believe is condemned already, because he has not believed in the name of the only begotten Son of God" (John 3:18).

Salvation is offered to all. But to experience it and to benefit from all its rich and enjoyable blessings, we must accept it. —R.W.D.

Salvation is free—but we must receive it.

Wednesday

**But He was wounded for our transgressions,
He was bruised for our iniquities (Isaiah 53:5).**

Underscore this truth: The death of Jesus Christ on the cross of Calvary was substitutionary—He died in our place, the Just for the unjust, and He is our only hope for eternity.

A Christian woman visiting a mortally wounded soldier had just finished praying when a nurse entered and said to him, "You have no need to worry over your sins; anyone who willingly gives his life for his country is all right." The soldier smiled weakly, but shook his head and said, "That is a mistake. When I lay out there on the battlefield, I knew I had given my all. I hadn't failed my country. But that didn't help me to face God. I wasn't fit to die, and I knew it, and it has troubled me every day since. But just now, as I heard this woman's prayer, I realized that the Lord Jesus was punished for all my sins, and a great peace has come into my soul. I'm not afraid to die now, because He has forgiven me."

Although that nurse meant well, she spoke in tragic ignorance. But the soldier grasped the foundation of the gospel—that Jesus died for our sins. A poet wrote: "O Christ, what burdens bowed Your head, / My sins You had to face; / You took my load, died in my stead, / Gave Your life in my place, / A sacrifice—Your blood was shed! / You saved me by Your grace."

We need to pause frequently and thank the Lord Jesus for dying on the cross and paying for our sins. He alone did it, and He did it alone. —P.R.V.

**The only valid passport to heaven
is signed in Jesus' blood.**

Thursday

JOHN 12:44–50

**Christ Jesus came into the world to save sinners
(1 Timothy 1:15).**

If a man who couldn't swim fell into deep water and called for help, would you throw him a book called *Five Easy Swimming Lessons*? Shout encouragement? Or jump into the water and yell, "Just follow my example. I'll teach you to swim"? None of those actions would save the drowning man. He doesn't need a book, a motivational speech, or swimming lessons. He needs a savior, someone to reach him where he is, pull him out of his life-threatening circumstances, and deliver him to safety.

Our spiritual condition demands the same kind of action. The Bible says "all have sinned" (Rom. 3:23), and "the wages of sin is death" (Rom. 6:23). Everyone born into this world is a sinner doomed to destruction. We cannot redeem ourselves by reading books about religion, by trying harder to do right, nor by following the example of others. Our only hope of escape from sin's deadly embrace is Christ, who stooped down in grace to redeem the dying.

The Bible says that "the Son of man has come to seek and to save that which was lost" (Luke 19:10). He redeems all who trust in Him for salvation. Just as a drowning person must cease struggling and relax in the arms of his rescuer, we too must trust in the Lord Jesus.
—R.W.D.

Christ believed is salvation received.

Friday

"If anyone thirsts, let him come to Me and drink"
(John 7:37).

How simply our Lord presented the gospel. He often depicted the sinner's response to the salvation He offered in terms of everyday activities like eating, drinking, and receiving.

During a gospel meeting in a town in Ohio, a man was greatly convicted of his need of the Lord Jesus. He concealed his feelings even from his wife, who was a lovely Christian. One evening when she was away, he became so anxious about his condition that he began pacing the floor. His daughter, noticing her father's agitation, asked him what was wrong. "Oh, nothing," he replied, trying in vain to relieve his pangs of conviction. The youngster, with the profound simplicity of childhood, said, "Daddy, if you were thirsty wouldn't you go and get a drink of water?" Her words startled the father. He thought of his thirsty soul, so parched and empty. Then he remembered what he had heard in the meeting—that the gospel was like a freely flowing fountain. He resisted no longer. That night he asked Jesus to save him.

Nothing can quench our spiritual thirst but Jesus. The wells of the world only make us more thirsty. Jesus said, "Whoever drinks of the water that I shall give him will never thirst" (John 4:14). —P.R.V.

No matter how much we drink from the wells of
wealth and achievement, we will only become more thirsty.

Saturday

Whoever desires, let him take the water of life freely (Revelation 22:17).

Concerned Christians asked evangelist George Needham to visit a rich and socially prominent man, but when he arrived at the man's house he found him to be very busy. Needham apologized for the intrusion but asked the man if he had time for one quick question. Receiving permission to ask, Needham said, "Are you saved?" "No," replied the rich man, "but I am trying to be a Christian." "How long have you been trying?" Needham asked. "For twelve years," he answered. To that, the evangelist responded, "Permit me to say that you have been very foolish." Taken back by the statement, the man asked Needham what he meant. Needham calmly explained, "You have been trying for so many years, yet you haven't succeeded. If I were you, I would give up trying and start trusting."

That evening, to Needham's surprise, the man came to the church where he was preaching. His face reflected a look of peace and joy that the evangelist hadn't seen earlier in the day. After the meeting, the visitor said to Needham, "I have been foolish indeed, wasting twelve precious years of life vainly trying, when salvation could have been mine by simply trusting."

The Bible does not tell us to work or do or try to be saved. The apostle Paul said, "But to him who does not work but believes on Him who justifies the ungodly, his faith is accounted for righteousness" (Rom. 4:5). The only way to receive eternal life is to stop trying and start trusting Jesus. —P.R.V.

Salvation is not try, but trust; not do, but done.

Week 16

GOD CALLS SAMUEL

While Samuel was lying down . . . the LORD called Samuel. . . . And Samuel answered, "Speak, for Your servant hears." Then the LORD said to Samuel: "Behold, I will do something in Israel at which both ears of everyone who hears it will tingle" (1 Samuel 3:3–4, 10–11).

THEME

HEARING GOD

On March 10, 1876, Alexander Graham Bell transmitted the first sounds over a single wire. He called to his assistant, "Mr. Watson, come here, I want you."

God has been sending similar messages to humanity ever since He called to Adam in the garden. Sometimes people respond quickly to God, but most often we play deaf.

In the Old Testament the original words for *hear* and *obey* were the same. A person who truly heard was one who also obeyed.

Samuel had a sensitive ear. He not only physically heard God's voice; but as an act of his own will, he obeyed God.

Equestrians call attentive horses ear-brisk. They hear and obey the rider's command.

At the end of His mountainside sermon, Jesus described people who are both hearers and doers as wise builders because they construct a solid life on the rock foundation of God's Word.

God earmarks those who perceive and perform His will.

Sunday

1 SAMUEL 3:1–10

"Speak, for Your servant hears"
(1 Samuel 3:10).

Several years ago when I was in Florida, I would awaken each morning to the cheerful sounds of a mockingbird outside my window. At first, the beauty of his melodies thrilled me, but soon my ears became accustomed to his songs. Then I grew preoccupied and I no longer heard his voice. I had begun to take that feathered songster's sunrise concerts for granted. The fact that I no longer heard them was my own fault. The Mockingbird still sang every morning, but I no longer listened.

A similar situation occurs when we "hear" God speak to us through Scripture. When we are first saved, we faithfully read the Bible and study it diligently. Our hearts are thrilled as we see God's plan unfold throughout its pages. But in time, reading His Word becomes routine and we no longer give our full attention to its message. We become slow in obeying its commands. Sometimes we neglect it entirely. As a result, we no longer "hear" God speak to us. This tragic pattern can develop so slowly that its weakening effects go unnoticed at first. Then one day we suddenly realize what we've been missing. How much better to be like Samuel, who remained attentive and said, "Speak, for Your servant hears" (1 Sam. 3:10).

Setting aside time each day to read Scripture, giving full attention to its teaching, and blocking out all distractions will increase our awareness of God's voice and will keep it from becoming mundane.
—R.W.D.

The more we read the sacred pages,
the better we know the Rock of Ages.

Monday

1 SAMUEL 3:1–15

**"Today, if you will hear His voice,
do not harden your hearts" (Hebrews 3:7–8).**

One summer an annoyed senior citizen from Richmond Heights, Missouri, hung up on President Reagan. He did it not just once but half a dozen times. The elderly gentleman didn't knowingly refuse to talk to the Chief Executive; he just didn't believe that the President was calling him. He was sure it was a prank. But the Southwestern Bell operator and a neighbor finally convinced him it was for real. As a result, the man had the privilege of chatting with Mr. Reagan for about fifteen minutes.

Many centuries ago a young Israelite named Samuel also received a call from a surprising source. He didn't realize who was calling, even when it was repeated. It came from one greater than a president. At first Samuel was perplexed, but when Eli told him God was trying to get through to him, he listened.

We Christians sometimes have the same response when God speaks to us. Deep down in our awareness we may have a thought or conviction that we cannot understand. At first, we may not recognize it as God's voice. Then, when we're convinced it's Him, we're surprised that He would want to speak to us. But God is personal. He wants us to know Him. He has spoken through His written Word, the Bible, and through the living Word, Christ. In addition, He indwells us in the person of the Holy Spirit who enables us to "hear His voice."

God is always trying to get through to us. That means we must always be listening. —M.R.D.II

**There are two kinds of Christians—those who
wait on the Lord and those who keep the Lord waiting.**

Tuesday

Power belongs to God. Also to You,
O LORD, belongs mercy (Psalm 62:11–12).

Disappearing quickly from the news communication world, the Tele-type machine is being replaced by high-speed electronic printers. Un-til recently, the da dacka-dack dak-dak-dak of the Teletype was a common sound in newsrooms and radio stations everywhere. An urgent bulletin was preceded by the sound of ten bells, which signaled a newsflash of highest priority. A columnist writing in the *Washington Journalism Review* said, "The Teletype said it all, and when its bells chimed out a 'bulletin' or 'flash,' it was like God clearing His throat."

Sometimes we become so busy and preoccupied with the things of this life that we do not hear God's voice. It's as if He has to shout at us through drastic circumstances to get our attention. How much better to remain spiritually alert so we can hear what God is saying to us at all times. The psalmist was like that. He was attuned to the voice of God. That's why he could say, "Twice I have heard." First, he came to understand that "power belongs to God" for judgment; and second, he found that mercy belongs to Him for salvation.

Today, God speaks to us through the written Word and through the Living Word. The writer of Hebrews said, "God . . . has in these last days spoken to us by His Son" (1:1). As we read of Jesus in the Word, may we be sensitive to the voice of God. If we ask the Spirit to enlighten us, we will "hear" what God is saying to us. —P.R.V.

**There needs to be more fear that we will not hear
the Lord than that He will not hear us.**

Wednesday

Be still, and know that I am God
(Psalm 46:10).

Some people can't stand silence. They turn on the radio the minute they're up in the morning and the instant they get into the car. They sit in front of a blaring TV set all evening or have music booming through the house. They have become so adjusted to noise that quietness makes them uncomfortable. As a result, they never hear the sweet, tranquil melodies of nature in the early morning. They never hear the still, small voice of God.

Psalm 46 expresses the blessedness of silent interludes in a noisy world. The writer opens with an affirmation of confidence in the protection of God in the face of destructive forces beyond our power. The psalmist spoke of erupting volcanoes, angry tidal waves, and powerful earthquakes that send great masses of rock tumbling into the sea. Next, he portrays a softly flowing river that distributes its life-giving water throughout the land. This scene is followed by a portrait of violent, antagonistic world powers raging against the Lord but being destroyed. After reviewing God's majestic triumph, the writer then says, "Be still, and know that I am God." The whole psalm is an eloquent call to silence so that we may sense that the Lord is at work amid the clamor and tumult of our restless world.

We can hear God's voice in the soft sounds of nature and in the comforting promises of His Word. He wants to let us know that He is present and in control. But we must be quiet. —H.V.L.

God still speaks to those who take time to listen.

Thursday

HEBREWS 5

And do not grieve the Holy Spirit of God, by whom you were sealed for the day of redemption (Ephesians 4:30).

Sensitivity to the prompting of the Holy Spirit, even in little things that seem harmless, marks the mature Christian. While preaching in a small church in Florida, a young evangelist noticed that his gold wristwatch sparkled in the light. He wrote, "I saw people looking at it. The Lord said to me, 'Take it off. It's distracting.' I said, 'Lord, I can surely wear a wristwatch that my daddy gave me.' But it was sensitivity that God was teaching me—to be sensitive to the little things. I took it off and . . . never wore it in the pulpit again."

It's not always easy to know when God is speaking, because inner urgings may arise from fear, selfish desire, or Satan. Yet if we learn biblical principles through reading the Word, and if we daily yield ourselves to the Holy Spirit, we will gradually come to recognize His gentle prompting. The writer of Hebrews said that mature believers have had their senses "exercised to discern both good and evil" (5:14). Whatever exalts Christ over self comes from God, and we can obey with confidence. But whatever is unkind, unloving, and self-seeking grieves the Spirit. When we do something like this, we must confess our disobedience to God at once to restore our fellowship with Him.

"Lord, make me sensitive" is a prayer that should always be on our hearts. —D.J.D.

When we yield ourselves to the Spirit's control, we do not lose our self-control.

Friday

HABAKKUK 2:15–20

Be still, and know that I am God
(Psalm 46:10).

A group of British miners in Australia heard the sweet song of a thrush one evening as they worked. The lovely sound hushed these hardened men into absolute silence. In the stillness their hearts became tender as memories of their boyhood days in their beloved England swept over them. Similarly, when we are quiet, God speaks to us most clearly and effectively.

Stepping into the stillness of a cold winter morning and gazing upon fields and buildings coated with dazzling frost or covered with sparkling snow have been unforgettable experiences. During the night, the silvery frost had come silently, its unseen fingers deftly touching the landscape. Or feathery snowflakes had descended without awakening a single soul. The silence of such a moment brings to mind the words of Psalm 46:10: "Be still, and know that I am God." I would also think of Habakkuk 2:20, "The LORD is in His holy temple. Let all the earth keep silence before Him."

God speaks to us during other times of silence as well. Sooner or later we lie sleepless as a result of illness, grief, or anxiety. These can be precious moments of quiet solitude when we tell the Lord we love Him and want Him to speak to us. In the stillness we can learn lessons we'd learn in no other way. We experience a new peace—a fresh sense of His presence. But we need not wait for a sleepless night! —H.V.L.

The quiet hour is the power hour.

Saturday

2 PETER 1:16–21

**All Scripture is given by inspiration of God
(2 Timothy 3:16).**

The apostle Peter wrote two books of the New Testament, yet he realized that he was merely an instrument through which God transmitted His message to people. Peter told his readers that "prophecy never came by the will of man, but holy men of God spoke as they were moved by the Holy Spirit" (2 Peter 1:21).

In *Thoughts for the Quiet Hour,* C. H. Spurgeon wrote, "The Bible is the writing of the living God." He explained that though "Moses was employed to write his histories with his fiery pen, God guided that pen. It may be that David touched his harp and let sweet psalms of melody drop from his fingers, but God moved his hands over the living strings of his golden harp. Solomon sang canticles of love and gave forth words of consummate wisdom, but God directed his lips and made the preacher eloquent. If I follow the thundering Nahum, when his horses plow the waters; or Habakkuk, when he sees the tents of Cushan in affliction; if I read Malachi, when the earth is burning like an oven; or the rugged chapters of Peter, who speaks of fire devouring God's enemies; if I turn aside to Jude, who launches forth anathemas on the foes of God—everywhere I find God speaking. It is God's voice, not man's."

"All Scripture is given by inspiration of God." But more than that, it is God Himself speaking to us. —R.W.D.

**The Bible is the only book whose Author
is always present when it is read.**

Week 17

SAUL REIGNS OVER ISRAEL

When David was returning from the slaughter of the Philistine, . . . the women sang . . . : "Saul has slain his thousands, and David his ten thousands." Then Saul was very angry, and the saying displeased him; . . . So Saul eyed David from that day forward (1 Samuel 18:6–9).

THEME

JEALOUSY

"Every time a friend succeeds," railed novelist Gore Vidal, "I die a little."

Novelists are not the only people who experience jade-green jealousy. Saul was extremely jealous of David's popularity. Young, handsome, and valiant, David charmed the crowds. Saul feared being deposed, and his jealousy haunted his whole reign.

Jealousy is the emotional response to the fear of losing something or someone we love. In the case of Saul, his apprehension about losing the throne probably led to extreme paranoia.

We understand Saul's situation because we have all felt jealousy. It is not as simple to comprehend righteous jealousy, but there is such a thing. Exodus 34:14 says that Jealous is one of God's names. God was jealous of anyone or anything that stole the affection of His people.

Holy jealousy has no selfish motives; it seeks only the best for every person. Paul promised the Corinthians to Christ, and he had a godly jealousy when they strayed (2 Cor. 11:2).

God's holy jealousy sent Jesus to the cross. In Old Testament terms, God was jealous because we had taken other lovers. He knew we could find happiness only in loving Him. The pure jealousy of Calvary was really the genuine love of a holy God.

Sunday

NUMBERS 12

Some indeed preach Christ even from envy and strife
(Philippians 1:15).

When the famous sculptor Michelangelo and the painter Raphael were creating works of art to beautify the Vatican, a bitter spirit of rivalry rose up between them. Whenever they met, they refused to speak to each other. Yet each was supposedly doing his work for the glory of God.

Jealousy often parades behind the facade of religious zeal. Miriam and Aaron criticized their brother Moses for marrying an Ethiopian. But God's anger revealed that it was actually jealousy that prompted their criticism. Out of jealousy, Saul sought to kill David, whom God had chosen to succeed Saul as king. And when the apostle Paul was in prison, some people were so jealous of the way God was using him that they preached Christ in order to add to the apostle's distress.

We can overcome this harmful attitude, but first we must identify it. Jealousy believes that someone else is getting what we deserve—whether money, popularity, wisdom, skill, or spiritual maturity. Second, we must confess it. Call it what it is—sin. And third, we must give thanks. The moment we see someone enjoying any advantage, we must accept it with gratitude. We can keep jealousy in check by refusing to compare ourselves with others.

As we learn to find our satisfaction in God, His grace enables us to rejoice with those who rejoice. When we do that, we have little room for envy. —D.J.D.

**When we turn green with jealousy,
we are ripe for trouble.**

Monday

JAMES 3:11–18

Jealousy as cruel as the grave;
its flames are flames of fire (Song of Solomon 8:6).

The very nature of jealousy is to turn on those who harbor it; and it will ultimately destroy them. The Old Testament word for *jealousy* means "to burn or to inflame"—an apt description of what goes on inside the person who allows jealousy to smolder.

A legendary Burmese potter became jealous of the prosperity of a washerman. Determined to ruin him, the potter induced the king to issue an order requiring the man to wash one of his black elephants white. The washerman replied that according to the rules of his vocation he would need a vessel large enough to hold the elephant, whereupon the king commanded the jealous potter to provide one. Though carefully fashioned, it crumbled to pieces beneath the weight of the giant beast. He made many more vessels, but each was crushed in the same way. Eventually the potter was ruined by the very scheme he had devised to defame the man he envied.

In a similar way, Saul's jealousy eventually caused his own destruction. In Proverbs 6:27 we read, "Can a man take fire to his bosom, and his clothes not be burned?" The coals of jealousy quickly become a raging fire that will burn us severely. Unless we douse it with confession and repentance, it will eventually consume us. —P.R.V.

As a moth gnaws a garment,
so jealousy consumes a man.

Tuesday

JAMES 3:13–4:6

**Where envy and self-seeking exist,
confusion and every evil thing will be there (James 3:16).**

In the summer of 1986, two ships collided in the Black Sea, causing a tragic loss of life. The news of the disaster was further darkened when an investigation revealed the cause of the accident that hurled hundreds of passengers into the icy waters. The blame did not belong to defective radar or thick fog but to human stubbornness. Both captains were aware of the other ship's presence and could have taken evasive action to avert the collision. But according to news reports, neither wanted to give way to the other. Each was too proud to yield the right-of-way.

Even greater havoc and loss can be created in human relationships for much the same reason—"envy and self-seeking." We prefer to blame the world's problems on religious or political differences, but James says that the root problem is pride and self-centeredness. It caused the archangel Lucifer to fall from the heavens (Isa. 14). And our first parents, Adam and Eve, lost their innocence for the same reason.

The only way to keep jealousy and envy from turning into major disasters is to draw on the wisdom that comes from above, wisdom that is pure, peaceable, gentle, willing to yield, and full of mercy and goodness. That will mark the beginning of harmony—not havoc.

—M.R.D.II

**Some troubles come from wanting to have our own way;
others come from being allowed to have it.**

Wednesday

JAMES 2:9–11; 3:13–18

Who is able to stand before jealousy?
(Proverbs 27:4).

Inequality seems to cause jealousy. When we see someone with more wealth than we have or with qualities we lack, we become jealous.

While recording interviews for a radio program, I asked people on the street in New York City if they believed all men are created equal. Most of them answered no. They cited our differing abilities, appearances, and environments. One man complained that he had to eat hotdogs for lunch while others ate in fancy restaurants. Only one person showed a deeper understanding of the question. She said, "Under God we are all equally human."

The Bible teaches that all people are created in the image of God, that they are all accountable for what they do with whatever He has given them, and that someday they will all die. So, "under God" there is equality—but only under God. Apart from Him and His plan to bring about eventual justice, we see much in life that is not fair.

Christians are in the best position to keep the right perspective. They have all come to God as sinners and have found forgiveness in the cross of Christ. Therefore, the rich person and the poor person stand together on the common ground of Calvary. The rich rejoice that they have discovered the emptiness of material wealth, and the poor rejoice that they have discovered eternal riches. And according to James, this is the wisdom that enables us to avoid the pitfall of jealousy. —M.R.D.II

No one can take from us the gifts that God gives us.

Thursday

"Has the LORD indeed spoken only through Moses?
Has He not spoken through us also?" (Numbers 12:2).

In the world of technology, friction is an enemy of efficiency. That's why auto engineers put so much emphasis on aerodynamics, easy-rolling tires, and short-stroke engines. They want to reduce the friction caused by air resistance, road contact, and moving parts.

In Numbers 12, we read about a form of friction that creates discord, makes everybody uneasy, diminishes our witness, weakens our worship, and hinders the Spirit's work in our lives. Miriam's jealous revolt against her brother Moses brought God's rebuke and slowed the Israelites' progress. The energy-robbing friction she caused was not unlike personality problems among jealous church members today.

Probably all of us have felt the sting of cruel verbal barbs shot at us by "envious archers." But the greatest pain caused by envy is felt by the person who harbors it. A God-centered, loving attitude is at the heart of the believer's life and health, but envy eats like a consuming disease into the bones and marrow of a person's moral fiber. That's why Socrates called envy "the soul's saw."

Whenever we begin to feel friction due to our envy or jealousy, we must confess it as sin and ask the Lord for His help. Then we must forgive those who have wronged us or apologize to those we have wronged. The friction will disappear, and we'll once again become spiritually energy-efficient. —H.V.L. & H.G.B.

We cannot be jealous and efficient at the same time.

Friday

GALATIANS 5:19–26

"For wrath kills a foolish man,
and envy slays a simple one" (Job 5:2).

No one is more miserable than someone filled with jealousy or envy. They rob us of happiness and make our good accomplishments seem bad. Furthermore, they exact their own punishment.

On the wall of a chapel in Padua, an old city in northeastern Italy, hangs a painting by the Renaissance artist Giotto. The painter depicted envy with long ears that could hear every bit of news of another's success. He also gave to Envy the tongue of a serpent to poison the reputation of the one being envied. But if you could look at the painting carefully, you would notice that the tongue coils back and stings the eyes of the figure itself. Not only did Giotto picture Envy as being blind, but also as destroying itself with its own venomous evil.

Jealousy was one of the sins hurting the church at Corinth. The people had divided into factions because they were jealous of one another's gifts. Each believer strove for preeminence. Paul therefore instructed them to follow the "more excellent way" of love (1 Cor. 12:31), telling them that "love does not envy" (1 Cor. 13:4).

If we resent the success and accomplishments of others and find ourselves striking out at them with damaging words or insidious innuendoes, we have a problem with jealousy. But God wants to administer the antidote of love. That alone will keep us from becoming jealousy's victim. —D.C.E.

If we shoot arrows of jealousy at others, we wound ourselves.

Saturday

ACTS 13:44–52

But when the Jews saw the multitudes,
they were filled with envy (Acts 13:45).

Envy and jealousy are feelings of discontent and resentment aroused by thinking about another person's desirable qualities or possessions and wanting them for ourselves. Here are some classic examples: Rachel envied Leah because she bore children (Gen. 30:1); Joseph's brothers resented him for his dreams (Gen. 37:11); Korah, Dathan, Abiram, and two hundred fifty princes envied Moses (Num. 16:1–3); Saul was jealous of David because the women praised him (1 Sam. 18:7–9); and in Acts 13:45, the Jews opposed Paul's preaching for the same reason—envy.

Any advantage held by another—intelligence, good looks, a slim figure, popularity, a good job, or even a person's spiritual insight—may trigger this feeling. The most devout Christian is not immune to its subtle attack. When F. B. Meyer first held meetings at Northfield, Massachusetts, large crowds thronged to hear his stirring messages. Then the great British Bible teacher G. Campbell Morgan came to Northfield, and the people flocked to hear his brilliant expositions of Scripture. Meyer confessed that at first he was envious. He said, "The only way I can conquer my feeling is to pray for Morgan daily—which I do."

A negative reaction toward anyone who possesses what we lack quenches the Holy Spirit's work in our hearts. That's why we must root out all envy and jealousy from our lives. We know we are gaining victory when we desire good for the one we envy. —R.W.D.

A daily dose of Christlike love will heal the disease of jealousy.

Week 18

DAVID KILLS GOLIATH

Then David put his hand in his bag and took out a stone; and he slung it and struck the Philistine in his forehead, so that the stone sank into his forehead, and he fell on his face to the earth (1 Samuel 17:49).

THEME

FAITH

Frustrated with the Queen, Lewis Carroll's Alice exclaimed, "There's no use trying . . . one *can't* believe impossible things."

"I daresay you haven't had much practice," said the Queen. "When I was your age, I always did it for half-an-hour a day. Why, sometimes I've believed as many as six impossible things before breakfast."

Believing the impossible, as the Queen said, does take practice; few achieve trust proficiency. Friends playing baseball lure us from the piano bench. Ridicule from peers makes us abandon our goal. The people of David's day were trustbusters. They belittled young David's belief in the unbelievable. They couldn't comprehend the incredible—that a mere child could kill a monster of a man.

Doubt did not deter David, and his faith marked him as a man after God's own heart. Faith means that we accept who God is, what He has done, and what He will do. God delights in those who practice faith regardless of circumstances.

Faith doesn't look to see how many follow when it walks up the hill, breaks through the crowd, rushes to the bloody beam, and proclaims, "He is the Christ."

Sunday

1 SAMUEL 17:32–54

"I come to you in the name of the LORD
of hosts, . . . whom you have defied" (1 Samuel 17:45).

I grew up believing that David accomplished his spectacular victory over the giant Goliath only through God's special help. But not long ago I read a report by two "experts" who said their study of 1 Samuel 17 and their knowledge of science led them to conclude that Goliath was weak and half-blind. They attributed his great size to a glandular disease called gigantism and claimed that he was especially vulnerable to the stone from David's sling because of tunnel vision caused by a brain tumor.

The author of 1 Samuel did not present Goliath as a weakling. He said Goliath wore armor that weighed about 125 pounds and wielded a spear with an iron point that weighed about 15 pounds. A person with gigantism walks with difficulty and isn't as strong as a small, healthy man, so if Goliath had been a victim of this disease he would have had a hard time carrying himself, much less the additional weight of the armor. Furthermore, if Goliath hadn't been a first-class warrior he would not have frightened the Israelites, nor would the Philistines have made him their champion. Indeed, without special help from God, David could not have killed Goliath. And without faith in God, David would not have dared to confront the giant.

As the Lord's followers, we are not involved in physical battles with human giants, but we are engaged in a war with Satan, a supernatural being far more powerful than Goliath. But we can have faith; God is all-powerful. He who helped David kill the giant can help us defeat the devil. —H.V.L.

**We may face situations beyond our reserves,
but never beyond God's resources.**

Monday

Now faith is the substance of things hoped for, the evidence of things not seen (Hebrews 11:1).

Songwriter Oscar Eliason wrote, "Got any rivers you think are uncrossable? Got any mountains you can't tunnel through?" He responded to these questions by saying, "God specializes in things thought impossible."

Every Christian faces obstacles along life's pathway, and walking in God's will doesn't guarantee that our way will be easy. But no matter how difficult, we can trust God and go forward in faith.

At the entrance to a local hospital is an automatic gate designed to rise when a car activates a hidden sensor near the entrance. When I drive up the ramp toward the gate, it remains down, blocking the entrance. But as I get closer, the arm swings up, allowing me to proceed. If I were to park my car a few yards from the entrance, the gate would stay closed. Only when I move forward does it open.

Someone said, "If God built a bridge a yard ahead, it could not be a bridge of faith." It's the first step into the unseen that proves we have faith. Abraham, for example, "went out, not knowing where he was going" (Heb. 11:8). He obeyed God and relied on Him to clear the path.

When we walk in obedience to the Lord and come upon a closed gate, we can confidently take the next step of faith. As we move forward we will see God open the way. —P.R.V.

Faith is the gate between our peril and God's power.

Tuesday

TITUS 1

I left you in Crete, that you should set
in order the things that are lacking (Titus 1:5).

Golf teaches us, among other things, that we can't always take the easy way out of a difficult situation. When a ball rolls off the fairway and into the rough, the golfer isn't permitted to pick it up and place it where it will be easier to play. He must hit the ball from the rough.

Young Titus found himself "in the rough." He had been left in Crete, charged with the task of building up the Lord's work there. But he encountered problems. The Cretans were generally deceitful, immoral, and lazy, and this spirit had invaded the churches. Problem people were causing division. Paul realized that his friend needed encouragement, so he wrote to him. He began his letter by saying, in essence, "Yes, things are bad in Crete. But that's exactly why I left you there. God can use you to bring about great and necessary changes." Titus listened, and he succeeded. Although the Bible doesn't record the results of this encouraging letter from Paul, archeologists have found the remains of stately churches that had the name "Titus" inscribed on their cornerstones.

Whenever we are in a difficult place, we don't help ourselves by looking for the easy way out. Instead, by exercising our faith in God and facing the challenge, we can battle our way through the problem. We'll become better people, and we'll discover that God can make us victorious. —H.V.L.

The greater the problem,
the greater our opportunity to tap God's power.

Wednesday

EPHESIANS 5:8–17

By faith the walls of Jericho fell down after they were encircled for seven days (Hebrews 11:30).

As a sculptor showed a visitor some marble figures displayed in his studio, an unusual sculpture caught the guest's attention. It had two peculiar features. Where the statue's face normally would have been, the sculptor had chiseled a covering of hair, and on both feet were wings. "What is the name of this one?" asked the visitor. "Opportunity," the artist answered. "Why is its face hidden?" "Because," said the craftsman, "we seldom know opportunity when he comes to us." "And why does he have wings on his feet?" "Because he is soon gone, and once gone, he cannot be overtaken."

The apostle Paul spoke of the quickly passing nature of opportunity in Ephesians 5:16. The word *time* used in this verse can also be translated "opportunity"—suggesting occasions for accomplishing high and noble purposes. But what are these opportunities? They are brief moments of personal contact—the passing incident, the turn of a conversation, or the "chance" meeting of an old acquaintance. Such times present golden opportunities for caring, for witnessing, for eternal good. Alexander MacLaren, the noted Baptist preacher from England, said, "Every moment of life is granted us for one purpose: becoming like our dear Lord. That ultimate, all-embracing end is reached through a multitude of near and intermediate ones."

Like the young shepherd David, when our faith is strong we will have the wisdom and courage to see every obstacle as an opportunity.
—P.R.V.

To believe only possibilities, is not faith, but mere Philosophy. —Sir Thomas Browne

Thursday

JAMES 1:1–4

We ourselves boast of you among the churches of God for your . . . faith in all your persecutions (2 Thessalonians 1:4).

A University of Michigan microbiologist tells his students that the human body is made up of ten trillion cells, which are home to some 100 trillion bacteria. He supports this claim by citing studies conducted by University of Pennsylvania researchers who once estimated that a dime-sized patch of skin may hold up to two million bacteria.

The presence of all those little critters might seem to be an overwhelming threat to our health. But scientists who have come to understand and appreciate the role of bacteria say that we would actually be sicker without them than we are with them. They apparently help ward off other bacteria that cause diseases.

This is not an argument for careless personal hygiene. But it is an interesting parallel to the setting in which Christians are called to live. Contrary to what we might think, we can actually benefit from a hostile environment.

God calls His children to show patience, love, and faith in a world polluted by sin and opposed to righteousness. Many of the troubles we encounter can help us avoid greater problems of independence, self-sufficiency, and pride that set in so quickly when all goes smoothly. The problems in our lives can help us to realize the need for dependence on the Lord and faith in His Word. Obstacles can contribute to our health if we'll see them as tests of our faith and as opportunities to develop endurance. Until Jesus comes, we can be healthier with them than without them. —M.R.D.II

The difficulties of life are intended to make us better —not bitter.

Friday

JAMES 2:14–26

**But do you want to know, O foolish man,
that faith without works is dead? (James 2:20).**

In nature, lightning and thunder present a striking illustration of the relationship between faith and works. When lightning flashes across the sky, we know that the roar of thunder will follow. Without lightning, there would be no thunder, because the one is the cause of the other. Likewise, good works always accompany saving faith, because one causes the other.

We must keep before us the clear truth that we are saved by grace and grace alone. Ephesians 2:8–9 says, "For by grace you have been saved through faith, and that not of yourselves; it is the gift of God, not of works, lest anyone should boast." But many believers who glibly quote this passage ignore the verse that follows: "For we are His workmanship, created in Christ Jesus for good works, which God prepared beforehand that we should walk in them" (v. 10). In the same manner that thunder contributes nothing to lightning, good works add nothing to our salvation. Rather, they are the "sound" of faith and will follow every genuine conversion experience. The one without the other is not the real thing.

Genuine faith is always evident by what follows—a life of good works. —R.W.D.

**Faith without works is presumptuous;
faith with works is precious.**

Saturday

Preserve me, O God, for in You I put my trust
(Psalm 16:1).

Some people touring a mint where coins are made came to the smelting area. As they stood before the caldrons filled with molten metal, the tour guide explained that if a person were to dip his hand into water and then have someone pour the hot liquid over his hand, he would neither be injured nor feel any pain. Picking out one couple, he asked if they would like to prove what he had just said. "No, thank you," the husband quickly said. "I'll take your word for it." But his wife responded eagerly. "Sure, I'll give it a try." Matching action to her words, she thrust her hand into a bucket of water and then held it out as the molten metal was poured over it. The hot liquid rolled off harmlessly just as the guide had said it would. The host turned to the husband and remarked, "Sir, you claimed to believe what I said. But your wife truly trusted."

When it comes to the promises in the Bible, many Christians react like the husband. They claim to believe them, but they don't really trust God. Consequently, they never experience them firsthand. They live a kind of second-hand Christianity—always relying on someone else's experiences with God to give validity to their beliefs. In Psalm 16, David spoke of having a goodly heritage, a glad heart, stability, hope, and the assurance of "pleasures forevermore." He knew the meaning of faith, and he proved it as a young boy when he dared to face the giant Goliath.

If we only claim to believe God's promises but never act on them, we will miss out on His marvelous blessings. —R.W.D.

To trust is to triumph.

Week 19

DAVID SINS

Have mercy upon me, O God, according to Your lovingkindness; according to the multitude of Your tender mercies, blot out my transgressions. Wash me thoroughly from my iniquity, and cleanse me from my sin. For I acknowledge my transgressions (Psalm 51:1–3).

THEME

CONFESSION

Thinking back over his life of lust, Augustine cried out to God, "I want to call back to mind . . . the carnal corruptions of my soul, not because I love them, but so that I may love you, my God. It is for the love of your love that I do it."

For King David, passionate plots overruled holy devotion, and a murderous coverup overshadowed his kindhearted commitment. He hid his sins from both God and Israel. The prophet Nathan diagnosed David's heart rot and confronted him with his sin. David had the authority to kill Nathan for his audacity. But rather than add another sin to the already heaping pile, he repented. In Psalm 51, David admitted his guilt to God and the whole nation.

True confession acknowledges who we are and what we have done. God obviously already knows, but such soul surgery heals our relationship with Him. In opening ourselves up, we allow God's purging power to clean out the corruption, cure our disease, and make it possible for us to love and talk to Him again.

God is not nearly so outraged at our sin as He is at the destruction sin does to our selves; for when we destroy ourselves, we can no longer reach out to Him.

On the cross Jesus died completely. Cut off from His Father in His hours on the cross, Christ sacrificed His own emotional bond to restore ours. Though our sin continues to break our bond with God, confession renews it and makes us emotionally strong.

Sunday

PSALM 51:7–13

Create in me a clean heart, O God
(Psalm 51:10).

By His sovereign grace, God can bring good out of our failures, and even out of our sins. J. Stuart Holden tells of an old Scottish mansion close to where he had his summer home. The walls of one room were covered by sketches made by distinguished artists. The practice began after a pitcher of soda water, spilled accidentally on a freshly decorated wall, left an unsightly stain. At the time, a noted artist, Lord Landseer, was a guest in the house. One day when the family went to the moors, he stayed behind. With a few masterful strokes of a piece of charcoal, the ugly spot became the outline of a beautiful waterfall, bordered by trees and wildlife. The artist turned a disfigured wall into one of his best depictions of Highland life.

David's sins of adultery and murder were ugly, disfiguring stains, but instead of casting David aside, God turned the ugliness into a thing of beauty by inspiring David to write two psalms of repentance and forgiveness. These psalms, 32 and 51, have brought comfort and hope to repentant sinners for centuries.

God never condones sin, nor does He spare His chastening rod. But when we confess, He begins a new work in our hearts. He does more than the artist did with the stain on the wall. God removes the blot of sin entirely and cleanses us. Then He makes us stronger and more useful than we were before. —P.R.V.

**As long as we have the grace of God,
failure is not final.**

Monday

My wounds are foul and festering because of my foolishness. I am troubled (Psalm 38:5–6).

Our dog had fleas. For a while they just about drove him crazy. When we realized what his problem was, we bathed him with flea shampoo, dusted him with flea powder, and fumigated his bedding with flea spray. Then, just when we thought we had them beat, they showed up again. What was happening? Was he getting them from his food? From his bedding? From us? No, he had recently come of age and was determined to run after new loves whenever we left the door open a crack. We yelled and threatened him, but he was deaf to our calls. Once I even swatted him with a copy of *Leadership* magazine, but it didn't do any good. He was bound to run whenever he could. And he brought back problems, for him and for us.

In a much more serious sense, David faced the discomfort of problems that resulted from his own willfulness. When he felt the hand of his Master pressing down on him, he knew why (Psalm 38:2). God was trying to rid him of the consequences of his own foolishness.

When a dog runs away and causes problems for himself, we can do little to stop him. He's just following his instincts. But when we run from God and bring trouble on ourselves, we can get help. Like David, we can recognize God's correcting hand and make a new start. Better yet, we can avoid chastening by coming to the Lord before He must correct us. To run from God is never the solution. —M.R.D.II

A small step of obedience is a giant step to blessing.

Tuesday

PSALM 51:7–13

Restore to me the joy of Your salvation, . . .
Then I will teach transgressors Your ways (Psalm 51:12–13).

It isn't easy to make a forty-foot, forty-five-ton, untrained whale do what you want it to do, even if it's for its own good. That's what well-wishing friends found out when a humpback whale, affectionately named Humphrey, made a wrong turn during his migration along the California coast. The wayward mammal became a national celebrity when he turned into San Francisco Bay, swam under the Golden Gate Bridge, and managed to navigate seventy miles upriver. For more than three weeks, Humphrey defied all efforts to get him back to salt water. Finally, marine biologists lured him with recorded sounds of feeding humpbacks. It worked. Humphrey responded to the "happy humpbacks" and followed the sounds back to the Pacific.

The lure of happy sounds works not only with lost whales but also with lost people. God makes the lives of His saints appealing to those who don't know Him. His Spirit brings conviction and creates a desire for what Christians have. In the case of repentant King David, once his joy was restored he could lead others to God (Ps. 51:13). And in the New Testament, we read that a Christian wife can draw her unsaved husband to the Lord by the power of a "gentle and quiet spirit" (1 Pet. 3:1–6).

The appealing qualities of love, joy, and peace belong to those who feed on the goodness of God. And they generate the "sounds" that lead the lost to the freedom found in God's ocean of infinite grace.

—M.R.D.II

The sweet sound of singing saints
calls sinners to salvation.

Wednesday

PSALM 32

**I will guide You with My eye. Do not be like
the horse or like the mule (Psalm 32:8–9).**

David felt like a new man. God had lifted the crushing weight of guilt that made his bones old (v. 3) and drained his vitality (v. 4). He had acknowledged his adultery with Bathsheba and his murder of Uriah (v. 5). Blessed beyond words by forgiveness, David urged any believer who strays or falls into sin to pray instantly for cleansing (v. 6). He also cautioned us not to wait for God to use tribulation to make us aware of His displeasure (v. 6).

God will guide us with His eye, David said, and then added, "Do not be like the horse or like the mule . . . which must be harnessed with bit and bridle." This was David's way of saying that God has two ways of bringing us back to Himself: the eye and the bit.

Earthly parents use the same two methods. When a youngster disobeys, one look from Dad conveys disapproval. And a speedy and sincere turnabout by the child assures renewed fellowship. But if the child disregards the gentle rebuke of the eye, Father must intervene with a stern word or a firm hand.

God wants us to confess and renounce our sin the moment we feel conviction about a thought, a word, an attitude, or a deed. He does not want us to be like animals that have no understanding, that need to be controlled by bits and bridles. God loves us too much to let us continue in our waywardness, but He prefers to guide us with His eye.
—D.J.D.

**The closer we walk with God,
the clearer we see His guidance.**

Thursday

I acknowledge my transgressions,
and my sin is always before me (Psalm 51:3).

Jason had misbehaved, so his mother sent him to his room. A short time later he came out and said to his mother, "I've been thinking about what I did and I said a prayer." His mother, pleased with his attitude, encouraged his behavior. "That's wonderful. If you ask God to make you good, I know He will help you." "But I didn't ask Him to help me be good," Jason said. "I asked Him to help you put up with me."

Prayers like Jason's are not uncommon. We don't like to admit that we may be to blame for the problem, so we petition the Lord to change other people or our circumstances. In doing so, we focus on secondary problems and avoid the heart of the matter—our own heart. Praying about our circumstances is effective only when we first come clean with the Lord about our own sin. In David's prayer in Psalm 51, he first asked for mercy (v. 1). Then he acknowledged his sin (v. 3), asked for a clean heart (v. 10), and asked for a restoration of the joy of his salvation (v. 12). When David confessed the shameful deeds of adultery and murder (2 Sam. 11), he made no excuses.

God wants nothing less than our total honesty when we talk with Him. We may have to struggle with ourselves—that kind of praying is not always comfortable—but it's the most profitable. —D.J.D.

Until man has gotten into trouble with his heart,
he is not likely to get out of trouble with God. —Tozer

Friday

DANIEL 9:1–19

Let us draw near . . . having our hearts
sprinkled from an evil conscience (Hebrews 10:22).

While visiting in an Egyptian home, Bradford Abernethy saw a servant give a pitcher of water and a rug to a boy who lived there. Three times, the lad washed his hands, feet, face, neck, ears, and arms. Then he kneeled on the rug, bowed his head to the floor, and began to pray.

The Scriptures teach that a right relationship to God comes from being "justified in the name of the Lord Jesus" (1 Cor. 6:11). The outward washing of the body referred to in the Old Testament was a symbolic act to remind God's people that when they entered the Lord's presence their hearts were to be free from unconfessed sin. David declared, "If I regard iniquity in my heart, the Lord will not hear" (Ps. 66:18). And in another psalm he wrote, "He who has clean hands and a pure heart . . . shall receive blessing from the LORD" (Ps. 24:4–5). It is foolish for those living in sin to expect the Lord to hear and answer their prayers. It's the prayer of a "righteous man" that is effective (James 5:16).

The Word of God assures us, "If we confess our sins, He is faithful and just to forgive us our sins and to cleanse us from all unrighteousness" (1 John 1:9). A clean heart is necessary if we expect God to hear our prayers. —R.W.D.

**The words of our prayers are not as important
as the condition of our hearts.**

Saturday

LUKE 15:11–24

When I kept silence, my bones grew old. . . .
I acknowledged . . . and You forgave (Psalm 32:3–5).

A twelve-year-old boy killed one of the family geese by throwing a stone and hitting it squarely on the head. Figuring his parents wouldn't notice that one of the twenty-four birds was missing, he buried it. But that evening his sister called him aside and said, "I saw what you did. If you don't offer to do the dishes tonight, I'll tell Mother." The next morning she gave him the same warning. All that day and the next the frightened boy felt bound to do the dishes. The following morning, however, he surprised his sister by telling her it was her turn. When she reminded him of what she would do, he replied, "I've already told Mother, and she has forgiven me. Now you do the dishes. I'm free again."

Luke tells us that the prodigal son, concerned about his meeting with his father, decided to begin the conversation by confessing his sin. Then he planned to offer himself as a slave. But he never had to make that proposal. He had hardly begun his confession when his father forgave him and restored him to his status as a son. For that young man, as for the little boy, confession opened the door to freedom.

David discovered the same liberation after his sin. In Psalm 32 he declared that when he kept silent, mental depression and bodily distress kept him bound. But as soon as he confessed what he had done, he was forgiven. His spiritual joy and physical vitality returned. Repentance brings release from bondage. —H.V.L.

**We can't put our sins behind us
until we are ready to face them.**

Week 20

DEDICATING THE TEMPLE

"I have built You an exalted house, and a place for You to dwell in forever. . . . There is no God in heaven or on earth like You" (2 Chronicles 6:2, 14).

THEME

WORSHIP

Writing of our response to God, Thomas Carlyle, the nineteenth-century essayist, concluded, "The man who does not habitually worship is but a pair of spectacles behind which there is no eye."

Solomon, like Carlyle, recognized people's need to worship. With the help of more than 150,000 workers, he built the most magnificent praise house ever. Opulent in its use of gold, silver, bronze, and fine cloth, the temple dazzled the ancient world.

On dedication day hundreds of singers and musicians, including 120 trumpeters, praised the Lord. They sang of His goodness and enduring love.

The glory of God filled the temple, but the earthly structure could not contain Him. God cannot be put in a box; He is not a genie. Worshipful people declare who God is and what He has done, but they never try to bring Him down to human level or limit Him to a single place.

The thief on the cross truly worshiped Jesus, for he recognized who He was and what He could do. Many of us do not; we wear prescription lenses but have no eyes.

Sunday

PSALM 33:1–22

Sing to the LORD, bless His name; Proclaim the
good news of His salvation from day to day (Psalm 96:2).

Most people are interested in news only if it's fresh. We read today's
newspaper rather than yesterday's. We discuss only the latest sports
scores at office coffeebreaks.

The same need to remain fresh and up-to-date applies to our awareness of the good things God does for us. The Old Testament songwriter realized the importance of recognizing the wonder God displays
every day, so he called for a new song and a new description of the
world's most important and most timely news. He wasn't implying
that we are to restrict our reports of God's blessings to late-breaking
news. Rather, he wanted a new appreciation of what the Lord has done
for us in the past as well as what He is doing now. The psalmist said
that God is in control of the weather, international relationships, and
the deepest dimensions of human experience. God is watching, and He
shows a special kind of care for those who love Him.

The good news of God's power did not stop at our conversion. We
can enjoy the fresh perspective of the writer of Psalm 33, because God
is still doing great things today. To see them, we must renew our
understanding of the One who controls our ever-changing world, the
One who knows what to permit and how to bring it into judgment.
The manifestations of God's handiwork reveal His new song in nature
and in man. —M.R.D.II

Expressing our gratitude to God should be as habitual
as our reception of His mercies is constant.

Monday

PSALM 147

Praise the LORD! For it is good
to sing praises to our God (Psalm 147:1).

Some people live as if human beings were merely thinking, working machines. This was true of the famous nineteenth-century inventor John Ericson. Although he had been a boyhood friend of the world-renowned violinist Ole Bull, he never went to a concert, saying music was a waste of time. But Ole, undaunted by his friend's attitude, entered the inventor's shop one day and began playing his violin. Ericson objected at first, but saw his listening workmen drop their tools. Soon he too was enthralled. When Mr. Bull stopped playing, Ericson pleaded, "Don't stop! Go on! I never knew until now what has been lacking in my life!"

A similar kind of one-sidedness occurs in the lives of many Christians. They feed their spirit by reading the Bible, praying, and attending church, all of which are necessary. But they stop short of being everything God intends them to be. They fail to cultivate a wide range of interests. They don't listen to inspiring music, nor do they take time to appreciate the mysteries and beauties of God's creation. They are imbalanced people.

But not the psalmist. Having God always at the center of his thought-life motivated him to growth and maturity, making his life broad and complete. His words reveal that he took time to observe God's wonders in nature and that he found music to be a fitting means through which to worship and praise God. —H.V.L.

Some people see more in a walk around the block
than others see in a trip around the world.

Tuesday

Make a joyful shout to the LORD, . . .
Come before His presence with singing (Psalm 100:1–2).

An old Jewish legend says that after God had created the world He called the angels to Himself and asked them what they thought of it. One of them said, "The only thing lacking is the sound of praise to the Creator." So God created music, and it was heard in the whisper of the wind and in the song of the birds. He also gave man the gift of song. And throughout all the ages, music has blessed multitudes of people.

Music is one of those good things in life we take for granted. Yet, as is so often the case, the world has taken this good gift from God and used it for evil purposes. In our day we're especially aware of its misuse and the shameful behavior so often associated with it. But good music is a blessing from the Lord. It soothes troubled hearts and motivates us to live for Christ. And through it we lift our hearts in praise to the Lord.

When we join voices with fellow believers and lift our hearts in hymns of praise, we honor the Lord, edify our brothers and sisters in Christ, and bring joy to our own lives. —R.W.D.

**No music so pleases God
as the heartfelt praises of His saints.**

Wednesday

**He is the head of the body,
the church (Colossians 1:18).**

We can never exaggerate the greatness of Christ. Paul said that "He is the image of the invisible God" (Col. 1:15), that "by Him all things were created" (v. 16), and that "He is before all things" (v. 17). As the preeminent person in human history, Christ is worthy of our love and our praise.

In his classic book *The Pursuit of God*, A. W. Tozer paid tribute to Frederick Faber, the Englishman who wrote the song "Faith of Our Fathers." Tozer said, "His love for the person of Christ was so intense that it threatened to consume him; it burned within him as a sweet and holy madness and flowed from his lips like molten gold. In one of his sermons he said, 'Wherever we turn in the church of God, there is Jesus. He is the beginning, middle, and end of everything to us. . . . There is nothing good, nothing holy, nothing beautiful, nothing joyous which He is not to His servants. . . . No one need be downcast, for Jesus is the joy of heaven, and it is His joy to enter into sorrowful hearts. We can exaggerate about many things, but we can never exaggerate our obligation to Jesus, or the compassionate abundance of the love of Jesus to us. All our lives long we might talk of Jesus, and yet we should never come to an end of the sweet things that might be said of Him.'"

Christ deserves our loving adoration. He is truly the preeminent One. —R.W.D.

**When we submit to Jesus' lordship,
we'll give Him our worship.**

Thursday

PSALM 29

This is the day which the Lord has made;
we will rejoice and be glad in it (Psalm 118:24).

Blind and deaf from the age of two, Helen Keller was asked by a young boy, "Isn't it the worst thing in the world to be blind?" Smiling, she replied, "Not half so bad as to have two good eyes and see nothing."

Many people with sharp eyesight and acute hearing seem totally unaware of the beautiful sights and pleasing sounds all around them. They never notice the majesty of stately trees, the tranquility of a quiet lake, or the splendor of starry skies. They fail to hear the melodies of singing birds or the gentle rustling of leaves.

God is pleased when we delight in the wonders of His creation and praise Him for them. The Holy Spirit underscored this truth for us when He moved David to write a vivid description of an oriental storm (Psalm 29). Calling it the "voice of the Lord," the psalmist depicted it as coming from the west and sweeping over land, breaking the mighty cedars in the mountain ranges, and stripping bark off the bushes. Later, when chanting this psalm in the temple, awestruck worshipers, visualizing the storm, would cry out, "Glory," giving praise to God.

Stepping outside each morning and breathing the fresh air reminds us to stop a moment and thank God for life. And an approaching storm with its flashing lightning and rolling thunder displays the power of God, prompting us to worship. Observing the sights and sounds around us will motivate us to live for the Lord and to praise Him.

—H.V.L.

Learn to enjoy nature's beauty—
it's the handwriting of God.

Friday

PSALM 148

Praise the LORD! Praise the LORD,
O my soul! (Psalm 146:1).

A music critic for *The Grand Rapids Press* could not find enough good things to say about violinist Itzhak Perlman after he appeared with the Grand Rapids Symphony. The guest soloist had played Tchaikovsky's very difficult "Concerto for Violin and Orchestra in D Major" in a way that made it look easy. In his review, the columnist wrote, "He draws the bow up and down so naturally, yet so perfectly, that he can meet the music's rhythmic and expressive demands without appearing to give it any thought or effort. Regardless of the tempo, every note is perfectly clear, perfectly in place rhythmically, perfectly in tune, and perfectly uniform with every other. Every phrase was crafted meticulously and expressively to fit into an overall conception of the concerto which came out sounding alive and exciting. And he played with and against the orchestra in a fascinating dialogue, as he spoke and answered the other instruments in a clear musical conversation."

Such lavish praise bothers me a little. Not because of the honor it gave Perlman—he deserves it. It troubles me because I seldom hear anyone praise God with such soaring abandon. Shouldn't we who know Him speak of His majesty and wondrous works with that same enthusiasm and detail?

Surely our heavenly Father deserves as much praise for creating the violinist as the violinist deserves for displaying his God-given talent.

—M.R.D.II

**If Christians believed God more,
the world would doubt Him less.**

Saturday

PSALM 33:1–11

Rejoice in the LORD, O you righteous! . . .
Sing to Him a new song (Psalm 33:1, 3).

Singing has always played a vital role in reverence. Worshipers sang psalms in the temple, often in the form of beautiful antiphons. First, the soloist and the choir would respond to one another, then the choir and the worshipers would do the same. Jesus and His disciples sang a hymn after the Lord's supper (Matt. 26:30). Paul encouraged believers to address one another with "psalms and hymns and spiritual songs" (Eph. 5:19).

The purpose of singing is not simply to prepare worshipers for the sermon. If so, singing would be just a gimmick. Paul would have frowned on such an idea because he was convinced that the gospel alone, truthfully proclaimed, is "the power of God to salvation" (Rom. 1:16). We sing because it is an effective way to express our adoration, our supplication, or our testimony. Through song we praise our God and edify one another.

The writer of Psalm 33 called upon the worshiping Israelites to sing praise to God for His powerful word, His unfailing counsels, and His continual concern for His people. Paul and Silas, in prison with their feet in stocks and their backs raw from a brutal flogging, sang because they were filled with the joy of salvation.

If we truly love the Lord, we will join enthusiastically with others in praising Him through song. And when we are alone and our heart is full of praise, we can sing without concern for how it sounds. The Lord is pleased with any melody of praise that comes from the heart.

—H.V.L.

**Music expresses what we cannot put into words,
but about which we cannot keep silent.**

Week 21

SOLOMON'S REQUEST

And God said to Solomon: "Because . . . you have not asked riches or wealth or honor . . . but have asked wisdom and knowledge . . . wisdom and knowledge are granted you; and I will give you riches and wealth and honor" (2 Chronicles 1:11–12).

THEME

WISDOM

When offered one wish, Midas, a legendary Phrygian king, asked that all he touched might turn to gold. His golden desire granted, Midas realized as soon as he wanted to eat that the gift was a curse, not a blessing. Although he got what he wanted, he didn't want what he got.

King Solomon also was offered one wish. But he did not waste it on a selfish, greedy request. Instead, he asked for wisdom that he might judge God's people justly. In requesting wisdom above riches, Solomon revealed right reasons for wanting to be wise. He asked not for his own benefit.

Wise people know how to learn; they never seek knowledge for their own sake. They know how to talk; they speak the truth in love. They know how to act; they pursue justice and evade evil. Perceptive people balance their words and actions. They say and do the right things at the right time for the right reasons.

The discerning person soon realizes that biblical wisdom is more about practice than philosophy. Wise people live skillfully. They apply heavenly counsel to earthly conduct.

In sending His Son to the unwise world, God applied knowledge. As Paul said, Jesus is God's wisdom applied to the world's problems (1 Cor. 1:24). We do not always think like God; but as His image-bearers by creation and new birth, we can be more perceptive. He left us with a word to the wise—imitate the life of Jesus.

Sunday

"Now give me wisdom and knowledge, that I may go out and come in before this people" (2 Chronicles 1:10).

A Persian philosopher, when asked how he had acquired so much knowledge, answered, "By not being too proud to ask questions when I was ignorant."

Even though Solomon was Israel's mighty king, he too was willing to admit his ignorance. But he wanted more than mere knowledge. When the Lord said to him, "Ask! What shall I give you?" (v. 7), Solomon made only one request. He asked for the insight and ability to judge God's people righteously. God gave him this, and He added wealth and honor as a bonus.

Solomon had his priorities right. He kept the people's welfare, not his own, in mind. Too often we want wisdom in order to achieve wealth and honor, but God doesn't work that way. He gives it to those who will honor Him whatever may happen.

Teenagers stand on the threshold of becoming adults and agonize over the question, "What should I do with my life?" Adults face job changes, family responsibilities, and many other far-reaching decisions. In times like these we need to search our hearts and ask, "Why do I want wisdom?" When we get our priorities straight, we can claim the promise of James 1:5, "If any of you lacks wisdom, let him ask of God, who gives to all liberally . . . and it will be given to him." It's always appropriate to ask God for wisdom when our heart's desire is to honor Him and do what's right. —D.J.D.

They are wise who take God for a teacher.

Monday

JAMES 3

The heart of the wise teaches his mouth,
and adds learning to his lips (Proverbs 16:23).

Experts tell us that people often hide what they are trying to say behind a wall of words. This is a kind of doubletalk in which their words do not coincide with their feelings. Gerald Nierenberg, a New York lawyer, wrote a book about this problem called *Meta-Talk: Guide to Hidden Meanings in Conversation.* In it he gives 350 examples of verbal distortion.

A communication consultant who holds workshops on this subject says many people fear that honesty in speech will cost them friendships, love, or respect. So they either keep their lips zipped or say something other than what they mean. Shyness, lack of self-worth, fear of displaying ignorance, fear of criticism, and fear of hurting someone's feelings also may impede honest communication.

Christians are not immune to this problem. Trying to be both loving and truthful can be extremely difficult. The Bible, however, provides a balanced and optimistic approach to this dilemma. Being honest with people may hurt, but if we speak kindly and with compassion we give them the support they need to face reality.

The third chapter of James indicates that divine wisdom can help us talk effectively, for it is "first pure, then peaceable, gentle, willing to yield, full of mercy and good fruits, without partiality and without hypocrisy" (v. 17). Believers who let these characteristics govern their speech will not have to hide behind a wall of words. —M.R.D.II

Gentle words fall lightly, but they have great weight.

Tuesday

PROVERBS 3:13–20

Do not be wise in your own eyes; fear
the LORD, and depart from evil (Proverbs 3:7).

A cartoon in a New York newspaper depicted a young woman garbed in cap and gown, holding a diploma. With her head held high, she looks down her nose at Mr. World. "Well, what do we have here?" Mr. World asks in his cold, cruel, cynical way. "Certainly you know who I am. Cecelia Shakespeare Doaks, a graduate of Prestige College. I have my A.B." "How sad," replies Mr. World. "Come with me and I'll teach you the rest of the alphabet."

We wouldn't disparage the graduate for learning, nor downplay the desire to pursue an education. But four years of classroom instruction, even under the most competent teachers, doesn't make a student wise. The "school of hard knocks" often contributes more to wisdom than the "university of hard facts."

Get an education? Yes! But more importantly, seek the wisdom that is from above. The Scriptures tell us, "The fear of the Lord is the beginning of wisdom" (Prov. 9:10). Knowledge is the acquisition of facts; wisdom is the right use of those facts. Even with the best education and the broadest practical experience, a man or a woman knows nothing apart from God. The Bible says, "If any of you lack wisdom, let him ask of God, who gives to all liberally, . . . and it will be given to him" (James 1:5). This kind of wisdom never leads to arrogance. —R.W.D.

The heart of education is education of the heart.

Wednesday

In 1972, two oil tankers collided under the Golden Gate Bridge, spilling 840,000 gallons of crude oil into the bay. Dying birds, fish, and seals began washing up on the shore. The tragedy prompted a man who lived near the bridge to live a simpler life that would use less natural resources. First, he began walking everywhere. A year later, he decided to stop talking in an attempt to call attention to what was happening to the environment. During the next thirteen years, he talked only once: he called his parents to tell them his plans to begin a walking pilgrimage. Through nonverbal communication, he conveyed the idea that the longer he maintained silence, the more he could listen to what other people were saying. Furthermore, as a result of his silence, the press began to take note of his cause and his message.

What this man discovered holds true for us. Talking less can help us not only to hear more but also to be heard more. Often our silence on a subject is more eloquent and noteworthy than any words we could say.

Solomon emphasized this truth repeatedly. The wise person hears and is heard because he knows both when to talk and when to remain silent. And he has a way of speaking even when he says nothing. There is wisdom in talking less in order to say more. —M.R.D.II

**Silence can be beautiful;
don't break it unless you can improve it.**

Thursday

1 CORINTHIANS 6:1–11

God is love (1 John 4:16).
"Be holy, for I am holy" (1 Peter 1:16).

In a children's story popular during the middle 1800s, a small boy disobeyed his mother by taking a piece of cake when she wasn't looking. The book referred to him as "mean," "contemptible," and "without one particle of honorable or generous feeling." It asked, "And can anyone love or esteem a child who has become so degraded?" A description of "the deceitful child" at the judgment of the great white throne followed, and we learn of his harsh sentence, "Depart from Me, you cursed, into the everlasting fire prepared for the devil and his angels" (Matt. 25:41).

Unwise Christians get like that. They emphasize God's wrath so much that they lose sight of His mercy. On the other hand, some put so much stress on God's love that they lose sight of His holiness. Neither extreme is healthy. Wisdom keeps truth and love in proper balance.

The story disturbs me because it gives a distorted view of God. It was right in warning against disobedience, but it said nothing about forgiveness. How unlike 1 Corinthians 6:1–11. There we see the solemn warning about unrighteousness and immorality followed by the words, "And such were some of you. But you were washed, but you were sanctified" (v. 11).

We must take seriously God's holiness and wrath against sin. But we must not forget His love and grace. We will live right and guide others correctly only as we gain wisdom and learn to hold the truth in balance. —H.V.L.

We must be careful not to teach the wrath of God apart from the grace of God.

Friday

2 PETER 1:1–11

Grace and peace be multiplied to you
in the knowledge of God (2 Peter 1:2).

An early evening thunderstorm provided the setting for the most beautiful rainbow I'd ever seen. But when I tried to describe it to my wife, I became thoroughly frustrated, for its beauty defied my words. In an attempt to understand what I had observed, I read an article in the encyclopedia. It explained that a rainbow is an arc showing the colors of the spectrum, which is a display of light separated according to wavelengths. Each wavelength consists of a different color. Therefore the rainbow appears as a band of colors. The article increased my understanding, but it offered only cold facts. It didn't capture the rainbow's glory. Abstract knowledge adds to my intellectual understanding, but only seeing its beauty can reach my emotions.

Second Peter 1 mentions two different kinds of knowledge. In verses 5 and 6, the author used a Greek word for knowledge that means the abstract information needed for spiritual growth. But in verses 2, 3, and 8, he used the Greek word that denotes a more complete, practical knowledge of Christ, which is actually the goal of such growth. These two terms differ in the same way that reading about a rainbow differs from seeing its beauty. Job spoke of that distinction after his testing when he said to the Lord, "I have heard of You by the hearing of the ear, but now my eye sees You" (Job 42:5). As you increase your knowledge about God, pray that you may also grow in your knowledge of God. —M.R.D.II

True wisdom starts with a heart full of faith,
not a head full of facts.

Saturday

2 PETER 1:1–14

**Giving all diligence, add to your faith virtue,
to virtue knowledge (2 Peter 1:5).**

In an interview at Santa Monica College a few years ago, a student told me that he was extremely interested in finding out all he could about religion, that he enjoyed studying it, and that he was looking for truth. When I questioned him further about his desire to learn so much about religion, he explained that he wanted to expand his education. His curiosity drove him to find out what motivates religious people, but he said he was not the kind of person who gets up in the morning with a desire to do the will of God.

We are like this student when we want to learn more about the Bible for some reason other than to know God better and to do what He wants us to do. The apostle Peter said that we should increase our understanding for one primary purpose—to bring our faith to maturity. Our goal in pursuing knowledge should be self-control, perseverance, godliness, brotherly kindness, and love, which are marks of a wise Christian. This progression toward maturity results in a full experiential knowledge of Christ (v. 8).

God doesn't ask us to increase knowledge for the sake of knowledge. He asks us to grow in our understanding so that we can become God-centered, loving, productive people. —M.R.D.II

**Unless it leads to wisdom,
knowledge can be dangerous.**

Week 22

ELIJAH AT HOREB

Elijah . . . arose and ran for his life, and went . . . a day's journey into the wilderness, and came and sat down under a broom tree. And he prayed that he might die (1 Kings 19:2–4).

THEME

DEPRESSION

Adoniram Judson, the pioneer missionary to Burma who translated the Bible into Burmese and is considered one of the great early missionaries, had difficulty dealing with the death of his wife, Nancy. In deep depression, he said, "God is to me the Great Unknown. I believe in him, but I find him not."

We have all gone through times when the only certainty was uncertainty. Like Christian in *Pilgrim's Progress,* we have all faced Giant Despair. As Winston Churchill put it, we are sometimes overtaken by the "black dog of depression."

Jezebel scared Elijah with her death threat, and he ran for his life. He was so discouraged that he asked God to carry out Jezebel's pronouncement. Instead, God reassured Elijah with His presence and plan for the future.

Like Elijah, the two disciples from Emmaus were near despair. Their hope that Jesus would redeem Israel had been dashed, leaving them disappointed and puzzled—but only until the resurrected Christ appeared. With His presence came a bright light for the future.

Faith and doubt travel hand in hand, and doubt about God's goodness and care often leads to depression. Yet sorrow has a spur; depression can drive us to Him. If we do not find Him, He finds us; and we cry out for joy. He is alive and He loves us.

Sunday

1 KINGS 19:1–10

"Now, LORD, take my life, for I am
no better than my fathers!" (1 Kings 19:4).

A letter came to Radio Bible Class that bore no signature and no
return address. It read, "By the time you receive this letter, I will have
committed suicide. I accepted Christ two years ago. Lately my world
has been crumbling around me. I can't take it anymore. I can't fall
again or be 'bad' anymore. God and I have drifted apart. . . . Lord, help
me. Could you take a moment and say a prayer for me, a teenager?
Lord forgive me!"

Even Christians can get so desperate that they want to take their
own life. In 1 Kings 19 we read that Elijah was so physically and
emotionally exhausted that he asked God to take his life. Although
that's not suicide, his request arises from the same feelings of despair.
But God brought Elijah out of his depression. He lifted him up by
strengthening him with food, restoring him through sleep, listening
to his complaint, gently correcting him, reassuring him in a still,
small voice, giving him new work to do, and telling him that all was
not lost.

Most people who take their own lives do so when they are deeply
depressed. Reality has become distorted, and they can't see the selfish,
sinful nature of their act. But God wants to restore and uphold them.
Sometimes He speaks hope directly to the soul, but more often He
uses sensitive, caring people who come alongside to help. We can be
God's hope to others. With a word, a smile, or a helping hand we can
say to those who are cast down, "In Christ there is hope." —D.J.D.

When we are most ready to perish,
God is most ready to help us.

Monday

PSALM 34:1–7

Behold, the eye of the LORD is on those who fear
Him, . . . To deliver their soul from death (Psalm 33:18, 19).

William Cowper, though a Christian, had sunk to the depths of despair. One foggy night he called for a horsedrawn carriage and asked to be taken to the London Bridge on the Thames River. He was so overcome by depression that he intended to commit suicide. After two hours of driving through the mist, Cowper's coachman reluctantly confessed that he was lost. Disgusted by the delay, Cowper left the carriage and decided to find the London Bridge on foot. After walking a short distance, he discovered that he was at his own doorstep. The carriage had been going in circles. Recognizing the restraining hand of God and convicted by the Spirit, Cowper realized that the way out of his troubles was to look to God, not to jump into the river. With gratitude he sat down and wrote these reassuring words: "God moves in a mysterious way His wonders to perform; He plants His footsteps in the sea, and rides upon the storm. O fearful saint, fresh courage take; the clouds you so much dread are big with mercy, and shall break in blessings on your head." Cowper's hymn of gratitude has comforted many of God's people since the eighteenth century.

The psalmist said, "The eye of the Lord is on those who fear Him." Our need is always His concern. —H.G.B.

No life is hopeless unless Christ is ruled out.

Tuesday

PSALM 77:1–15

"This is my anguish; but I will remember the years of the right hand of the Most High" (Psalm 77:10).

After a long and hard winter, the bright and balmy days of spring were again invaded by a renegade polar air mass. Winter seemed to be starting all over again. Those with cabin fever started to panic. Others, worn out from shoveling snow, slumped back into their chairs and worried about another high heating bill. But nobody concluded that the age-old order of the seasons had come to an abrupt end, or that the solar system had reversed its cycle. Looking back reminded them that late-season storms have happened before and reassured them that spring would eventually come.

Likewise, looking back on past blessings can restore our hope and give us reason to look ahead. The author of Psalm 77 had sunk so low that all hope seemed gone. He was so troubled he couldn't sleep. He was so depressed he couldn't even talk about it. He was so low that the fleas of the field had to get on their knees to bite him. But then something happened. He remembered his forefathers. They had gone through similar troubles before the Lord delivered them. Remembering the Lord's faithfulness to them renewed his faith.

The Bible reminds us that we are not the first to walk this way. Men and women of God have seen dark times before, but the forecast of faith is always bright. —M.R.D.II

Judge God's love by His promises, not by His providences.

Wednesday

JOHN 9:1–7

"Rabbi, who sinned, this man or his parents, that he was born blind?" (John 9:2).

When illness strikes someone, we tend to think of it as the result of sin. Since all our woes can be traced to man's original sin, we reason that sin must also be the immediate cause of sickness. Apparently this was how the disciples analyzed the case of the man born blind. But Jesus' reply, "Neither has this man nor his parents," undercuts all pat answers to affliction.

Perhaps emotional illness, more than any other kind of suffering, is subject to shortsighted, judgmental responses. Most physical diseases are socially acceptable, but a stigma still hangs over most psychological disorders. In her book *God's Remedy for Depression*, Vivian Clark tells of a discussion on the topic "Is Depression Sin for the Christian?" One person said, "Because it can't coexist with the fruit of the Spirit, which is joy, it must be a sin." Another added, "There is no reason for Christians to be depressed." Just then, a sad-faced woman slipped away from the group. For days she had been despondent and unable to gain victory. Those remarks added to her depression.

Some emotional problems may indeed be caused by wrong attitudes or secret sins. But all of us transgress, and yet not everyone breaks down. The causes of depression and mental illness are so varied and complex that we must not engage in simplistic solutions. To help someone, we shouldn't immediately ask, "Who sinned?" Rather, we should pray, "Lord, help me further Your work in this person's life."
—D.J.D.

**Compassion invests everything necessary
to heal the hurts of others.**

Thursday

**For my soul is full of troubles
(Psalm 88:3).**

Walking with the Lord is more fulfilling than anything this world offers, but it is not an uninterrupted stroll of peace, joy, and praise. Nowhere does the Bible say that God's people are exempt from physical pain or even great mental and spiritual darkness.

During his ministry, C. H. Spurgeon, one of England's finest preachers, frequently fell into deep depression. In a biography of the "prince of preachers," Arnold Dallimore wrote, "What he suffered in those times of darkness we may not know . . . even his desperate calling on God brought no relief. 'There are dungeons,' he said, 'beneath the castles of despair.'"

Psalm 88, written by a godly man named Heman, stands alone in the psalter for its unrelenting sorrow and gloom. Unlike David, whose despair usually gave way to hope, Heman's psalm ends with the word *darkness.*

But how can such a woeful psalm encourage us? First, it confirms that some of God's people do undergo great spiritual misery. Second, it shows the way out. Heman poured out his anguish to God even though no answer came. Some Bible scholars see in his mental agony a parallel to Christ's. Looking back to Calvary, we know that when He bore our sin He was actually forsaken by God. He died in our place. Therefore, we who trust Him will never be abandoned. God promises that deliverance is certain, even when there is no relief in sight.

—D.J.D.

**God is with us in the darkness
just as surely as He is with us in the light.**

Friday

PROVERBS 12:17–28

Anxiety in the heart of man causes depression, but a good word makes it glad (Proverbs 12:25).

Ken's friends invited him to their home for dinner. The food was superb—except for the apple pie. It wasn't bad; it just didn't measure up to the rest of the meal. Even so, Ken went out of his way to find some good things to say about it. Later, he visited the home again and stayed for dinner. On this occasion, the hostess topped off the meal with a cherry pie that was absolutely delicious. But Ken didn't say one word about it. This bothered the hostess, so she finally blurted out, "I don't understand. The last time you were here, I served a pie that I was ashamed of, yet you were very complimentary. Tonight I've given you what I think is the best pie I've ever made, and you haven't said a word about it." Ken smiled and replied, "I agree that the cherry pie tonight was fantastic, and that the apple pie you served last time was not as good as this one. But you see, the first one needed the praise!"

Our relationship with people is like that—some need more encouragement than others. Everyone who deserves praise should be recognized, and we should never say that something is good when it's really bad. Yet no matter how imperfect a person may seem or how poor the performance, we can almost always find something commendable to praise.

Discouraged people surround us—perhaps even in our own homes. But using a little imagination, we can find creative ways to give them the encouragement they need. —R.W.D.

If you see people without a smile today, give them one of yours.

Saturday

Now may the God of hope fill you
with all joy and peace in believing (Romans 15:13).

The English poet Alexander Pope said, "Hope springs eternal in the human breast, man never is but always to be blessed." As Christians, we know there is only one sure and abiding source of hope, and that is God. If hope originated in ourselves, we would be cast into the depths of despair because life's complex problems have a way of squeezing every last ounce of it from our hearts. But when we trust God, hope abounds by the power of the Holy Spirit.

In his book *Live With Your Emotions,* Hazen G. Werner quotes part of a letter from a woman who had run out of hope. She wrote, "A vile and ugly sin had dogged my way for years. My soul had been eclipsed in darkness. I began to feel I would never be emancipated from its grasp. Then one evening in the midst of my despair, I felt the impulse to say, 'Thank you, God, anyway,' and for a moment it was light. I said to myself, 'That must be the way.' I began to thank Him still more, and the light continued and grew, and for a whole evening I was relieved of my burden."

What that woman seemingly stumbled onto by accident, the psalmist knew from experience. The power of gratitude can lift the weight of the most pressing trial. Turning the gaze of his soul heavenward, he saw God as an inexhaustible source of hope.

When we get discouraged, we can talk to ourselves as David did: "Why are you cast down, O my soul? . . . Hope in God" (Psalm 42:5). No matter how dark the path, thank God for Himself. It will open a window to heaven and let in a ray of hope. —D.J.D.

Hope, like an anchor, is fixed on the unseen.

Week 23

ELISHA STOPS AN ARMY

And Elisha prayed, and said, "LORD, I pray, open his eyes that he may see." Then the LORD opened the eyes of the young man, and he saw. And behold, the mountain was full of horses and chariots of fire all around Elisha (2 Kings 6:17).

THEME

GOD'S PROTECTION

One of the purposes for forming the United States of America was "to provide for the common defense." It has not always been easy. At the Constitutional Convention one of the delegates moved to restrict the standing army to five thousand men at any one time. George Washington sarcastically asked one of the other delegates to suggest an amendment—no enemy could invade at any time with more than three thousand troops.

As we all know, whether in war or in everyday life, we cannot control the enemy. In Elisha's day, the Syrian army marched to the city of Dothan at night and surrounded it. Elisha's servant was afraid until the Lord opened his eyes to the heavenly army encircling the Syrians. Elisha prayed for protection, and the Lord blinded rather than killed the enemy.

Much of the Old Testament is about God protecting His people. God did not create the world and then retire to a long winter's night sleep. He has involved Himself in the humdrum and the humdinger.

Many years after He blinded Elisha's enemies, He sent One who gave sight to the blind and called them to follow Him across the battleground to safety. In the upper room Jesus told His followers that they were protected from Satan by the very power of His name. Those of us today who fly His colors can be assured that our enemies never outnumber His troops.

Sunday

2 KINGS 6:8–23

"Those who are with us are more
than those who are with them" (2 Kings 6:16).

In the subway in New York City, two youths moved through an underground train and robbed a well-dressed man who appeared to be asleep in his seat. Suddenly the whole car came alive. The victim turned out to be a decoy, and the passengers who jumped up from their seats were police officers. Like lightning, they converged on the young pair and arrested them. Although these officers were "unseen" at first, they provided ample security for riders on that subway car.

We see a similar picture of protection in 2 Kings 6. In a manner more dramatic than what happened on that New York subway, Elisha's servant saw why his master could be so confident in the face of what seemed to be impending disaster. We read that "the LORD opened the eyes of the young man" and he saw an amazing sight (v. 17). An invisible army "of horses and chariots of fire" surrounded Elisha, ready to protect the Israelites from the Syrian army.

Divine protection is not just an Old Testament provision. As God's children, we can put our faith in His mighty defense as we do His will. We can therefore move ahead with confidence, eager to fight the foe. Even when the battle seems to be too great and it appears that we face defeat, we must still trust the Lord. We can encourage ourselves by thinking of Elisha's message to his servants, "Those who are with us are more than those who are with them." —M.R.D.II

With God behind us and His arms beneath us,
we can face whatever lies ahead of us.

Monday

PSALM 59

You have been my defense and refuge
in the day of my trouble (Psalm 59:16).

Growing up in a tough Bronx neighborhood, Jerry and Jeff Monroe developed an interest in self-defense early in life. As they got older, they became experts in the martial arts, and they opened a kung fu school in 1978. Later, after several members of their family had fallen victim to street crime, the brothers fought back by forming the Shaolin Protectors to patrol the streets of their neighborhood. Eventually they merged with another vigilante group and formed with Curtis Sliwa the now-famous Guardian Angels.

One day a fellow member of the Guardian Angels walked up to Jerry, pointed his finger at him as if it were a gun, and said "You're good at kung fu. Bang!" Jerry got the point. His skill at self-defense was no match for a loaded gun. Then the other Angel asked, "Where will you spend eternity if you're blown away on patrol?" Jerry admitted he had never thought about that. When Jerry mentioned the incident to his brother, they both realized their need for God in their lives. Today Jeff and Jerry are Christians, and they use their kung fu demonstrations to tell others about the ultimate defense, the kind David celebrated in Psalm 59.

In today's society, we are vulnerable to everything from viruses to nuclear weapons. We need divine protection. We must depend on God, who is our defense and refuge in the day of trouble. —M.R.D.II

When troubles call on us, we can call on God.

Tuesday

The LORD is . . . my shield and the horn
of my salvation, my stronghold (Psalm 18:2).

On a visit to the National Air and Space Museum in Washington D.C.,
I marveled at the small capsules that carried our first astronauts into
space. In particular, the heatshields fascinated me. These protective
layers of special material were all that kept the men inside from being
burned up as the spacecraft sliced through the atmosphere on its way
to splashdown.

The Detroit News carried an article about another kind of shield
that I find even more amazing—the vast magnetic field that sur-
rounds the earth. Generated by the sun, it is so large that Pioneer 10,
which has traveled more than twenty-three trillion miles, has not yet
passed out of its protection. Called the heliosphere, this magnetic
force shelters our entire solar system from harmful cosmic rays. Without it, life on earth would end.

Recalling the astronauts' heatshield and reading about our solar
system's heliosphere made me think of the greatest protective shield
of all—God Himself. David wrote, "The LORD is . . . my shield and . . .
my stronghold." He knew that the Lord could keep him secure in a
hostile world. We too can know that same confidence. Even though
Satan may attack us and evil may surround us, the Lord is our protector. Whenever we are frightened by circumstances or feel that the
forces against us are too much, we can take comfort in knowing that
God's protective shield is more powerful than anything man or nature
can provide. —D.C.E.

**God is no security against life's storms,
but He is perfect security in life's storms.**

Wednesday

PSALM 27:1–6

The eternal God is your refuge, and underneath are the everlasting arms (Deuteronomy 33:27).

As I read Deuteronomy 33, I recalled an old song written by Ada Habershon. "When I fear my faith will fail, Christ will hold me fast; when the tempter would prevail, He can hold me fast."

A woman facing difficult trials and troubling circumstances came to W. B. Hinson at the close of a sermon and said, "I'm very much afraid I might fall." Hinson replied, "Well, why don't you do it?" "But Preacher," she protested, "where would I fall to?" "You would fall down into the everlasting arms of God," he replied. Then he said, "I have read in the Bible that His everlasting arms are underneath His children. And you know, I believe that if you fall down upon those everlasting arms, it is sure and certain that you will never fall through them." Without question, the believer can rest in the unfailing strength and support of the omnipotent Father. God bolsters this assurance with a progression of truth in Isaiah 41:10 when He says through the prophet, "I am with you." "I will strengthen you." "I will help you." "I will uphold you with My righteous right hand." And in John 17:11 we read this prayer of our Lord: "Holy Father, keep through Your name those whom You have given Me." His request will not be thwarted because our Savior has given every believer into the keeping, safeguarding power of the Father. So even when we stumble, we fall into the everlasting arms of His grace. —P.R.V.

When we get to the place where there's nothing left but God, we find that God is all we need.

Thursday

PSALM 139:1–12

"Am I a God near at hand," says the LORD, . . .
"Do I not fill heaven and earth?" (Jeremiah 23:23–24).

A legendary man went to a beggar and asked, "Why do they say God is everywhere? I don't see Him anywhere." The beggar picked up a clod of dirt and hit the other with it. When the man complained that it hurt, the beggar said, "You say you have pain in your head. Show it to me and I will believe it."

He made his point. By reminding the man that he didn't have to see pain to know it existed, he helped him understand that neither do we have to see God with our eyes to know He is everywhere present.

The promise of God's omnipresence comforts and encourages the Christian. Scottish preacher Thomas Chalmers wrote long ago, "When I walk by the wayside, God is along with me. When I enter into company amid all my forgetfulness of Him, He never forsakes me. In the silent watches of the night, when my eyelids are closed and my spirit has sunk into unconsciousness, the observant eye of Him who never slumbers is upon me. I cannot flee His presence, go where I will. He leads me and watches me and cares for me. And the same Being who is now at work in the remotest dominions of nature and of providence is also at my hand, to give to me every moment of my being, and to uphold the exercise of all my feelings and of all my faculties." We can rest in the assurance that the unseen God is always near. Wherever we go, He walks with us to lead us, assist us, comfort us, and bless us. —D.C.E.

A skeptic once asked a Christian, "Where is God?"
The Christian answered, "First tell me where He is not."

Friday

PSALM 119:113–120

**You are my hiding place and my shield;
I hope in Your word (Psalm 119:114).**

In a State of the Union address in the early 1960s, President John F. Kennedy said that each day was drawing us nearer to the hour of maximum danger. And now, over a quarter of a century later, perils such as a nuclear holocaust are a greater possibility than ever. In fact, at the end of 1980, the editors of the *Bulletin of Atomic Scientists,* who use a "doomsday clock" to gauge human history by a twenty-four-hour measurement of time, moved the hands to four minutes to midnight. The escalating nuclear arms race led them to make this change. They reasoned that if an atomic war were to take place, the total destruction of mankind would be inevitable.

In his book *No Place to Hide,* Dr. David Bradley, who monitored the radiology of early atomic bomb tests, wrote, "When one considers that one-millionth of a gram of radium contained within the body may be fatal, one is inclined to turn from calculus to Christianity." Yes, that is the best possible answer, for the Christian can be secure in the presence and love of God. Psalm 91 speaks of the Lord as a secret place, a shadow (suggesting nearness), a refuge, a fortress, a protector, and a deliverer. We are always safe in him.

Whether our danger comes from the threat of war, disease, family crisis, or satanic attack, God is our fortress. Whatever the circumstances—even in a nuclear age—we have a place to hide. —D.C.E.

**No danger can come so near the Christian
that God is not nearer.**

Saturday

Be my rock of refuge . . . and my fortress
(Psalm 31:2–3).

Protection comes in many forms. A rabbit dives for his hole. A squirrel clings to the backside of a branch. A deer runs for the dense cover of a swamp. A two-year-old runs for his dad's pantleg. A teenager looks for the security of friends. A marine digs in under cover of friendly guns. But what does a Christian do? Where do we hide when surrounded by danger?

David had the answer to that question. When he wrote Psalm 31, things were not going well for him. He was hurting, tired, and weak. His mind was distressed, his heart broken. His enemies were chasing him, and his friends had let him down. Though vulnerable, he was not defenseless. David had a refuge that those who didn't trust Jehovah knew nothing about. He knew that in God is the safest place, and that the wisest defense strategy is having a right relationship with Him. So that's where he found his security. Just as a small child might find confidence in using his older brother's name when threatened by a bully, David called upon the name of God. Because he was living in fellowship with Him, he hid himself in the security of the One who had helped him so many times before and who loved him with an unfailing love.

Are we wise? Are we as quick to seek that same security? We can trust God. He who was a sure hiding place for David is also the One we should cling to for our protection. —M.R.D.II

**Christians find safety not in the absence of danger
but in the presence of God.**

Week 24

JOSIAH RESTORES WORSHIP

Then the king stood by a pillar and made a covenant before the LORD, to follow the LORD and to keep His commandments. . . . And all the people took their stand for the covenant (2 Kings 23:3).

THEME

THE POWER OF GOD'S WORD

On June 15, 1215, in the grass field of Runnymeade, one document of sixty-three paragraphs changed the course of a whole nation. That charter of human rights, called the Magna Carta, became the rallying point for the British for generations to come.

God gave Israel some words on a mountaintop that were far more powerful than those ratified in an English field two millenniums later. But evidently Israel did not find God's words important; they lost some of them for at least half a century. Finally, in 622 B.C., Hilkiah the high priest found a portion of God's Word, perhaps Deuteronomy, in the temple. He gave the sacred section to Josiah the king, and the holy words changed the rest of Josiah's reign. The people destroyed their heathen idols and began to worship God again.

Whenever people in biblical times read and followed God's Word, it changed their lives. As they remembered what God had said, they moved back to the main road. But soon their memories faded, and they once again sauntered down side streets.

To correct mixed-up memories and homemade maps, God gave one final Word—Jesus Christ, the fullest expression of His mind. Christ's Words and life have become not only a precious memory and a spiritual centerpiece, but also the only sure way to find God at the end of the road.

Sunday

2 KINGS 22:8–20

When the king heard the words of the Book of the Law . . .
he tore his clothes (2 Kings 22:11).

Complex family problems divided an Alabama family. In the turmoil, a young boy went to live with his father and came to believe that he belonged there. Later, he recognized himself on a special television program about missing children. Realizing that he belonged with someone else, he told his babysitter, who then called authorities. Before long, the child was in his mother's arms.

This reminded me of what happened to King Josiah in 2 Kings 22. He had assumed that he and his nation were where they belonged spiritually. But one day Hilkiah the priest found the long-lost law of God and read it to Josiah. The king suddenly realized that sin had separated him and his people from their God. He tore his clothes in personal repentance and concern for his people. As a result, the nation repented and returned to the God to whom they belonged (2 Kings 23). It all came about because Josiah saw himself and his people in the words of the Scriptures.

We sometimes assume that we are where we belong spiritually, when in fact we have unconfessed sin in our lives. To keep this from happening, we must read the Bible as God's personal message to us. He gave it to us so that we could see ourselves in it, recognize our sin, and confess. Then, when we repent, we will be "reunited" with Him.

—M.R.D.II

**Other books were given for our information;
the Bible was given for our transformation.**

Monday

PSALM 119:9–16

**Your word I have hidden in my heart,
that I might not sin against You (Psalm 119:11).**

Michael Billester, a Bible distributor, visited a small hamlet in Poland shortly before World War II and gave a Bible to a villager who read it and was converted. The new believer then passed the Book on to others. The cycle of conversions and sharing continued until two hundred people had become believers through that one Bible. When Billester returned in 1940, this group of Christians met together for a worship service and asked him to preach the Word. He normally asked for testimonies, but this time he suggested that several in the audience recite verses of Scripture. One man stood and said, "Perhaps we have misunderstood. Did you mean verses or chapters?"

The villagers had not memorized a few selected verses of the Bible but whole chapters and books. Thirteen people knew Matthew, Luke, and half of Genesis. Another person knew the Psalms. That single copy of the Bible given by Billester had done its work. Transformed lives bore witness to the power of the Word.

Most people in the United States have easy access to Bibles. Many homes have several on their shelves. So we often take the Scriptures for granted. To experience for ourselves the Bible's transforming power, we must read and memorize it and apply its truth daily. Like the psalmist, we must hide the Word in our hearts. In the soul, not on the shelf, is where it takes root and produces godly lives. —P.R.V.

**Too many people put the Bible on the shelf
instead of into their hearts.**

Tuesday

ACTS 4:32–37

You are . . . His own special people, that you may proclaim the praises of Him who called you (1 Peter 2:9).

As newsman Clarence W. Hall followed American troops through Okinawa in 1945, he and his jeep driver came upon a small town that stood out as a beautiful example of a Christian community. He wrote, "We had seen other Okinawan villages, . . . down at the heels and despairing; by contrast, this one shone like a diamond in a dung heap. Everywhere we were greeted by smiles and dignified bows. Proudly the old men showed us their spotless homes, their terraced fields, . . . their storehouses and granaries, their prized sugar mill."

Hall saw no jails and no drunkenness, and divorce was unknown. He learned an American missionary had come there thirty years earlier. While he was in the village, he had led two elderly townspeople to Christ and left them with a Japanese Bible. These new believers studied the Scriptures and started leading their fellow villagers to Jesus. Hall's jeep driver said he was amazed at the difference between this village and the others around it. He remarked, "So this is what comes out of only a Bible and a couple of old guys who wanted to live like Jesus."

The great power of God's Word leads to salvation through faith in Christ, creating a "special people," a community of believers who love one another, exhort one another, and serve God together. We need to pray that our churches will be an example of God's power to a watching world. —H.V.L.

The world at its worst needs the church at its best.

Wednesday

PSALM 119:41–48

For our gospel did not come to you in word only,
but also in power (1 Thessalonians 1:5).

First-century believers communicated the gospel verbally while it was being put into written form. In each generation since, believers have taken the truths of the Word of God with them as they moved about, proclaiming them openly in church services and whispering them in secret. Christianity has taken root and grown strong because God's Word has brought salvation and hope to people of every station in life. The written Word of the living God was given to all mankind, and its impact on our world is immeasurable.

American clergyman and author Henry van Dyke expressed the broad influence of the Book of books in this way: "Born in the East and clothed in oriental form and imagery, the Bible walks the ways of all the world with familiar feet and enters land after land to find its own everywhere. It has learned to speak in hundreds of languages to the heart of man. It comes into the palace of the monarch to tell him that he is a servant to the Most High, and into the cottage to assure the peasant that he is a child of God."

Kings and peasants have read the Bible and believed, nations have been altered, and cultures have improved because of its message. The Bible makes a difference wherever it goes, and it makes a difference in our lives when we read it, meditate upon its truth, and apply it to our lives. The Book for everyone has a special message for each of us.

—D.C.E.

The Bible, like a bank, is most helpful when it's open.

Thursday

PSALM 119:25–32

For the word of God is living and powerful
(Hebrews 4:12).

One Sunday evening at church a short-term missionary reported on her overseas experiences and told about crossing into a communist country. At the border, the guards asked, "Do you have any guns, drugs, or Bibles?"

Although they probably hadn't read it, those communist border guards apparently believed Hebrews 4:12. To them, the Bible was as dangerous as guns and drugs. Guns injure and kill the body. Drugs alter and distort the mind. The Bible exposes and destroys falsehood. But the Bible threatens more than their religion of atheism. It threatens their place of power and control over the people because it gives to the people what no government can. The Bible enriches lives, instills hope, and frees the human spirit, which makes it as threatening to an atheistic government as guns and drugs.

In Psalm 119, the psalmist refers to some of the powerful effects of the Word of God on his life. It revives his soul (v. 25); it imparts inner strength (v. 28); it guides him into truth (v. 30); and it enlarges his heart (v. 32).

We who are blessed with both the Old and New Testaments have God's full and final written revelation of Himself. When we meditate on the truths of this powerful book, we experience its impact on our lives by the indwelling Holy Spirit, who makes it real to us.

Guns, drugs, and the Bible all wield power, but only the Bible destroys what is false and builds what is true. —D.J.D.

**No weapon in Satan's arsenal can destroy
the sword of the Spirit, which is the Word of God.**

Friday

JOHN 15:1–7

"You are already clean because of the word which I have spoken to you" (John 15:3).

The Word of God has cleansing power. One of the surest ways to live a victorious Christian life is to bathe ourselves daily in the purifying principles of the Bible—by reading it, studying it, and obeying it.

A woman in a pagan area of the world became a believer and began attending Bible classes taught by the missionary who had led her to Christ. The teacher soon became discouraged because the new convert seemed to forget everything she was taught. One day the missionary remarked impatiently to the young Christian, "Sometimes I wonder what's the use trying to teach you anything. You forget it all anyway. You remind me of a strainer. Everything I pour into your mind runs right through." The student quickly responded, "I may not recall everything, but just as water passes through a strainer and makes it clean, what you have taught me from the Bible helps make me clean. I need that. That's why I keep coming back." The forgetful new Christian may not have retained all of the missionary's instruction, but as the truths of the Bible "poured through" her mind, she felt its cleansing effect.

It's important for us to be in God's Word every day—but even more important for the Word to be in us, where its purifying power can do its most effective work. —R.W.D.

**If we pore over God's Word,
His cleansing power will pour through us.**

Saturday

"The secret things belong to the LORD . . . but those things which are revealed belong to us" (Deuteronomy 29:29)

At lunch one day, W. Wilbert Welch, chancellor of the Grand Rapids Baptist College and Seminary, told a story about one of his professors, Dr. Brokenshire, a godly and gifted scholar with a thorough knowledge of Scripture. "I remember our first day in class," Welch recalled. "The professor didn't know us by name yet, so he referred to some cards in his hand. Looking up, he said, 'Mr. Green?' The student identified himself. 'Mr. Green, do you have any problems with the Bible?' 'No, sir,' replied the confident new student. Brokenshire replied, 'Then why don't you read it? You will.'"

A thoughtful reading of the Bible will raise questions. Peter said that Paul's writings contained "some things hard to understand" (2 Pet. 3:16). Sometimes we see only one side of a truth, or we come across what seems like a contradiction. Then there are the bigger problems—divine election and human freedom, the origin of evil, the reason for pain and suffering. But these perplexities need not undermine our confidence in the Bible.

God wants us to study the Bible, and a questioning mind is fertile soil for learning. Some things, however, will remain a mystery, and we must humbly accept God's right to withhold knowledge from us. No matter what problems we have in understanding the Bible, we can thank Him that He has revealed sufficient truth to win our hearts, guide our steps, and bring us to heaven. —D.J.D.

Our difficulties in understanding the Bible are not due to divine error but to human ignorance.

Week 25

REBUILDING THE TEMPLE

When the adversaries of Judah and Benjamin heard that the descendants of the captivity were building the temple. . . . They troubled them in building, and hired counselors against them to frustrate their purpose (Ezra 4:1, 4–5).

THEME

PERSEVERANCE

In August, 1857, Cyrus Field and his company, Atlantic Telegraph, attempted to lay a telegraph cable from England to North America, but the cable broke at twelve thousand feet under the ocean surface and could not be recovered. During the next nine years, Field and his men made three more unsuccessful attempts. Finally, in July, 1866, they succeeded in laying hundreds of miles of cable across the Atlantic.

Field's task took nine years, but Israel spent almost twenty-one years rebuilding the temple. The work began in 537 B.C. and was finally completed in 516 B.C. Israel's enemies continually stopped the work; one period lasted as long as seventeen years. People of less perseverance might have given up, but Israel had a deep desire to worship God.

Paul wrote about Christ's patience, or, more exactly, His perseverance, in his second letter to the Thessalonians (3:5). We may not understand why an all-powerful God demonstrated patient determination in His humanity, but we are to follow His pattern of perseverance.

We may not give up family and home as He did, but dare we cling too tightly? We may not hunger, but should we be fat and spoiled? We may not suffer and die, but why are we unwilling? Disciples persevere; they are willing to lose life to gain it.

Sunday

EZRA 3:8, 4:1–5

**Now the temple was finished . . . in the
sixth year of the reign of King Darius (Ezra 6:15).**

Many people fail to reach a worthy goal because they become weary
and discouraged. They give up, not realizing that success is within
reach.

Zerubbabel and his work crew encountered constant delays and
discouragements while they rebuilt the temple. How easy it would
have been to give up. Yet they knew God had ordered the work they
were doing, and this gave them confidence.

This verse cleverly illustrates the reward of perseverance.

> Two frogs fell into a deep cream bowl;
> The one was wise, and a cheery soul;
> The other one took a gloomy view,
> And bade his friend a sad adieu.
> Said the other frog with a merry grin,
> "I can't get out, but I won't give in;
> I'll swim around till my strength is spent,
> Then I'll die the more content."
> And as he swam, though ever it seemed,
> His struggling began to churn the cream,
> Until on top of pure butter he stopped,
> And out of the bowl he quickly hopped.
> The moral, you ask? Oh, it's easily found.
> If you can't get out, keep swimming around!

Doing God's will is not always easy. But when the going gets tough,
"keep on swimming." —R.W.D.

We conquer by continuing.

Monday

GALATIANS 6:9–18

In due season we shall reap if we do not lose heart (Galatians 6:9).

If God has called us to a task, quitting is never fitting. Yet who hasn't trudged through the lowlands of discouragement, looking to every side road for an opportunity to leave a difficult and frustrating work. Satan is quick to suggest that we might as well give up, go elsewhere, or let someone who is more talented do the job. But we are where we are by God's appointment. If we're in this kind of situation, the noblest expression of faith is a dogged determination to go on with the task.

A minister had been pastoring a church for some time with seemingly little results. Then one night he had a dream in which he was trying to break a large granite rock with a pickax. Hour after hour he labored, but made no progress. At last he said, "It's no use. I'm going to quit." Suddenly a man appeared by his side and asked, "Weren't you appointed to do this task? Why are you going to abandon it?" The minister told him that the work was futile; he could make no impression on the granite. "That is not your concern," replied the stranger. "The work is in your hands; the results are in another's. Work on!" Taking up the ax again, the minister struck the rock; and at his first blow the granite flew into hundreds of pieces. When he awoke from his dream, a valuable lesson had been impressed upon his heart.

The "rocks" in our lives may seem harder than steel. Yet, if we are in God's will, they will one day yield. —D.J.D.

Perseverance comes not only from a strong will but also from a strong won't.

Tuesday

HEBREWS 10:32–39

**Run with endurance the race that is set before us
(Hebrews 12:1).**

On a warm summer afternoon, three young people and I decided to hike along a five-mile stretch of the picturesque Tahquamenon River in Michigan's Upper Peninsula. We started out with energy and vigor, taking the first few hundred yards with ease. But then the path began to twist and turn as it followed the river's course. We trudged through low, muddy areas and scrambled up steep ridges. Fallen trees blocked the path, and we had to climb over or crawl under. To cross some of the creeks that flowed into the river, we either jumped or walked gingerly along narrow logs. We weren't sure how far we had to go or what lay ahead. Yet we knew our friends would be waiting at the end of the trail, so we had to keep going.

When we did stop for a brief rest, we talked about some parallels between our obstacle-ridden walk and the Christian life. We usually begin our Christian walk with great vigor, excited about our salvation. But it isn't long before we come upon the twists and turns of temptations and trials. We can get mired in the mud of mediocrity or plunge from the peaks of pride. All sorts of dangers and difficulties block our path. We aren't sure what's ahead, and we get weary and discouraged. But we know what awaits us in eternity, so we "run with endurance" the path that is set before us.

All of us get discouraged and tired at times. How pleasant it would be to stay where we are. When that temptation hovers, we must take a deep breath of the Spirit and keep moving on. For rich rewards await us at the end of the trail. —D.C.E.

**Falling drops at last will wear the stone.
—Lucretius**

Wednesday

PHILIPPIANS 1:1–11

**He who has begun a good work in you will complete it
until the day of Jesus Christ (Philippians 1:6).**

Occasionally when I walk along the beach in Florida, I see the remains of partially built sand castles. Apparently the sculptors got distracted or bored and left their castles unfinished. There is something sad about these ruins. Like the unfinished painting, the half-built house, or the incomplete manuscript, they are a haunting reminder of our human tendency to leave things undone.

In his book *Intercepted Letters,* William Marshall wrote: "It is a great trial to one who is naturally fond of bringing a thing to completion, to see how many fragments—unfinished bits of life—are left over. He asks himself, 'What do I have to show for my labor?' Our trust must be that God will take up what is incomplete and wrap around it His completeness. 'He cannot fail.'"

What a difference between man and God! The Creator always finishes what He has started. All of His masterpieces, planned in eternity past and begun in time, will be brought to fulfillment in eternity future. That's when each believer will be completely conformed to His image.

As we struggle now to be more Christlike, we can be confident that one day we will reach that goal. God is molding us into trophies of grace, fashioned like His Son. He leaves nothing undone. —P.R.V.

**The conversion of a soul is the miracle of a moment;
the growth of a saint is the work of a lifetime.**

Thursday

HEBREWS 12:1–4

**Looking unto Jesus, the author
and finisher of our faith. . . . (Hebrews 12:2).**

Every workman takes pride in a project completed and well-done. I thought of this recently when I visited the site of a new house my friend was building. The foundation had been laid, the walls erected, and the wiring and plumbing installed, but the structure still wasn't a house. It needed the finishers. Without the woodworkers, the cabinetmakers, the carpet layers, and the painters, the building was incomplete.

We as Christians need a "finisher" too. The sanctifying work of the Holy Spirit in our lives, which began at conversion, must continue until the One who began the transformation finishes it. And that can happen only by trusting and obeying Jesus, "the author and finisher of our faith," the One to whom we are being conformed.

At one point the psalmist must have felt that God had stopped working in his life, for he cried, "Has God forgotten to be gracious?" (Psalm 77:9). We feel that way too sometimes. We think perhaps that progress has stopped; that plans have been rolled up and tucked away; that construction has been halted. But God does not give up on His children. We are all "under construction," and He will add the finishing touches in His own time.

God is not the architect of incompleteness. The Bible says, "He who has begun a good work in you will complete it until the day of Jesus Christ" (Phil. 1:6). Our part is to stay in fellowship with Him. He'll do the rest. —P.R.V.

**Keep in step with God;
He has planned every step of the way.**

Friday

LUKE 9:57–62

"No one, having put his hand to the plow, and
looking back, is fit for the kingdom of God" (Luke 9:62).

When Deborah, Israel's fourth judge, sang her song in celebration of Israel's victory over the Canaanites (Judges 5:2–31), she mentioned the people of the tribe of Reuben. They had "great resolves of heart," she said; but, she noted with dismay, they were content to sit "among the sheepfolds." They had not turned their plans into action.

The tribe of Reuben was like the boy who sat at his mother's desk, carefully drawing a picture. Soon he laid down his pen and proudly showed his mother his sketch of the family dog. She commented on the fine likeness, then noticed that something was missing. "Where is Rover's tail?" she asked. "It's still in the bottle," the boy explained.

Many important things in the Christian life are left undone because we don't put our plans into action. We decide to devote more time to the reading and studying of the Word of God, then get sidetracked by other activities. We resolve to be more faithful in praying for others. And for a while we do just that. Then, gradually, other things take priority.

No matter how noble our plans, no matter how good our intentions, they can't glorify God if they are "still in the bottle." —P.R.V.

**We may be on the right track,
but we won't get anywhere if we just sit there.**

Saturday

HEBREWS 5:13–6:3

Therefore, leaving the discussion of the elementary
principles of Christ, let us go on to perfection (Hebrews 6:1).

When autumn comes and the leaves drop from my neighbor's trees, I
can look out of my back window and see a forlorn sight—a weather-
beaten building surrounded by weeds. In the mind of the designer,
this structure was to have been a health club complete with swimming
pool, handball courts, and sauna. But somewhere along the way the
planners and builders encountered difficulty—perhaps lack of funds—
and they abandoned the project. So instead of being a center of activity, the structure is an unfinished and useless eyesore.

In a sense this is what the writer to the Hebrew Christians was
warning them about in Hebrews 5—a warning we must heed. We are
not to stop when we have laid the foundations of repentance and
salvation; we are to go on to the maturity that God, the architect of
our faith, has planned for us. He knows what the result of the building
of our faith should be: a center of activity that glorifies Him. So when
obstacles arise, when the needed resources of time, study, and energy
run out, when we encounter opposition, we are not to let the project
come to a screeching halt. We must continue construction.

God chose us to "be holy and without blame before Him" (Eph. 1:4),
and He provides us with the resources—the indwelling Holy Spirit
and His Word—for the process of sanctification to be completed.

—J.D.B.

So often we try to alter circumstances to suit ourselves,
instead of letting them alter us.

Week 26

REBUILDING THE WALLS

I did not demand the governor's provisions, because the bondage was heavy on this people (Nehemiah 5:18).

THEME

LEADERSHIP

When asked the secret to his success, restaurateur and chef Andre Soltner of the famed Lutèce in New York replied, "I cook from my heart, with love. It must be the same with service. The waiter must serve with love. Otherwise the food is nothing. . . . Many times, I leave my kitchen and go to the tables to take orders myself. It starts right then and there . . . there is nothing mysterious about Lutèce. I put love in my . . . serving. That is all."

Nehemiah knew how to put love in his serving. Under his leadership, the Israelites successfully rebuilt the wall of Jerusalem after they returned from captivity. Nehemiah organized the people, encouraged them, and artfully handled all opposition. Yet his greatest achievement may have been his loving leadership. He worked alongside the people, and to identify with them in their great need he refused to take the food that was due him as governor.

The kings of ancient near-eastern countries normally ruled with harshness and cruelty. The Romans of New Testament times often treated their subjects unfairly and brutally. And leaders today sometimes consider their own interests and finances before that of their followers. In contrast to these unloving, me-first forms of leadership, Jesus called leaders to give up their own rights, to serve instead of dictate, and to risk everything for others.

We like being the head pin, but falling first is not our game. Mark says that Jesus took the blame for us. And in so doing, He demonstrated loving leadership (10:45). All would-be leaders should fall in behind Him.

Sunday

NEHEMIAH 1:1–6; 2:11–18

I went out by night . . . and viewed the walls of Jerusalem which were broken down (Nehemiah 2:13).

The Chicago newspapers reported a rash of gang-related slayings in a large inner-city housing project. The police seemed unable to stop the violence. For several weeks Jane Byrne, mayor of Chicago, wrestled with the problem. Then, to everyone's surprise, she announced that she and her husband were moving into that apartment complex. Immediately she gained widespread community support for her action. Soon even her critics admitted that her bold leadership and example had made a significant difference.

Mayor Byrne's action reminds me of Nehemiah, that man of God who was instrumental in rebuilding the walls of Jerusalem. As a Jewish exile serving in a high-ranking position under the king of Persia, he received word that the remnant of his people in Jerusalem were in great danger. The walls of the city had been knocked down; the gates had been burned. Heartbroken, Nehemiah wept, fasted, confessed his sins, and prayed for several days to the God of heaven. Then, as the Lord directed him, he left the security of his position and moved into the violence-racked city. He stayed there until the walls were rebuilt and order was restored.

Whatever position of authority we hold, there's a lesson in this for us. We must be willing to identify with human need so that God can use us in troubled areas. That's leadership that leads. —M.R.D.II

**People who doubt what we say
may change their minds when they see what we do.**

Monday

NEHEMIAH 5:1–16

Be an example to the believers . . . in love, in spirit,
in faith, in purity (1 Timothy 4:12).

Believers exert a positive influence on others by setting a good example with the consistency of their lives. Will Houghton, president of Moody Bible Institute during the 1940s, was such a person.

Before Houghton became president of Moody, he pastored a church in New York City. An agnostic living there was contemplating suicide, but he decided that if he could find a minister who lived what he professed, he would listen to him. Since Will Houghton was a prominent figure in the city and a pastor, the man chose Houghton for his case study. He hired a private detective to watch him. When the investigator's report came back, it revealed that Houghton's life was above reproach. The agnostic went to Houghton's church, accepted Christ, and later sent his daughter to Moody Bible Institute.

Nehemiah was another believer who dramatically affected the lives of those around him. Even rich nobles and high officials listened respectfully as he rebuked them. Why? Because of the quality of his life. Whatever he asked of others, he was willing to do himself. And because Nehemiah joined in the hard work and refrained from using his position to accumulate wealth, the leaders couldn't help but listen to what he said.

An exemplary life awakens spiritual and moral sensitivity in those who observe us, and it gives power to our words of witness. —H.V.L.

**We can preach a better sermon
with our lives than with our lips.**

Tuesday

MATTHEW 7:15–20

"Therefore by their fruits you will know them"
(Matthew 7:20).

Throughout history, ungodly people have attained power and influence through their strong personalities or their spectacular deeds. But natural qualities and remarkable feats do not provide the kind of spiritual leadership that God desires and approves. A classic example is the Russian "clergyman" Rasputin.

Rasputin gained a foothold in the home of Czar Nicholas II because he seemed to possess a supernatural power to help the czar's hemophiliac son. Rasputin's "prayers" appeared to do far more for the boy than the efforts of all his doctors. Thus, the "holy man" achieved great influence in the government by telling the czar and his wife that their son would live only as long as they listened to his advice. As time went on, Rasputin became openly cruel and immoral, maintaining his position through intimidation and fear.

Charlatans can be clever and winsome. They may even perform counterfeit miracles. But observed closely, their lives give no evidence of the fruit of the Spirit. Their works are as worthless as apples tied on an apple tree to make it look productive.

Fitness for spiritual leadership comes from the inside, not the outside, and includes the qualities of love, joy, peace, longsuffering, goodness, faithfulness, gentleness, and self-control (Gal. 5:22–23).

—H.V.L.

A good leader is one who knows the way,
goes the way, and shows the way.

Wednesday

JAMES 3

Let not many of you become teachers, knowing that we shall receive a stricter judgment (James 3:1).

Author Mark Twain was often outspoken about his bitterness toward the things of God. Sadly, church leaders were largely to blame for his becoming hostile to the Bible and the Christian faith. As Twain grew up, he knew elders and deacons who owned slaves and abused them, and he knew ministers who used the Bible to justify slavery. He heard men use foul language and saw them practice dishonesty during the week after speaking piously in church on Sunday. Although he saw genuine love for the Lord Jesus in some people, including his mother and his wife, he was never able to understand the bad teaching and poor example of certain church leaders.

Leadership is a privilege, and with privilege comes responsibility. God holds teachers of His truth doubly responsible because they are in positions where they can either draw people toward Christ or drive them away from Him.

Serving as an elder, a deacon, a Sunday school teacher, or a Bible club leader is an awesome responsibility. Those who are called to these positions are responsible to lead people *to* the Savior rather than away from Him. According to James 3, they can do this by exemplifying true wisdom, which is "pure, then peaceable, gentle, willing to yield, full of mercy and good fruits, without partiality and without hypocrisy" (v. 17). —H.V.L.

The best kind of leadership produces fellowship.

Thursday

JAMES 5:13–20

**If we say that we have no sin, we deceive ourselves
(1 John 1:8).**

In his book *Helping Those Who Don't Want Help*, Marshall Shelley told of a pastor who was backing out of his garage when he heard a "snap." When he got out to look, he discovered his favorite fishing pole in two pieces. "Who was using my fishing pole?" he asked. "I was, Dad," said his five-year-old son. "I was playing with it and I forgot to put it away." The pastor wasn't pleased, but he said to his son, "Well, thank you for telling me," and said no more about it. Two days later, while shopping with his mother, the boy said, "Mom, I got to buy Dad a new fishing pole. I broke his other one. Here's my money." And he handed her his total life savings—two dollars. "You don't have to do that," said his mother. "But I want to, Mom," the boy said. "I found out that Dad loves me more than he loves his fishing pole."

Later, the pastor told his congregation about the incident. "When I heard what my son said, I felt great. I felt that for once I had done something right." After the service, several men told the pastor that they appreciated what he had said about doing something right for once. They had the idea that pastors always did everything right.

This is a good lesson for other leaders also. We don't always have to appear to be "on top of it." We need to admit that we struggle sometimes; we need to reveal some of our own faults and failures. When leaders are open and honest about their own lives, others will be helped and encouraged by what they say. —D.C.E.

We should acknowledge our own sins—not our neighbor's.

Friday

PSALM 15

Who may dwell in Your holy hill?. . . He who swears
to his own hurt and does not change (Psalm 15:1, 4).

At the University of Santa Clara, California, a researcher conducted a study of 1500 business managers to determine, among other things, what workers value most in a boss. The survey revealed that employees respect leaders who are competent, have the ability to inspire, and are skillful in providing direction. But there was a fourth quality they admired even more—integrity. Above all else, workers wanted managers who kept their word, who were honest, who were trustworthy.

While this finding holds special significance for Christian managers, it also says something to all who name the name of Christ. Integrity is a trait that applies to all believers, no matter what their position. According to Psalm 15, it should be at the very heart of every word and deed of every godly person. Since the God of the Bible always keeps His word, it follows that godly people should also be known as those who do what they say they will do.

Personally, I find this truth to be somewhat unsettling. Although I have not had an especially difficult time avoiding conscious lies, I have found it easy to forget good intentions or to fail to keep a promise. Sometimes it's difficult to do what I said I would do.

Maybe we all need to be more careful about our integrity. Do those around us admire us for our honesty? Does the Lord above? Does He see us as doing what we said we would do—even if it hurts?

—M.R.D.II

Those who are on the level can rise to the highest place.

Saturday

GENESIS 43:1–12

Whatever things are true, whatever things are honest, . . . think on these things (Philippians 4:8 KJV).

Our society needs a good dose of old-fashioned honesty, particularly among its leaders. In business, in politics, in school, in the home, and even in the church, we are seeing less and less of this vital quality—especially in money matters. Under-the-table deals, unrecorded transactions, padded expense accounts, forgotten debts, and unpaid traffic fines are the order of the day. The rule seems to be, if you can get away with it, do it.

We need to recapture something of the spirit and moral character of the sixteenth President of the United States. Throughout Lincoln's professional life as a lawyer he always had a partner. Frequently, Abe would go out on a circuit to handle legal matters while his colleague stayed at home. When he completed a case, Lincoln often collected the fee before he returned to the office. He always divided the money in his billfold, carefully wrapping his partner's half in a piece of paper on which he wrote his name and the case for which it was received. In this way, if anything happened to him before turning over the money, no one could dispute the amount and for whom it was intended. This practice may seem trivial, but it was totally in keeping with the man we have come to know as "Honest Abe."

We all should make it our goal to live in such a way that the word *honest* sounds right in front of our name. —D.J.D.

Don't talk *cream* and live *skim milk.*

Week 27

JOB LOSES EVERYTHING

"Behold, God works all these things . . . with a man, . . . That he may be enlightened with the light of life" (Job 33:29–30).

THEME

HOPE IN SUFFERING

"Years ago I used to commiserate with all people who suffered," wrote Bill Wilson, cofounder of Alcoholics Anonymous. "Now I commiserate only with those who suffer in ignorance, who do not understand the purpose and ultimate utility of pain."

Unable to understand the purpose of his pain, Job, with the help of three friends, probed the mind of God. The same answer popped up repeatedly—Job had sinned and God was punishing him. Yet this answer didn't match the circumstances. Another speaker, the youth Elihu, though making the same judgment, finally broke the connection between pain and punishment. He suggested that God may use suffering solely to teach people about life.

Suffering is like a hot, May day in a classroom. We want to escape it; we want to play hooky. We do not see the link between heat and Harvard. But schoolwork sweat does more than lower body temperature; it changes who we are and how we think. So does suffering; it has its own built-in reward.

Jesus knew physical aches and emotional anguish, and the writer of Hebrews says that He learned obedience through His suffering (5:8). If Jesus could learn from the traumas of life, then it is time for us to go back to school.

Sunday

"I have heard of You by the hearing of the ear,
but now my eye sees You" (Job 42:5).

The other evening a robust seventy-six-year-old man responded to my comment about his fine physical condition by saying, "Good health is the greatest of all blessings." I replied, "Are you sure you really mean that? A man told me recently that he is thankful for illness because that's how he and his wife learned to depend on God's presence and power." Smiling, my friend said, "You're right. Trusting God is a far greater blessing than good health. If it takes sickness and pain to think about the glory of God and heaven, I say, praise the Lord for sickness and pain."

The psalmist wrote, "It is good for me that I have been afflicted" (Ps. 119:71). Many believers agree wholeheartedly with that statement, for it was in a time of trouble that they too discovered the tenderness of God and experienced the reality of His presence. Although they saw no form of the Almighty as some Old Testament saints did, nor did they hear an audible voice from a whirlwind as Job did, they knew God was with them. They would rather not go through the difficulty again, but they look back upon it as worth every bit of hurt they endured.

Good health and financial prosperity are great blessings, and we should be thankful for them. But we need not get discouraged when we encounter illness or adversity. Through them we can come to know God better, and we can say with Job, "I have heard of You by the hearing of the ear, but now my eye sees You." And that is the greatest of all blessings. —H.V.L.

**God sometimes puts us in the dark
to show us that He is the light.**

Monday

JOB 19:13–27

"That in my flesh I shall see God, whom . . .
my eyes shall behold" (Job 19:26).

Children of God can rise above every trouble and trial of life if they anticipate the glories of heaven and the joy of being there with the Savior.

I received a letter from a severely handicapped man who possessed the sense of victory that comes from a forward look of faith. He had survived a long, delicate cranial operation, but he suffered some brain damage, partial blindness, some deafness, and mild paralysis. In addition, he spent several months on dialysis after both kidneys failed. He went through an unsuccessful transplant operation and endured another period of dialysis before receiving a replacement kidney. He admitted that he felt pretty low at times, but he didn't stay down in the dumps. He fully believes that God has a loving purpose in everything He allows, and he said he was looking forward to the glorified body awaiting him. He closed his letter by saying, "I can live with my problems because I know all of these things are preparing me for heaven."

In Job 19 we read not only Job's bitter lament but also his beautiful expression of hope. He bewailed his loneliness, for in addition to losing his health and wealth he had lost his sons and daughters and all his friends had abandoned him. Even little children would have nothing to do with him. Yet he found consolation. Deep within, he believed that on the other side of death he would see God as His Friend and Savior. With that hope he could triumph over everything—and so can we. —H.V.L.

No one is hopeless whose hope is in God.

Tuesday

1 PETER 1:1–9

That the genuineness of your faith . . . may be found
to praise, honor, and glory (1 Peter 1:7).

The abrasive experiences we encounter each day help to prepare us for heaven. God uses all of life's troubles to polish and perfect our character. If we accept our trials with the right attitude and recognize that the heavenly Father is working through them, we will someday shine with splendor before Him.

In the rough, a diamond looks like a common pebble, but after it is cut, its hidden beauty begins to emerge. The stone then undergoes a finishing process to bring out its full radiance. A skilled craftsman holds the gem against the surface of a large grinding wheel. No other substance is hard enough to polish the stone, so the wheel is covered with diamond dust. This process may take a long time, depending on the quality desired by the one who will buy it.

This is similar to the way God works with us. The procedure is not pleasant, nor is it intended to be. The Divine Workman, however, has our final glory in view. We may be "grieved by various trials," as Peter said, but when we understand what is behind them we can rejoice even in adversity. God has one goal in mind during the refining process: that our faith "may be found to praise, honor, and glory at the revelation of Jesus Christ." Knowing this enables us to look beyond the unpleasantness of "polishing" to see the outcome. —P.R.V.

**A gem cannot be polished without friction,
nor a man perfected without adversity.**

Wednesday

HEBREWS 12:1–11

**My son, do not despise the chastening of the LORD,
nor detest His correction (Proverbs 3:11).**

Scientists tell us that the seeds of certain types of desert bushes must be damaged by a storm before they will germinate. Covered by hard shells that keep out water, these seeds can lie dormant on the sand for several seasons until conditions are right for growth. When heavy rains finally bring flash floods, the little seeds are banged against sand, gravel, and rocks as they rush down the slopes. Eventually they settle in a depression where the soil is damp several feet deep. Able to absorb water through the nicks and scratches they acquired on their downhill plunge, they finally begin to grow.

Sometimes Christians are like those seeds. We need bad weather to stimulate our spiritual development. We do not take life seriously until something drastic happens. Although the heavenly Father never allows His children to suffer needlessly, sometimes He lets us experience nicks and scratches that let the water of His Word seep in and soften our hearts.

An unexpected stay in the hospital, stacks of unpaid bills, or family disruption can quickly awaken a sleeping saint. Such difficulties hurt for a while, but if we yield to the Lord we will find that life's bruises can mark the beginning of spiritual advances. Occasionally God will let us be roughed up to grow up. We may prefer to remain seeds, but He wants us to become fruitful trees. —M.R.D.II

There are no gains without pains.

Thursday

The LORD will strengthen him on his bed of illness;
You will sustain him on his sickbed (Psalm 41:3).

Crutches kept Roger, a disabled high school student, from being physically active, yet he excelled in his studies and was well liked by his
peers. They sometimes felt sorry for him, but for a long time nobody
asked him any questions about his illness. One day, however, his
closest friend asked. "Polio," Roger answered. The friend responded,
"With so many difficulties, how do you keep from becoming bitter?"
Tapping his chest with his hand, Roger replied with a smile, "It never
touched my heart."

I suppose there are people who have never known affliction. But for
most of us, sickness—whether physical, mental, or emotional—
crowds into our lives sooner or later. The natural and proper response
is to seek relief. The Bible does not guarantee a life free from illness or
disability, nor does it assure us that every prayer for recovery will be
answered—though many are. But it does promise a spiritual wholeness far more desirable than physical health.

If we suffer from a long-term illness that God does not remove, we
need not give in to bitterness, rebellion, self-pity, or guilt. When those
emotions well up, as they surely will, we can be honest with God. He
understands. He will make us a channel for His love and power. If we
keep our lives open to Him, affliction will never touch our hearts.

—D.J.D.

**There is nothing suffered by the body
from which the soul may not profit.**

Friday

**The testing of your faith produces patience
(James 1:3).**

While visiting an inlet of the sea that reached deep into land, leaving a sheltered bay, I noticed that the pebbles on that protected beach were rough and jagged—not smooth and polished. But out on the open shore where fierce waves break over the rocks, the pebbles were sleek and round.

The same is true of Christian character. Just as the harsh treatment of the ocean waves makes the rough stones smooth, our trials, difficulties, and testings can produce in us the luster of Christian maturity. When circumstances become difficult, we can rest assured that God has only one design in view—the perfection of our character. That's why the psalmist could testify, "It is good for me that I have been afflicted, that I may learn Your statutes" (Ps. 119:71). Echoing that statement, Scottish pastor Samuel Rutherford declared that he "got a new Bible" through the furnace of adversity. The Scriptures took on fresh meaning for him when his faith had been tested and his character enriched.

The popular idea that bad things happen because we are being punished is contrary to what God says. The Word of God indicates that troubles can be a badge of honor for the Christian. Through them we can see that God is at work in us to produce the patience that James said would help us become mature, lacking nothing (James 1:4). Through the rough seas of trouble, God "rounds" the stone of our character and conforms us to the likeness of His Son. —P.R.V.

God sends trials not to impair us but to improve us.

Saturday

Praise the LORD . . ., fire and hail, snow and clouds;
stormy wind, fulfilling His word (Psalm 148:7–8).

The psalmist brings glory to the Lord by exhorting all of creation to lift its voice in praise to His name (148:7–12). He recognized that the powerful elements of weather, such as hail and snow and great storms, are sent by God to do His bidding. Not only do they nourish and sustain life, but they also mold and shape it.

I thought about this as I looked at a gigantic beech tree near our cabin in northern Michigan. I've long admired the way its trunk rises thick and tall to the ceiling of the forest, and how its limbs, twisted yet sturdy, reach out in all directions. The weather, doing God's bidding, has made that tree what it is. A merciless summer sun has beaten down on it. Then, in the shortening days of autumn when its leaves turn brilliant yellow, the cold strong winds of Lake Superior have whipped its branches and left them bare. The winter ice coats its limbs, and it must carry the weight of heavy northern snows. Then come the spring rains, and wild thunderstorms toss the tree to and fro with mighty gusts.

The storms and winds and hail that fulfill God's Word are like the stresses and pressures of my own life. They too are sent to do God's bidding, to mature and strengthen me, and to make me what I am.

All kinds of weather—summer sun and winter storms—come from God, and He will shape us into His likeness as we yield to Him.

—D.C.E.

God will take care of what you go through;
you take care of how you go through it.

Week 28

ISAIAH PREDICTS CAPTIVITY

The LORD of hosts, Him you shall hallow; Let Him be your fear, and let Him be your dread (Isaiah 8:13).

THEME

FEAR OF GOD

On June 6, 1944, five thousand ships departed England for the Normandy coast and the greatest invasion of World War II. From this military event comes the story of the skipper who lectured his crew on fear, and said, "Fear is a very healthy thing." A third-class yeoman yelled in reply, "Captain, you're looking at the healthiest sailor in the United States Navy."

During Isaiah's time, King Ahaz and the people of Judah trembled like trees in a wind storm because of the Syrian and Ephraim alliance. Isaiah warned Ahaz and Judah about their misplaced fear; Syria and Ephraim were just two smoldering wood stubs that Assyria would put out in 722 B.C. Judah should fear a holy God, and in so doing, other fears would go away like the frequent east wind.

We tend to associate fear with punishment and danger, but that shows our limited understanding of it. Perfect fear comes from our sense of awe and wonder as we get glimpses of God. John says, "Perfect love casts out fear" (1 John 4:18). Fear, for the Christian, is not so much about punishment as love. God-fearing people are God-loving people.

Fear can be healthy; but God must be the focus. In fearing God, we express not only awe but also trust and love. This frees us from rival and lesser fears and makes us both fearsome and fearless.

Sunday

ISAIAH 51:7–16

The fear of man brings a snare, but whoever trusts in the LORD shall be safe (Proverbs 29:25).

Fear of what others may think about us can play an important role in the way we act. The American Indians recognized this and used scorn and ridicule to promote social order. For instance, when a child of the Fox tribe was taught the do's and don'ts of Indian life, his elders didn't hold over his head an abstract rule of morality. Nor did they threaten him with punishment now or in the hereafter. Instead, they said to him, "The people of the village may say things about you."

Isaiah 51 also recognizes the power of peer pressure—but not as a motivation for right conduct. Whereas the Indians used fear of ridicule to induce good behavior, the Lord warned His people Israel that the "reproach of men" could be their downfall. Their concern with what others said about them could cause them to seek unholy human alliances and to make compromises. Instead, God called them to trust the Lord and seek only His approval.

This is also good advice for us, because "the fear of man" snares many Christians. If we order our conduct only by the approval or disapproval of others, we will be frustrated and left with a painful sense of insecurity.

When we find our fulfillment in doing what pleases God, the crippling terror of what others think will give way to the confidence of a healthy fear—a reverence for God that frees us to live for His approval. —M.R.D.II

The fear of God can deliver us from the fear of men.

Monday

Render therefore to all their due: taxes to whom taxes . . . fear to whom fear (Romans 13:7).

One night I heard a radio preacher say that we should fear only God. But I don't agree. Peter exhorted servants to be subject to their masters "with all fear" (1 Pet. 2:18), and Paul said that wrongdoers should be afraid of civil authorities (Rom. 13:4). A hierarchy of fear is an integral part of living on our sin-cursed planet. Our moral responsibility is to put the things we fear in their proper place.

A boy whose friends urged him to experiment with illicit drugs told me he was afraid they would think of him as a coward, but he resisted because he was more frightened of the consequences. A young man who volunteered for dangerous military duty admitted he was scared of being wounded or killed, but he had a greater concern about what would happen if the enemy won the war. Both of these young men did what was right because they recognized the priority of certain fears.

The Bible teaches that our greatest fear should be of displeasing God. A believer who is told that he must either commit evil or face the firing squad should be more concerned about disobeying the Lord than being shot. That's what Jesus meant when He said, "Do not fear those who kill the body but cannot kill the soul. But rather fear Him who is able to destroy both soul and body in hell" (Matt. 10:28).

Fear is part and parcel of life here on earth. But this strong emotion can serve us well if we let our fear of God be supreme. —H.V.L.

Shame arises from the fear of men, conscience from the fear of God. —Samuel Johnson

Tuesday

ISAIAH 51:1–16

"Who are you that you should be afraid of a man who will die, and . . . who will be made like grass?" (Isaiah 51:12).

Phobias are nothing new to most Americans, but "cyberphobia" is. It's one of America's newest phobias. According to a team of business professors at George Mason University, a large number of people have cyberphobia—a serious fear of computers. Just being in the same room with one causes some to feel panic, have irregular heartbeat, breathing difficulties, dizziness, and trembling. One therapist says that these individuals have more than the normal fear of failure while learning to work with computers. They become so anxious that they fear passing out, going crazy, or losing control. This doesn't make sense to most of us, but then no phobia makes much sense. Yet the fear is real.

Many of us have another phobia that can be equally debilitating— the fear of the opinions and actions of others. Sometimes we think and act as if our fate and well-being rested solely in the hands of other people. Isaiah told us how it looks to the One who is in control when we become so afraid of people that we panic and forget to trust entirely in Him. He said that fearing the reproach of people is foolish because they are dying creatures who have little more real strength and longevity than grass (51:12). The Lord knows what great harm people can do to us (vv. 13–14). But He has the last word. Our future and everlasting well-being depend on Him and Him alone. —M.R.D.II

Faith can break the stranglehold of fear.

Wednesday

ISAIAH 6:1–5

But they, measuring . . . and comparing themselves among themselves, are not wise (2 Corinthians 10:12).

A little boy announced to his mother, "I'm like Goliath. I'm nine feet tall." "What makes you say that?" asked his mother. The tyke replied, "Well, I made a little ruler and measured myself with it, and I am nine feet tall!"

Although the child's measurements were accurate, his ruler was defective. He was like many people who fail to see their need of salvation because they measure themselves by a faulty standard. By looking at their peers and comparing their own behavior with others who have done worse than they have, they conclude that they are not so bad after all. But such pride is demolished when people compare themselves with a perfect standard of righteousness.

When the prophet Isaiah saw the Lord in all His glory, he exclaimed, "Woe is me, for I am undone! Because I am a man of unclean lips, . . . For my eyes have seen the King, the Lord of hosts" (Isa. 6:5). And according to Romans 3:23, we all have sinned and fallen short of God's glory. These two verses reveal how we measure up spiritually in God's sight.

Those who have never given their lives to Christ, and who recognize how far short of God's standard they fall, can place their trust in Christ and enjoy the true righteousness found in Him. When we measure our morality against that of other sinners, we are "not wise." We are using the wrong standard of measurement. —R.W.D.

**If we could merit our own salvation,
Christ would not have died to provide it.**

Thursday

ISAIAH 8:11–22

So will I . . . bring their fears on them; because, when
I called, no one answered (Isaiah 66:4).

Many people like to be scared, but only in the world of make-believe. They keep going to horror movies, but they don't like to be faced with legitimate causes for fear. A writer who depicts the threat of communism in Central America is accused of using scare tactics. A Christian leader who dares suggest that some diseases may be God's judgment on sin is scorned. The general attitude is: "Never say anything about God's judgment to scare people into doing what's right."

Isaiah didn't hesitate to use fear in addressing God's people. Already afraid of the Assyrians, they accused him of treason because he warned the king against making an alliance with this nation. He responded, in essence: "You have far more reason to be afraid of what God will do than of what Assyria will do." He told them that if they made an alliance with Assyria God would punish them. The Almighty would become a rock to make them stumble, and a trap to take away their freedom.

The Bible declares that those who reject Jesus and continue in their wicked ways will find God to be their enemy. If this frightening thought motivates a person to trust Him for salvation, it has served a good purpose. Similarly, if fear causes a Christian to serve the Lord with new zeal, it has fulfilled a positive function. The fear of God is good because it leads to right living—even if it scares us. —H.V.L.

Fear God and you will have nothing else to fear.

Friday

Walk worthy of the Lord, fully pleasing Him (Colossians 1:10).

A strong desire to please God is the highest incentive for doing His will and shows a true understanding of godly fear. We may have other worthy motives, such as the inner satisfaction of doing what's right or the anticipation of heavenly rewards. But we bring the greatest glory to God when we obey and serve Him because we long to do what brings Him delight.

Craig, a first-grader, beamed with satisfaction as he handed me a spelling test on which his teacher had written a large "100—Good work!" Craig said, "I showed this to Dad and Mother because I knew it would please them." I could just see him riding home on the bus, hardly able to wait for the moment when his parents would express their excitement with how well he had done. His desire to make Dad and Mom happy obviously was a strong motivating factor in his life.

When Paul used the simile of a soldier serving with single-minded devotion to please his commanding officer (2 Tim. 2:3–4), he wanted Timothy to know the supreme reason for serving God, even when the going gets tough. Wholehearted devotion, marked by hard work and careful attention to God's rules, brings the greatest glory to the Lord when it comes from a yielded, loving heart. Our Savior, who in His humanity shrank from the prospect of being made the sin-offering for mankind, nevertheless prayed, "Not My will, but Yours, be done" (Luke 22:42). Our motive, like His, should be the desire to please the Father. —H.V.L.

Man weighs the deeds; God weighs the intentions.

Saturday

MATTHEW 10:24–33

**"Fear Him who is able to destroy both soul and body"
(Matthew 10:28).**

All sorts of fears obsess believers. Although some may be legitimate, most are vague, nameless feelings of apprehension. They rob us of confidence and joy, and keep us from spiritual health and effectiveness. The Bible has the solution to this problem. When we learn the fear of God, we will not be controlled by earthly terrors.

A young boy living in Holland when it was occupied by the Nazis during World War II, wrote the following in his journal: "Last week three German officers stopped my dad in the hallway. They held him at gunpoint and forced him to open the steel door leading to the basement. One of them ordered Dad to show the crawl space under the hallways. He said if he didn't tell where the hidden weapons are, he will be shot. Dad usually is not a great hero. He's even afraid of the dentist. But this time he is not afraid at all. One of them cocked his Luger and held it against my Dad's temple. Dad recited the Bible verse that was on his mind, 'And fear not them who kill the body, . . . but rather fear Him who is able to destroy both body and soul in hell.' The Germans looked at each other, shrugged their shoulders, and then left. The steel heels of their boots made a clanging noise on the iron stairway."

This boy's father feared God more than he did the enemy. Having that kind of attitude will help us put all our fears in perspective.

—D.C.E.

**We need not fear the darkness of this world,
for we have Christ the light.**

Week 29

ISAIAH PROPHESIES FUTURE

"Behold, the former things have come to pass, and new things I declare; before they spring forth I tell you of them" (Isaiah 42:9).

THEME

PROPHECY

Girolamo Cardano, a renowned sixteenth-century astrologer, predicted the hour of his own death. When the day came, he was healthy and safe. Lest he be branded a charlatan, he killed himself.

In Isaiah's day, humbuggery abounded. Isaiah spoke out against the fraud of street-corner prognosticators by showing how God's predictions always came to pass. He not only spoke of the past, but he predicted two future deliverers—Cyrus and Christ. Cyrus would rescue Israel from the Babylonians, and Christ would release Israel and all peoples from spiritual bondage.

Isaiah's prophecies about Christ are some of the most startling in the Bible; he foretold His death, burial, and resurrection hundreds of years before the actual events. The Gospels confirm Isaiah's detailed descriptions.

Christ made a few predictions Himself as He castigated the religious quacks of His day. Some considered Him a great Prophet, but many saw Him as nothing more than a wood-and-hammer man from Nazareth. Most inexplicable to His disciples was His forecast of His own death; somehow they had missed the point of Isaiah.

Christ was no impostor; He willingly gave up His life as a surety of His word and our future.

Sunday

JEREMIAH 6:9–17

"From the prophet even to the priest,
everyone deals falsely" (Jeremiah 6:13).

Scientists have a reputation for wanting to get the facts. Yet within the last few years some have shown themselves vulnerable to deception. One newspaper, for example, uncovered serious problems in the findings of a research team whose work had been influential in a controversy over alcohol. The experts studied whether or not persons once dependent on the substance could resume drinking without falling back into addiction. They claimed it was possible. Investigative reporting, however, later produced contrary evidence from patients who had been involved in the research. Those "cured" alcoholics who started drinking again were having extremely difficult problems. Some had even committed suicide. Apparently, those researchers were not so trustworthy after all.

Religious leaders, even more than scientists, should always be above making false claims. But Jeremiah cites evidence to the contrary. He shows that the priests, the prophets, and the preachers of his day were not speaking the truth. They told the people what they wanted to hear. They didn't want to learn about judgment, repentance, and their own lack of godliness. But their message of hope and peace was nothing more than a bag of lies.

We, too, sometimes fall into the trap of listening only to voices that tell us what we want to hear. We too easily assume that all preachers and leaders tell the truth. We need to make sure that we judge their message by the whole counsel of God. The Spirit and the Word will alert us to false claims. —M.R.D.II

The first point of wisdom is to know the truth;
the second, to discern what is false.

Monday

HABAKKUK 2:1–8

"Behold the proud, his soul is not upright in him; but the just shall live by his faith" (Habakkuk 2:4).

Speaking to the graduating seniors of New Zealand Bible College, Brian Smith said, "How well I recall the remark of a senior missionary in India when he was reflecting on the phenomenon we call Hinduism. 'When you see its temples and hear the throb of its drums and smell the fragrance of its incense, and realize the tremendous hold it has upon the land, your heart sinks. And the consolation I have is this: This too, this mighty construction of religion and faith and worship, will disappear, like all those systems of the past. Where now are the ancient gods of the Assyrians, the Egyptians, and the Romans? Where now Artemis, "great goddess of the Ephesians, she whom Asia and the whole world worships"? These are no more.'"

As Habakkuk wrote about the powerful Chaldean armies (1:6), he no doubt despaired over their seeming invincibility. A similar feeling must have swept over European Christians in the 1940s when they saw their homelands overtaken by the Nazis. And today the same is surely true of believers in atheistic countries. But for those who trust God, there is always hope. That's why the prophet Habakkuk affirmed that the just shall live by faith. God's people have the assurance that they will triumph—if not here, then in eternity.

Ungodly philosophies and false religions seem overwhelming at times, but they will not last. God has promised that righteousness will prevail. —D.C.E.

**That which does not begin with God
ends in failure.**

Tuesday

"Bethlehem Ephrathah, . . . out of you shall come forth to Me the One to be ruler in Israel" (Micah 5:2).

Isaiah, Micah, and many of the other prophets foretold many details of Jesus' birth, life, and death hundreds of years before they were fulfilled. The likelihood of these events occurring exactly as they were prophesied is too remote to explain away the phenomenon by calling it coincidence.

In *Science Speaks,* Peter Stoner applies the modern science of probability to just eight prophecies. He said, "The chance that any man might have . . . fulfilled all eight prophecies is one in 10^{17}. That would be 1 in 100,000,000,000,000,000." Stoner said that if we took that many silver dollars and laid them across Texas they would cover the state two feet deep. Then, to emphasize his point, he said, "Mark one of these silver dollars and stir the whole mass thoroughly. . . . Blindfold a man and tell him he can travel as far as he wishes, but he must pick up [that one marked silver dollar.] What chance would he have of getting the right one?" Stoner concludes, "Just the same chance that the prophets would have had of writing those eight prophecies and having them all come true in any one man, . . . providing they wrote them in their own wisdom."

Since Christ's first coming was the exact fulfillment of many prophecies, we can expect the same of His second coming.

We can thank God for sending his Son to die and rise again. But we can also rejoice that He's going to send Him back to earth to reign. Bethlehem's Babe will return as creation's King, just as prophets foretold long ago. —D.J.D.

Prophecy is history written ahead of time.

Wednesday

"Lest I come and strike the earth with a curse"
(Malachi 4:6).

Last words are powerful. Malachi 4 expresses God's final words to Israel under the Old Testament dispensation. For four hundred years He would remain silent until they would hear "the voice of one crying in the wilderness: 'Prepare the way of the Lord'" (Matt. 3:3). Although Malachi 4:6 appears to be a curse, it really is not. It does not close the door on hope. On the contrary, it was God's last appeal of love. The threat of a curse, expressed by the word *lest,* was aimed at averting the natural consequence of disobedience.

G. Campbell Morgan noted that from Malachi's time until Christ's, rabbis did not end their reading of Malachi with verse 6. Skipping from verse 4 to 6, they then reverted to verse 5, "Behold, I will send you Elijah the prophet before the coming of the great and dreadful day of the LORD." And in the Greek Old Testament, verse 4 is put at the end. Thus the Jews regarded God's final words as spoken in love, not in anger.

God's final prophetic words to believers in the New Testament are also filled with hope: "He who testifies to these things says, 'Surely I am coming quickly.' Amen. Even so, come, Lord Jesus! The grace of our Lord Jesus Christ be with you all. Amen" (Rev. 22:20–21).

God's last words to Israel and to the church can give us hope. The assurance of His grace and the warnings from His love will keep us living close to Him. —D.J.D.

The Christian's future is as bright as the promises of God.

Thursday

The LORD will take vengeance on His adversaries
(Nahum 1:2).

Nahum means "consolation, full of comfort." And that's what Nahum's message of doom upon Nineveh and Assyria brought to the people of Judah. Mighty Assyria had made Judah a vassal state, extracting heavy taxes and inflicting harsh slavery on them. With their security constantly threatened by pillaging raiders from Nineveh, God's people were asking, "Has Jehovah forsaken us? Why does an evil nation prosper while we suffer?" Against this background—Assyria's pride, cruelty, and seemingly invincible power in contrast to Judah's forlorn hopelessness—Nahum thunders his prophecy: "Nineveh will fall! God has not forsaken His people."

Translating the prophet's message into today's language, it might sound something like this: "Might does not make right. Countries with the most nuclear weapons and the biggest armies are not exempt from divine wrath. Any nation that thwarts justice and oppresses people will ultimately fall into ruin—whether it be Libya, Russia, China, Great Britain, Germany, or the United States."

The next time the evening news shows a dictator living in luxury while the people languish in poverty or innocent victims suffer under the cruelty of tyrants, recall the message of Nahum. The sovereign Ruler of this world will have His day. Justice will prevail. What a Nahum. What a consolation. —D.J.D.

**The highways of history are strewn with
the wreckage of nations that forgot God.**

Friday

"As you have done, it shall be done to you;
your reprisal shall return upon your own head" (Obadiah 15).

Among others, many prominent entertainers and respected educational leaders reject God and deny the existence of an absolute moral standard. They say we can determine for ourselves what is right and wrong. They laugh at words like patriotism, duty, loyalty, and godliness. But now their influence is reaping a bitter harvest—multiplied abortions, heartbreaking divorces, violent crimes, teenage suicides, and disturbing payoffs by foreign agents for military secrets. Discussing an unprecedented rash of Americans spying for other countries, Charles Colson said that the U.S. is reaping what it has sown.

Obadiah warned the Edomites that they would reap what they had sown. Using the past tense but speaking about the future, he portrayed the lighthearted drinking of their wild parties and said that their derisive fun would soon give way to somber drinking from the cup of God's wrath. His prophecy was fulfilled. Within a few years Edom was destroyed by Gentile powers.

We must remember the reaping principle. Woven into the fabric of life, it applies to individuals as much as to nations. It's both a warning and a promise. When we do evil, we reap judgment. But when we do good, we reap the blessing of God's approval. —H.V.L.

Those who plant thorns cannot expect to gather flowers.

Saturday

I will punish the world for their evil,
and the wicked for their iniquity (Isaiah 13:11 KJV).

The problem of compulsive gambling may be foreign to most of us, yet the obsession is all too real. Some studies estimate that between one and six million Americans are psychologically addicted to the habit. Hoping to get rich fast, gamblers bet against high odds. Gambling gives excitement but almost always ends in defeat. It is indeed a temporary pleasure.

Some Christians have a similar problem—spiritual gambling. They bet against God. Hoping to enjoy worldly pleasure, they bet against God's prophecies about future punishment for sin.

Even though we know there is no such thing as luck, we often dabble in sinful pleasures as if it were possible to ignore the will of God and still come out ahead. We seem to be addicted to the excitement of risk. We apparently think that just because we won't lose our soul in hell we need not be concerned about a life of spiritual defeat.

God did not give us five-to-three odds that He would keep His word. The odds are not even one thousand-to-one. We can be absolutely sure that what He promised will come true. That's why it is foolish to trust our own wisdom, instincts, or desires. We must trust in the reliable word of the Lord rather than take our chances with the temporary excitement of sin. —M.R.D.II

Whatever God prophesies He performs.

Week 30

JEREMIAH WARNS JUDAH

"I will not remain angry forever. Only acknowledge your iniquity, that you have transgressed against the LORD your God" (Jeremiah 3:12–13).

THEME

HYPOCRISY

George Jeffreys, a sixteenth-century English judge infamous for his cruelty and ruthlessness, once pointed his cane at a man about to be tried, denouncing him, "There is a rogue at the end of my cane." The accused glared at Jeffreys. "At which end, my lord?" he demanded.

Although Jeremiah warned Judah of its sin for more than four decades, the people refused to acknowledge their waywardness. They dropped their sins at the temple door and picked them up again when they left. They were spiritual streetwalkers, giving their souls to other gods. Doing an about-face at the steps of justice, they cheated widows, orphans, and strangers. Because of their hypocrisy, God led them to the slaughterhouse in 586 B.C., the year of the final thrust against Jerusalem by the Babylonians.

In Greek theater the "hypocrite" held a painted mask in front of his face to portray a character. Today, hypocrites are those who try to disguise their true identity; they say they are one thing, but their actions prove otherwise.

Peter, who played the phony at Christ's trial, tells Christians to put aside hypocrisy if they want to grow close to Jesus (1 Peter 2:1–5, 22). Those who know themselves live in humility and honesty—never pointing canes.

Sunday

"Judah has not turned to Me with her whole heart,
but in pretense" (Jeremiah 3:10).

Humorist Sam Levenson told the story of a driver who put a note under the windshield wiper of a parked car that read, "I have just smashed into your car. The people who saw the accident are watching me. They think I'm writing down my name and address. I'm not. Good luck."

In Jeremiah 3, we read of another clever bit of pretense. Judah pretended to return to the Lord, but the hearts of the people remained far from Him. They called God "Father," but they continued doing all the evil they could get away with (vv. 4–5).

As this situation in Jeremiah indicates, putting on a false front is a very old practice. But I doubt that any is more up-to-date. And I can't think of a problem I'm more concerned about in myself than a failure to respond from the heart to the Lord who has made Himself so real and so knowable in Christ. It is easy to say, "Yes, yes, He is our Lord and Savior. He has died for our sins and deserves our worship and service." But it's not so easy to remember our commitment to Him when the pressure is off and no one is watching how we live.

Let's not kid ourselves. We're smart enough to look good in public and say the right things about the Lord when it's in our best interest to do so. But what about our heart relationship with the Lord? Can we look Him in the face without shame? Looking good in the eyes of others is not enough. —M.R.D.II

The harder we work at what we should be,
the less we'll try to hide what we are.

Monday

LUKE 20:45–21:4

**"Man looks at the outward appearance,
but the LORD looks at the heart" (1 Samuel 16:7).**

The world's standard for measuring people differs radically from God's. The news and entertainment media, for example, pay homage to the rich and famous, showing little regard for their moral or spiritual qualities. The Almighty, on the other hand, delights in virtues like humility, meekness, sincerity, reverence, and unselfishness.

Sometimes, because we cannot see people's hearts and motives, we misjudge them, both positively and negatively. The Jewish people, because they could see only the actions of the scribes, held them in high regard. These well-educated religious leaders copied the Scriptures without charge while depending on their profession for their livelihood and on freewill gifts. This gave them every appearance of great piety. The Lord Jesus, however, saw the scribes as men who took advantage of their position to fleece the gullible and obtain red-carpet treatment everywhere. Moreover, He observed the humble sincerity of the widow who, out of love for God, deposited in the temple treasury two small copper coins, a gift that represented great sacrifice. Yet she received no recognition from the people.

As we set our own personal goals and make judgments about people around us, we must remember that God looks at our hearts. If we remain open to the ministry of the Holy Spirit and rely on Him, He will produce in us a lifestyle that will meet with Divine approval.

—H.V.L.

**If we have a distorted picture of the Christian life,
we've allowed the world to develop the film.**

Tuesday

I call to remembrance the genuine faith that is in you
(2 Timothy 1:5).

Several customers were waiting in line at a London cheese shop one day when the famous preacher C. H. Spurgeon came in to make a purchase. Not one to stand around calmly, he became a little fidgety as he stood behind the others and waited his turn. Noticing a fine block of cheese in the shop window, he couldn't resist touching it, and gently tapped the cheese with his walking stick. To his surprise, the "cheese" made an empty metallic sound—like the ring of a big bread pan. Spurgeon later recounted, "I came to the conclusion that I had found a very well-got-up hypocrite in the window."

People can be like fake cheese—they look like something they aren't. Many use the name *Christian* and make a rather pretty display on Sunday morning, yet they have the hollow sound of a hypocrite. A person may look like a Christian but lack genuine faith. When tapped with temptation or spiritual duty, the sham becomes evident. What seemed to be spirituality is a veneer of profession—without the substance of possession.

Not so with Timothy. His faith was genuine—so real that thinking of it filled Paul with joy. Satisfaction must have filled Timothy's heart as he read the apostle Paul's words (2 Tim. 1:5).

We must continually evaluate our faith and ask ourselves if what we profess will stand up under God's examination. —P.R.V.

Many give Christianity their countenance but not their heart.

Wednesday

PHILIPPIANS 3:1–11

I also count all things loss for the excellence of the knowledge of Christ Jesus my Lord (Philippians 3:8).

To be good is not necessarily to be godly. But to be godly is to be good. Failure to make this distinction leads to misunderstanding. Christians sometimes assume that just because their conduct is above reproach, they are right with the Lord. But this may not be true. The Bible says it is possible to be moral without relying on God or even knowing Him.

The Cheyenne, a group of native Americans who once lived in central Minnesota and northern South Dakota, were highly moral people. They practiced moderation, dignity, and generosity, and they manifested an almost unbelievable degree of self-control. Parents loved their children and gave them affection without spoiling them. They also taught them ethical values, so that most of them became dedicated, self-sacrificing, well-behaved human beings. Yet these people were not Christians.

Knowing that people can be good without being godly should cause us to inventory our own lives. If non-Christians can be moral in their own strength, so can we. But no matter how nice we may look on the outside, as long as we depend on ourselves, we displease the Lord. Being godly is a virtue that comes only through relying on Christ. Our goal should be goodness that comes from godliness. —M.R.D.II

Holiness is a journey that leads to godliness.

Thursday

GALATIANS 2:11–21

Now when Peter had come to Antioch, [Paul] withstood him to his face, because he was to be blamed (Galatians 2:11).

The apostle Peter, though a devoted follower of Jesus, made a serious mistake in separating himself from Gentile believers just to please his narrow-minded Jewish friends. So Paul rebuked him lest he lead others astray. He knew that even a dedicated Christian can err and bring great harm to the work of the Lord.

Hobart E. Freeman was a sincere pastor who helped many people find Jesus as their personal Savior. But when he spoke negatively of doctors as "medical deities" and urged his followers not to seek medical attention, he caused them needless suffering. Apparently some died from illnesses that could have been cured. The *Ft. Wayne News-Sentinel* claims to have documented evidence of eighty-six deaths among Freeman's people. A young mother who had been a member of his church said that both she and her baby would have died if she had followed his directions. A doctor told her that she should have a Caesarean section, but she and her husband decided to follow Freeman's counsel and not have a doctor on hand for delivery. But when it became obvious that both mother and baby would die without medical attention, they quickly changed their minds.

We must be careful whom we trust. Even when people seem devoutly religious, sincere, and honest, we should test their teaching by asking the Lord for guidance, searching the Scriptures, and talking with knowledgeable, trustworthy Christians. Sincere people can be sincerely wrong. —H.V.L.

Error is often dressed in the garb of truth.

Friday

Examine yourselves as to whether you are in the faith (2 Corinthians 13:5).

In these days when everyone is so good at role-playing, it's sometimes difficult to tell the difference between the impostor and the real thing. Even within the church, some behave as if they can satisfy God by skillfully acting out the part of a Christian.

They are like the goat who wanted more than anything else in the world to be a lion. He told himself that if he could learn to walk like a lion, talk like a lion, and go where lions go, he would be a lion. So he practiced stalking through the jungle and tried to swish his stubby little tail majestically. Then he tried to turn his pitiful little bleat into the deep, awesome roar of the king of beasts. He worked and worked on it. Finally convinced that he looked and sounded like a lion, he said, "Now, all I have to do to be a lion is to go where lions go." So he marched into lion territory one day about lunchtime.

Sometimes people who have learned to walk, talk, and act like Christians, think they really are. By outward appearances, they are. But if they have never personally placed their trust in Jesus Christ, they are phonies. They lack that "genuine faith," which alone brings true salvation (2 Tim. 1:5).

When we rely on church attendance, pious language, or good behavior to get us into heaven, we deceive ourselves. Only by trusting the Lord Jesus as Savior can we avoid the rude awakening on the day of judgment that faced the misguided goat when he walked into lion territory. —D.C.E.

We should work harder to be what we ought to be than to hide what we are.

Saturday

MATTHEW 23:25–33

"Even so you also outwardly appear righteous to men, but inside you are full of hypocrisy" (Matthew 23:28).

Our society encourages hypocrisy. Even before our children enter school they begin to master the art of artificiality. It isn't long until they become as sophisticated as their adult counterparts at the slick little deceptions of modern life.

This practice is bad enough in social circles, but it is even worse when it occurs in the church. When Sunday morning comes, we adjust our behavior to fit what others expect of a good Christian. We sit piously in our "Sunday best," hiding from everyone that we are selfish, stingy, unforgiving people.

In his book *Improving Your Serve,* Charles Swindoll tells of speaking at a singles retreat in a Rocky Mountain resort. He had purposely brought along a full-faced rubber mask that his children had given him as a funny present. One evening he wore it as he began to speak on authenticity. As expected, the crowd went wild with laughter. Each new sentence increased the effect. After removing the mask, he observed, "It's a funny thing, when we wear literal masks, nobody is fooled. But how easy it is to wear invisible ones and fake people out by the hundreds. . . . Servants who are 'pure in heart' have peeled off their masks. And God places special blessing on their lives."

We all struggle with the problem of hypocrisy. But when our hearts are pure, we will have no reason to cover our faces. —D.C.E.

A hypocrite is a person who isn't himself on Sunday.

Week 31

ISRAEL TAKEN CAPTIVE

"The children of your people say, 'The way of the LORD is not fair.' But it is their way which is not fair!" (Ezekiel 33:17).

THEME

BLAME

Rose Cipollone smoked for forty-three years and died of lung cancer at the age of fifty-eight. Her husband blamed the cigarette manufacturer and brought suit against it. A federal jury awarded her estate four hundred thousand dollars from the Liggett Group, the manufacturer of L&M cigarettes. James Kilpatrick, commenting on the case, wrote, "We have reared a generation of whiners and buck passers. . . . Nobody is at fault for anything."

Ezekiel, himself a captive in Babylon, must have tired of hearing the excuses of the exiles. They blamed their bondage on their parents, saying that God was judging Judah because of past sins. Ezekiel refuted this thinking. He said that people are individually responsible for their actions. If God punished the third and fourth generation of children, these sons and daughters brought God's wrath on themselves for following the corrupt ways of their predecessors.

The Jews in Christ's time had not changed; they were still making excuses for themselves. In the Parable of the Great Supper, they used family responsibilities and business transactions as excuses for neglecting spiritual service (Luke 14:15–24).

God knew from the beginning the minds of snivelers and whimperers, so He designed an excuse-proof plan. Creation itself reveals God and leaves us without excuse (Rom. 1:20).

God's people don't make excuses; they always draw themselves with faultlines.

Sunday

**"Behold, all souls are Mine; . . .
the soul who sins shall die" (Ezekiel 18:4).**

When salmon travel hundreds of miles up rivers and streams to spawn where they were hatched, they act on instinct. In a sense, they are driven by an uncontrollable force. People, on the other hand, are different. We cannot blame instinct for our actions. We are responsible. Even though we may feel driven, we make the choices that lead to our downfall.

A young convict who escaped execution through a last-minute decision from a Supreme Court Justice considers human conduct and animal instinct the same. Referring to the murders he committed and to his own fate, he said, "Things just happen." He apparently thinks some kind of force was responsible for his pulling the trigger and killing the two people who happened to be at the scene of the crime.

More than 2,500 years ago, some Israelites said essentially the same thing. They quoted a well-known proverb that placed the blame for their sins on their ancestors (Ezek. 18:2). But Ezekiel told them they were all wrong. He said that a good man will not be punished for the sins of a wicked son. Neither will a godly son be punished for the sins of his evil father.

No matter what our situation, we are responsible for what we do. We might as well stop making excuses for our sins and take the first step in exercising individual responsibility—acknowledge our guilt and then put our trust in Jesus Christ. —H.V.L.

Many people excuse their own foolishness by calling it fate.

Monday

Then the whole congregation . . . murmured against Moses and Aaron in the wilderness (Exodus 16:2).

Fred Grimm, a Christian probation officer, told of a father who made a scapegoat of his son by blaming him for family conflicts. Although the man and his wife had been fighting for years, the father told his son, "It's always because of your big mouth that your mother and I fight. If I leave you and your mother, it will be your fault." The youngster's problems were compounded when the father died suddenly from a stroke and the mother accused her son of having caused his father's death. The boy was devastated.

Blaming others for our problems is not only unjust and cruel, it's displeasing to the Lord. The children of Israel did this in the wilderness shortly after their deliverance from the land of Egypt. When food and water were short, they panicked and blamed Moses and Aaron for getting them into their predicament. They made scapegoats of their leaders. Yet God mercifully overlooked their lack of faith and unfair criticism of His servants in those two incidents. Later, though, when the Israelites committed the same sin again, He judged them severely (see Numbers 16).

Scapegoating can do great damage. Instead of looking for someone else to blame for our problems, we need to analyze our situation, acknowledge our failures, and ask God for forgiveness and help.

—H.V.L.

We won't get closer to God by passing judgment on others.

Tuesday

PROVERBS 30:5–13

**Every way of a man is right in his own eyes
(Proverbs 21:2).**

In an experiment years ago, researchers fitted people with special prismatic glasses that made things appear upside down, straight lines appear curved, and sharp outlines seem fringed with color. Even though the subjects continued to wear the glasses, within just a few days the unnatural shapes, tinted edges, and inverted landscapes gradually disappeared, and the world began to appear normal again. Their brains had overcome false data coming through the lenses. This adaptability in the physical realm is indeed a blessing.

Proverbs suggests, however, that the mind doesn't function very well in the spiritual realm. In fact, we are sinners whose deepest imaginations are evil, and our thought-life produces a world of illusions. We think of ourselves as pure, when in reality we are guilty before God. That is why, for example, many people shift the responsibility for their behavior to environmental factors or to faulty upbringing. They fail to see their own rebellion and selfishness and imagine themselves to be the helpless, innocent victims of circumstance. In this way, they justify thoughts, feelings, and actions that are obviously sinful. Their way is right in their own eyes.

As Christians, we should be aware of the deceptive nature of our hearts and allow the Holy Spirit to correct our vision through a knowledge of God's Word. —M.R.D.II

Salvation gives spiritual vision to sin-blinded eyes.

Wednesday

LUKE 6:37–42

There is one Lawgiver, who is able to save and to destroy.
Who are you to judge another? (James 4:12).

The seventeenth-century French churchman Fenelon said, "It is often our own imperfection which makes us reprove the imperfection of others; a sharp-sighted self-love of our own which cannot pardon the self-love of others."

Sometimes our own faults and imperfections make us see faults in others that don't even exist. A woman complained that her neighbor's windows were always dirty. One day, after complaining about them to a friend, the visitor encouraged her to wash her own windows. She followed the advice. The next time her friend visited, she exclaimed, "I can't believe it. As soon as I washed my windows, my neighbor must have cleaned hers too. Look at them shine."

Criticism also blinds us to the good that others accomplish. A man who built a large drinking fountain in a public square drew derogatory comments from an art critic about its design. Though somewhat hurt, the builder asked, "Is anyone drinking from it?" The builder was happy to learn that the fountain, even though the critic didn't like its design, was doing its job—and doing it well.

Instead of calling attention to others' imperfections, we should examine ourselves. What we don't like in someone else might be the same thing that's wrong with us. And instead of judging others, we should look for the good in them and love them in spite of their faults.

—R.W.D.

When criticizing, don't forget: God is listening.

Thursday

1 KINGS 21:17–29

Ahab . . . tore his clothes and put sackcloth on his body, . . .
and went about mourning (1 Kings 21:27).

John and Joe stole some money, but they reacted differently when confronted with the evidence. John broke down immediately, confessed his guilt, and offered to repay the money. But Joe refused to take any responsibility and blamed his companion. Later, with his parents supporting him, Joe claimed he was forced into this conduct because some of the young people in his church had never accepted him.

After more than thirty-five years of giving spiritual counsel, I can testify that people who try to cover their sins will not prosper, and that those who confess and forsake them find mercy (Prov. 28:13). Many people never realize that they become their own worst enemies by blaming others instead of facing up to their own faults.

In 1 Kings 21, we read that King Ahab wanted a vineyard belonging to Naboth, but the owner refused to sell it. So Jezebel, Ahab's wife, had Naboth executed. Although Ahab merely allowed her to use his name in signing the orders, he didn't blame his wife when confronted with his evil deed. Instead, he acknowledged his crime, expressed grief over it, accepted responsibility, repented, and received a merciful reprieve.

Whenever we do wrong, we are wise to face up to it, take responsibility for our actions, and ask God to forgive us. We will be better people when we learn to say, "I'm to blame." —H.V.L.

**Only those willing to take blame
can ever be trusted with responsibility.**

Friday

"Judge not, that you be not judged"
(Matthew 7:1).

For some reason, it is easier to jump to negative conclusions about people than it is to assume the best about them. When we do this, we ascribe to them bad intentions and evil purposes that may not be true. We also reveal something about ourselves, for the faults we see in others are usually a reflection of our own.

Bishop Potter "was sailing for Europe on one of the great transatlantic ocean liners. When he went on board, he found that another passenger was to share the cabin with him. After going to see the accommodations, he came up to the purser's desk and inquired if he could leave his gold watch and other valuables in the ship's safe. He explained that ordinarily he never availed himself of that privilege, but he had been to his cabin and had met the man who was to occupy the other berth. Judging from his appearance, he was afraid that he might not be a very trustworthy person. The purser accepted the responsibility for the valuables and remarked, 'It's all right, Bishop, I'll be very glad to take care of them for you. The other man has been up here and left his for the same reason'" (H. A. Ironside, *Illustrations of Bible Truth*).

We need to make sure we have all the facts before we speak and guard ourselves against making snap judgments about people. The standards we use to judge others will be used to judge us. —D.C.E.

It is much easier to be critical than to be correct.
—Disraeli

Saturday

"But the people took of the plunder . . .
to sacrifice to the LORD" (1 Samuel 15:21).

People come up with some very creative excuses for disobedience. A friend sent me the following list of statements made by motorists trying to explain their involvement in accidents:

- The other car collided with mine without giving warning of its intentions.
- A pedestrian hit me and went under my car.
- Coming home I drove into the wrong house and collided with a tree I don't have.
- I pulled away from the side of the road, glanced at my mother-in-law, and headed over the embankment.
- The pedestrian had no idea which direction to run, so I ran over him.

These excuses show how prone we are to evade responsibility for our wrong actions, but weak attempts to justify mistakes, errors, or blatant disobedience will not absolve us of blame.

We also make excuses when we fail to do God's will. If we could view our rationalizations from His perspective, we would see that they are as ridiculous as the statements of those motorists. Saul told God that the people would use the animals they had taken from the Amalekites as sacrifices. But he was merely covering up for disobeying God, who had told him to destroy everything.

If we seek every way possible to do God's will, we won't need to make excuses. —P.R.V.

Reasons that sound good aren't always good sound reasons.

Week 32

DANIEL'S STAND

The governors . . . sought to find some charge against Daniel; . . . but they could find no charge or fault. . . . Then these men said, "We shall not find any charge against [him] unless we find it . . . concerning the law of his God" (Daniel 6:4–5).

THEME

INTEGRITY

After the Civil War, a large insurance company offered Robert E. Lee the title of president and an annual salary of fifty thousand dollars. Lee protested that he was not worth that much. A representative explained that the company only wanted Lee's name, not his services. Lee firmly replied, "That is not for sale."

Daniel was not willing to worship God privately and sell his name to a heathen cause even if the fee was his own life. Disregarding his possible demise at the lions' club, he demonstrated that he was the real lion—courageous in his integrity against all odds.

People of integrity are sincere and honest; they avoid deception, artificiality, or shallowness of any kind. They are truthful and forthright at all costs. They know themselves and therefore are whole and complete.

Jesus was a man of integrity. He refused to endorse the corruption of the Pharisees, though they might have made Him a leading rabbi. He rejected the kingmaking desires of the populace, though they would have dressed Him in royal robes. He resisted the temptations of Satan, though he promised Him the world.

If we sing the praises of God's name, we will not be tempted to sell our own.

Sunday

**They could find no charge or fault,
because he was faithful (Daniel 6:4).**

A friend of mine, evangelist Herb Tyler, made a call from a pay phone after speaking one night. He told the operator his name and the number he wanted to call, deposited the money, and talked for a few minutes. When he hung up, all his coins came back. Calling the operator, Herb said, "I don't know if you are the one who took my call just now, but my coins came back." "I know," she said. "I was in your audience tonight when you spoke on integrity, and I wondered if you practice what you preach. So I flipped the lever and returned the coins. The so-called Christians that I know don't live like it." Tyler put the coins back in the box—but only after making an appointment to talk to the operator in person. As a result of their meeting, she trusted the Lord as her Savior.

The little details of our lives tell in forceful language how much integrity we have. Another good example of this is Daniel. His "excellent spirit" displayed itself in all of his actions. Under the scrutiny of more than 120 officials, he showed that he was a true follower of Jehovah by his everyday habits.

To show others that our faith is real, we must display integrity in the mundane happenings of life. If we conduct our affairs with integrity—at home, school, or work—people observing us will "find no charge or fault" against us. —P.R.V.

Those who are true to God will also be true to others.

Monday

DANIEL 1:1–8

Daniel purposed in his heart that he would not defile himself (Daniel 1:8).

An interesting thing to watch from an airplane is the winding path of a river. No two waterways are alike, but they all have one thing in common: they are crooked. And the reason is simple—rivers follow the path of least resistance. They flow around anything that blocks their eroding work. Rivers are crooked because they take the easy way.

Christians become crooked for the same reason. When we fail to overcome temptation, resist the devil, or tackle the enemy head-on, we deviate from the straight path God would have us follow. Unlike Daniel, who "purposed in his heart that he would not defile himself," we bend to worldly pressures and compromise what we know is right.

This shouldn't happen. Nothing is so strong that we need allow it to sidetrack us. Writing to Christians, John said, "You are of God, little children, and have overcome them, because He who is in you is greater than he who is in the world" (1 John 4:4). Believers can be "strong in the Lord" and press forward in "the power of His might." Rather than being overcome, we can be overcomers. Nothing should deter us in our Christian walk or divert us from our prescribed course. We don't have to give in to any temptation or foe.

Unlike rivers, which have no choice in the matter, we can remain straight by refusing to follow the path of least resistance. —R.W.D.

No one ever goes crooked who stays on the straight and narrow.

Tuesday

1 PETER 2:11–19

Finally, brethren, whatever things are . . . honest, . . .
meditate on these things (Philippians 4:8).

An office supervisor instructed her secretary to alter some questionable financial records. When the secretary refused, the supervisor
asked, "Don't you ever lie?"

For many people, both public and private honesty is an obsolete
virtue—a moral remnant of bygone days. Integrity is more complex
than simply refusing to lie. Integrity means speaking out when
remaining silent would convey the wrong impression, and it means
doing what's best for others even if it causes us harm.

Sa'ad, a sensitive, hard-working man who lives in Zarayed, one of
Cairo's garbage dumps, works long hours collecting trash. He is one of
thousands of Egypt's garbage collectors who struggle to survive, but
who seldom break out of their hopeless prison of poverty. Often he
clears little more than fifty cents a day. One day Sa'ad found a gold
watch valued at nearly two thousand dollars. He could have sold the
watch and made a better life for himself and his family. He could have
reasoned that he needed it more than the owner or that it was God's
justice that allowed him to find the watch. But he didn't. He returned
the watch to its owner. Sa'ad is a Christian and believes it's wrong to
keep what doesn't belong to him.

If this kind of honesty is not evident in our lives, we need to
reexamine ourselves. Jesus is the Truth. Truthfulness, therefore, must
be the way of life for all who follow Him. —D.J.D.

**Some people are honest only because
they have never had a good chance to steal anything.**

Wednesday

DANIEL 6:16–28

So this Daniel prospered in the reign of Darius and in the reign of Cyrus (Daniel 6:28).

Success comes in various forms. Some view it as the accumulation of great wealth gained through suffering and sacrifice. But for the believer, success comes only through doing God's will.

A young man named John W. Yates was so poor that he had to put cardboard in his shoes to cover the holes. Yet when he opened a bank account at the age of fifteen, he deposited his meager earnings under the name "John W. Yates and Company," acknowledging God as his partner and manager. He carried that practice into his business. In time, he became a multimillionaire.

Another young man, Oswald Chambers of Scotland, showed so much artistic promise that he was invited to study under Europe's greatest masters at age eighteen. But he declined the offer and enrolled in a little-known Bible school, where he eventually became a teacher. Later, he went to Egypt and ministered to the spiritual needs of British soldiers. Chambers died there when he was only in his forties, but he left to the world a rich legacy of devotional literature. Both men made doing God's will their prime objective; both achieved success.

Daniel began his career as a young captive in Babylon. Repeatedly he put his life on the line to remain faithful to the Lord. He refused to compromise, and God elevated him to a position of prominence. When we take that kind of attitude and accept whatever God has for us, we can be sure of success, no matter what form it takes. —H.V.L.

Outside God's will is no true success; in God's will, no failure.

Thursday

1 PETER 2:9–12

Providing honorable things, not only in the sight of the Lord, but also in the sight of men (2 Corinthians 8:21).

The first governor-general of Australia, Lord Hopetoun, inherited a brass-bound leather ledger that became one of his most cherished possessions. John Hope, one of his forebears, had owned it three centuries earlier and had used the ledger in his business in Edinburgh. When Lord Hopetoun received it, he noticed the prayer inscribed on the front page: "O Lord, keep me and this book honest." John Hope knew that he needed God's help to maintain his integrity.

Honesty is essential for the Christian. Shading the truth, withholding the facts, juggling figures, or misrepresenting something are dishonest activities that displease God. For this reason, and to demonstrate the new nature that comes through salvation, Christians should strive to live uprightly before God and man. The use of our time on the job, for example, must be above reproach. We should give an honest day's work to our employer. To do less will destroy our verbal witness and brand us as dishonest.

Speaking of a mutual Christian friend, an acquaintance of mine said, "He's true blue, all wool, and a yard wide," indicating that our friend was genuine, truthful, and trustworthy.

We too must strive to be honest in motive as well as in action and acknowledge our need of the Lord's help to do so by praying, "Lord, keep me honest." —P.R.V.

Honesty is the first chapter of the book of wisdom.

Friday

PROVERBS 2:1–9

He who walks with integrity walks securely, but he who perverts his ways will become known (Proverbs 10:9).

Personal integrity is often missing in today's society. Our world-system sees nothing wrong with people who shade the truth or make promises they don't intend to keep. The Christian, however, should be one "who walks with integrity."

In an article in *Moody Monthly,* John Souter wrote, "It was 11:00 P.M. I was sitting at the console of a sophisticated typesetting machine while an advertising man, a Christian, looked over my shoulder. He had roused me from bed to do a rush job for his client. Somehow I sensed I would never be paid for this job. But I swept those feelings aside. After all, this was a brother—a born-again Christian who would certainly pay his bills. But my fears were on target. I was never paid. Unfortunately, that experience has not been unique to me. I've learned there is often a big difference between what Christians say and what they actually do."

Apparently, many Christians have bought society's lie that integrity isn't important. As believers in Christ, though, we must follow the highest standards of personal honesty. When confronted with the temptation to compromise or to shade the truth, we must turn our backs on it and do what's right, regardless of personal cost.

If we have old bills to pay or promises to keep, we need to get things in order. Christians should be known for their honesty. —D.C.E.

A debt is never too old to pay.

Saturday

"Does He not see my ways, and count all my steps?"
(Job 31:4).

As professional golfer Ray Floyd got ready to tap in a routine nine-inch putt, he saw the ball move ever so slightly. According to the rule book, if the ball moves at all the golfer must take a penalty stroke. Floyd was among the leaders in a tournament offering a top prize of 108,000 dollars. To acknowledge that the ball had moved could mean losing his chance for big money.

Writer David Holahan described what some golfers might have done: "The athlete ducks his head and flails wildly with his hands, as if being attacked by a killer bee; next, he steps back from the ball, rubbing his eye for a phantom speck of dust, all the while scanning the playing partners and the gallery for any sign that the ball's movement has been detected by others. If the coast is clear, he taps the ball in for his par."

Ray Floyd, however, didn't do that. He assessed himself a penalty stroke and wound up with a bogey on the hole.

The patriarch Job also showed remarkable honesty in matters not seen by human observers. He maintained his integrity by fearing God and shunning evil. Job knew that the eyes of the Lord were on him at all times, and that was what really mattered to him.

The true test of our integrity comes when no one is watching us. If we remember that God sees what others don't and that it's His approval that matters, our integrity will improve. —M.R.D.II

**It is better to suffer for the truth
than to be rewarded for a lie.**

Week 33

HOSEA BUYS GOMER

Then the LORD said to me, "Go again, love a woman who is . . . committing adultery. . . ." So I bought her for myself for fifteen shekels of silver (Hosea 3:1–2).

THEME

FAITHFULNESS

Mary Ann Evans, better known as English novelist George Eliot, wrote on May 5, 1880, to her friend Barbara Bodichon about her marriage. "By the time you receive this letter I shall . . . have been married to Mr. J. W. Cross . . . who . . . sees his happiness in the dedication of his life to me."

Hosea continued to love Gomer, his adultrous wife. His love and faithfulness became God's object lesson to Israel. Although Israel had been a wayward wife and chased after other gods, God was still faithful and loving.

Stories of unfaithfulness to God abound; men and women continually seek intimacy with each other and with gods of their own making instead of with the One who truly cares.

The unfaithfulness of Judas must have hurt Jesus deeply. He had shared His life with him. At their last meal together, they dipped their bread into the bowl at the same time; their hands may have touched. Later, in the garden, Judas kissed Jesus, but it was a kiss of betrayal. Even though Judas double-crossed His loving friend for monetary gain, Jesus probably grieved when He heard that Judas hanged himself.

Like a faithful spouse, God listens for the phone to ring, for the sound of tires on gravel, for any sign that we have returned. When we finally come home, He quietly asks where we have been. He hugs us, tells us good night, and says, "I love you. I will always be here."

Sunday

You will guide me with Your counsel,
and afterward receive me to glory (Psalm 73:24).

When we reflect on the past, things often look much different than when they happened. For instance, a young woman cried when she broke up with a young man to whom she had been engaged. Yet later she told me that she looked back on that heartache with gratitude. Today she has a fine Christian husband, and the former suitor turned out to be irresponsible and has been divorced twice.

When Hosea wrote the book that bears his name, he saw the earlier events of his life quite differently than when he lived them. He had married a girl named Gomer, only to see her become unfaithful to him, bear children by other men, and sell herself into ritual prostitution. With a broken heart, he had continued his ministry while loving her and longing for her restoration.

The day finally came when he was able to purchase her freedom and bring her home. The Lord enabled Hosea to see his relationship with Gomer as a dramatic portrayal of God's relationship with His unfaithful people Israel. I believe that's why Hosea could say early in the book that the Lord, knowing all that would transpire, had in His wise providence directed the prophet to enter this marriage.

In heaven, we'll be able to look back and see God's purposes in the things that happened here on earth. With this assurance in mind, we can look forward in confidence, saying with the psalmist, "You will guide me with Your counsel, and afterward receive me to glory."

—H.V.L.

**Never be afraid to entrust an unknown future
to an all-knowing God.**

Monday

PSALM 107:1–15

His compassions fail not. They are new every morning; great is Your faithfulness (Lamentations 3:22–23).

Hudson Taylor, the founder of the China Inland Mission, wrote the following in his journal: "Our Heavenly Father is a very experienced One. He knows very well that His children wake up with a good appetite every morning. He always provides breakfast for them, and He does not send them supperless to bed at night. . . . He sustained three million Israelites in the wilderness for forty years. We do not expect He will send three million missionaries to China; but if He did, He would have ample means to sustain them all. . . . Depend on it. God's work done in God's way will never lack God's supply."

Hudson Taylor had an absolute trust in the faithful God, and the Lord marvelously blessed the work he established.

We may be weak, but our heavenly Father is all-powerful. Our feelings may fluctuate, but He never changes. Even creation is a record of His steadfastness. That's why we can sing, "Summer and winter, and springtime and harvest, / Sun, moon, and stars in their courses above, / Join with all nature in manifold witness / To Thy great faithfulness, mercy, and love."

"God is faithful, by whom you were called into the fellowship of His Son, Jesus Christ our Lord" (1 Cor. 1:9). Our strength for the present and our hope for the future are not based on our own perseverance, but on the fidelity of God. At every turn of the road we can count on the Father's faithfulness. —P.R.V.

He who abandons himself to God,
God will never abandon.

Tuesday

HEBREWS 6:7–12

**God is not unjust to forget your work
and labor of love (Hebrews 6:10).**

A. C. Dixon told the story of Johanna Ambrosius, the wife of a poor farmer who lived in the German Empire during the latter part of the nineteenth century. She and her husband spent many long hours in the fields, so she knew little of the outside world. But she had the soul of a poet. With her hope in God, she wrote down the thoughts that filled her heart. She had great sympathy for the struggling people around her, and her mother-heart expressed its joys and sorrows in poetry. Somehow, a bit of verse she had written found its way into print and later into the hands of the Empress of Germany. Impressed by the beauty of what she read, she asked that the author be located. On finding Johanna and learning of her meager lifestyle, the Empress expressed her love for the woman by supplying her immediate needs and by giving her a pension for life.

God calls many of us to serve Him in obscure places where no one expresses gratitude or even seems to notice what we do. But God observes everything we do to help bear the burdens of others, and He will reward us for our labors. He sees our struggles, knows the load we carry, and takes note of our faithfulness. He cares for us in our pilgrimage and will make it all worthwhile when He comes again.

Our eternal pension is guaranteed. God will not forget our "work and labor of love." —P.R.V.

**Work for the Lord—the pay may not be much,
but the retirement plan is out of this world.**

Wednesday

MATTHEW 24:42–47

**A faithful man will abound with blessings
(Proverbs 28:20).**

God's Word commends faithfulness. The parables in Matthew 24 and 25 about being ready for Christ's sudden appearing point out that those who faithfully do their tasks receive the Lord's approval. Day by day, in good fortune or in bad, whether feeling good or a little down in the dumps, we are to continue steadfastly doing the job God has given us.

After the tragic bombing of a marine base in Beirut in October 1983, the steadfastness of one young soldier moved and heartened the American people back home. He had been critically wounded in the explosion of the revamped hotel where he and his fellow marines had been staying. Many of his buddies had been killed. He was covered with bandages and a jungle of tubes was attached to his body. Unable to speak, he indicated he wanted to write something when visited by General Paul X. Kelly, Commandant of the Marine Corps. Painfully he wrote the words *semper fi,* a shortened form of the U.S. Marine Corps motto, *Semper Fidelis,* which means "Always faithful."

Those of us in the Lord's army can learn from this young man's example. We too may have come under heavy attack. Our "wounds" may be many. Some of our beloved fellow soldiers may fall in battle. Even so, we are to be faithful to the end. An attitude of determined loyalty should fill our hearts and drive us onward no matter what the circumstances. Yes, *Semper Fidelis,* "always faithful," is also the Christian's motto. —D.C.E.

The proof of our faith is our faithfulness.

Thursday

JOHN 19:25–30

**I have fought the good fight, I have finished the race,
I have kept the faith (2 Timothy 4:7).**

In 1981 Bill Broadhurst entered the Pepsi Challenge 10,000-meter road race in Omaha, Nebraska. Ten years earlier, surgery for a brain aneurysm left him paralyzed on his left side. But on a misty July morning, he stood with 1,200 lithe-looking men and women at the starting line. The gun cracked. The crowd surged ahead. Bill threw his stiff left leg forward and pivoted on it as his right foot hit the ground. His slow plop-plop-plop rhythm seemed to mock him as the pack disappeared into the distance. Sweat rolled down his face, pain pierced his ankle, but he kept going. Six miles, two hours, and twenty-nine minutes later, Bill reached the finish line. A man approached from a small group of bystanders. Bill recognized him from pictures in the newspaper. "Here," the man said. "You've worked harder for this than I have." With those words, Bill Rodgers, the famous marathon runner, put his newly won medal around Broadhurst's neck, proclaiming him a winner.

The sight of Jesus hanging "helpless" on a cross looked like a tragic defeat. But three little words from His lips amounted to a victory shout: "It is finished!" Three days later the truth of His words would be known. The empty tomb confirmed His claim. He had finished His work by defeating death and atoning for sin.

The Christian life is not a race to see who comes in first, but an endurance run to see who finishes faithfully. Remaining faithful to the finish makes us true winners. —D.J.D.

We are judged by what we finish, not by what we start.

Friday

Speaking in Edinburgh, missionary John Williams held his audience spellbound with thrilling accounts of God's work among the tribespeople of the New Hebrides Islands. A soft-spoken missionary followed Williams with a brief report of his work. In a low and trembling voice he said, "My friends, I have no remarkable success to relate like Mr. Williams. I've labored for Christ in a far-off land for many years and have seen only small results. But I have this comfort: when the Master comes to reckon with His servants, He will not say, 'Well done, thou good and successful servant,' but 'well done, thou good and faithful servant.' I have tried to be faithful!"

From Jesus' story in Matthew 25 we learn that unequal gifts exercised with equal diligence will receive equal reward. In the parable, talents represent God-given abilities to carry out God-assigned responsibilities. What's important is not how much we accomplish, but our motives and the quality of our labors. Alexander MacLaren wrote, "Christ rewards not action, but the graces that are made visible in the action; and these can be seen in the tiniest as in the largest deeds. A light that streams through a pinprick is the same that pours through the widest windows."

We need not feel inadequate if we have been diligent in serving Christ. Although it's rewarding to see large results, in God's eyes faithfulness that produces even small results is a job well done.

—D.J.D.

**Work done well for Christ will receive
a "well done" from Christ.**

Saturday

2 TIMOTHY 4:1–8

I planted . . . but God gave the increase
(1 Corinthians 3:6).

A deacon rebuked an elderly preacher one Sunday morning before the service. "Pastor," said the man, "something must be wrong with your preaching and your work. There's been only one person added to the church in a whole year, and he's just a boy." The minister listened, his eyes moistening and his thin hand trembling. "I feel it all," he replied, "but God knows I've tried to do my duty." On that day the minister's heart was heavy as he stood before his flock. As he finished the message, he felt a strong inclination to resign. After everyone else had left, that one new boy came to him and asked, "Do you think if I worked hard for an education, I could become a preacher—perhaps a missionary?" Again tears welled up in the minister's eyes. "Ah, this heals the ache I feel," he said. "Robert, I see the Divine hand now. May God bless you, my boy. Yes, I think you will become a preacher."

Many years later an aged missionary returned to London from Africa. People spoke his name with reverence. Nobles invited him to their homes. He had added many souls to the church of Jesus Christ, reaching even some of Africa's most savage chiefs. His name was Robert Moffat, the same Robert who years before had spoken to the pastor on that Sunday morning in the old Scottish church.

Our service for Christ may sometimes seem fruitless. We wonder if anything significant is happening. But if we are faithful, God will give the increase. —D.J.D.

**Faithfulness is God's requirement,
fruitfulness is His reward.**

Week 34

HABAKKUK'S IMPATIENCE

O Lᴏʀᴅ, how long shall I cry, and You will not hear?. . . Then the Lᴏʀᴅ answered me and said: . . . "At the end [the vision] will speak, and it will not lie. Though it tarries, wait for it; because it will surely come" (Habakkuk 1:2, 2:2–3).

THEME

WAITING ON GOD

"God, I hate being patient. I'm not a patient person. I want things to happen. I have a big project under way, and I'd like to have it be successful . . . now. There are a lot of things I need to know about life, and I'd like to know them . . . now. I'd like to have my letters answered, my questions answered. . . . Why do I always have to wait?" wrote Gladis DePree, author and world traveler.

The Old Testament prophets continually played the waiting game, wondering at times whether God would fulfill His Word. Habakkuk's frustration with God was representative of the prophetic dilemma— their own fire-and-brimstone preaching versus God's seemingly slow-train-to-nowhere actions. After the prophets recovered from the doldrums, they found that God did not have a deaf ear. He was simply teaching His messengers the value of waiting.

While waiting, people think about both God and themselves and find out again who they are and what they believe. In New Testament times, God promised Simeon that he would see the Savior. Simeon waited for the Messiah most of his life and evidently was near death when God rewarded his patient hope. Luke tells the touching story of Simeon carrying Jesus in his arms and praising God (Luke 2:28–32).

The waiting rooms of life are not always pleasant places, but the Great Physician eventually walks through the door with a message of hope.

Sunday

HABAKKUK 1:12–2:4

**They soon forgot His works;
they did not wait for His counsel (Psalm 106:13).**

A friend found it difficult to be patient during a long hospital stay. She was a Christian, but she feared that some sins from her past were too bad to be forgiven. I assured her that when she confessed them to God He forgave her. And her doctors reassured her that her depression would lift and she would get better. Still she found it difficult to wait for the light to break through.

Habakkuk was perplexed and impatient too. First he complained to God about the evils of the Israelites (1:2–4). The Lord responded by saying that He would use the Babylonians to scourge them (1:5–11). Then the prophet raised a new problem—Babylon was more wicked than Israel (1:12–17). Though frustrated, Habakkuk didn't act rashly. Instead, he showed reverence for God by declaring that he would wait for Him to make things clear. When God spoke to Habakkuk again, He assured the prophet that He would give him the answer. He commanded him to write it clearly so that he could proclaim it speedily. But He also told Habakkuk that he would have to wait awhile before seeing all the wrongs made right. This delay was a trying experience for Habakkuk, but the answer eventually came, and at just the right time.

When waiting for God to work, we must exercise patience and steadfast faith, leaving matters in His hands. God will reward us for our patience—but not too soon nor too late. —H.V.L.

Patience is a virtue that carries a lot of *wait*.

Monday

PSALM 62

My soul, wait silently for God alone,
for my expectation is from Him (Psalm 62:5).

The twentieth century is the age of the instant. We can make coffee, cook a meal, and even telephone overseas in less than a minute. We have become accustomed to immediate results. Perhaps that's why we often find it difficult to wait on the Lord. We want instant spiritual growth. We need to understand, though, that maturity comes as the years progress, not through some on-the-spot formula that gives it to us all at once.

A pastor from Detroit, W. G. Coltman, told of a woman who came to him for counsel about some serious marital problems. After weighing the situation carefully, he said to her, "There are two roads open before you. One is to take matters in your own hands and force the issue. . . . That will bring a speedier solution, but it will mean a broken home. The other road is that of God's ordering, of waiting upon Him and for Him. He may make you wait for some time before He works your problem out. Your patience may be severely tried, but in the end you will have a permanent and satisfactory solution." She heeded his words and began to trust the Lord. As a result, her faith was strengthened as she saw God intervene in the difficulties of her home.

To "wait" does not imply passive submission, but an attitude of patience. It expresses dependence upon God and brings quietness to the soul. When we face insurmountable problems and feel that we are on the precipice of panic, we can remember that our heavenly Father "acts for the one who waits for Him" (Isa. 64:4). —P.R.V.

We conquer by continuing.

Tuesday

ISAIAH 40:25–31

**Those who wait on the LORD . . .
shall run and not be weary (Isaiah 40:31).**

Lagging behind spiritually? Speed up! Still behind? Try harder! Go faster! Get more involved in church activities. Push yourself—run—keep on the go. You've got too much invested to slow down. To stop now would be to lose the ground you've gained, right? Wrong! The Bible says that being effective for the Lord comes from knowing how to slow down and wait on the Lord.

Astronaut Michael Collins described the problem of trying to link two orbiting space vehicles. When two airplanes rendezvous for an in-flight refueling, the plane behind simply increases speed until it catches the other aircraft. In outer space, however, the situation is quite different. Acceleration puts the trailing spacecraft into a higher orbit, causing it to move away and widen the gap. Therefore, the ship's commander must act against all natural instincts and slow down, dropping his craft into a lower orbit, which enables him to catch up, maneuver into position, and make contact at precisely the right moment.

So it is with the busy child of God. Taking on more activities can mean losing ground as a result of lost time with the Lord. To get ahead, we must slow down and wait on the Lord. As we do, we will have time to pray, to read God's Word, and to rearrange our priorities.

When we're behind, the only way to catch up is to slow down and wait for the will and work of God. —M.R.D.II

**Unless we come apart and rest awhile,
we may just plain come apart. —Havner**

Wednesday

Do you not know that . . . one receives the prize?
Run in such a way that you may obtain it (1 Corinthians 9:24).

A computer study of five thousand racehorses has revealed a way to predict whether or not a young horse will develop into a good runner. According to an article in *USA Today,* a professor at the Massachusetts Institute of Technology used computers and high-speed cameras to find out how a good horse runs. He discovered that the legs of a fast horse operate much like the spokes of a wheel. Each leg touches down only as the leg before it pushes off, resulting in peak efficiency. Later studies disclosed that a horse's manner of walking changes little after the first few months. Therefore, motion analysis when a horse is young can predict how well it will run when it matures.

In the Old Testament, Isaiah talked about running well in the course of life. He said that the people who run the best are the ones who learn to wait on the Lord. They don't waste energy trying to do things on their own. They make the Lord their strength and hope.

In the New Testament, the apostle Paul compares the Christian life to a race. He said that those who run well are characterized by efficiency of effort. For the Christian, this means running with control and self-discipline (1 Cor. 9:24–27). The author of Hebrews said that a good runner gets rid of anything that adds extra weight (Heb. 12:1).

To earn an imperishable crown we must wait on the Lord, practice self-control, and lay aside sinful burdens. These are the secrets of running well. —M.R.D.II

Those who wait on the Lord
will run without the weight of sin.

Thursday

ISAIAH 30:15–18

"In quietness and confidence shall be your strength"
(Isaiah 30:15).

In *The Uttermost Star,* author F. W. Boreham told about a farewell service for a minister who had pastored a church for twenty years. Several preachers attended, and each eloquently extolled the pastor's virtues. Boreham commented that he had forgotten everything said that day except for a simple statement made by a man who was not even scheduled to speak. The man had asked permission to say a word, and in a single sentence had paid his pastor this compliment: "I have seen him nearly every day of my life for twenty years, and I've never seen him in a hurry!" After the service, the minister said he considered that tribute to be the most gratifying. He took it as an indication that over the years he had truly learned to wait patiently upon the Lord—he had discovered the secret of Isaiah 30:15.

For many people, staying calm, cool, and collected under pressure is partly a matter of natural temperament or self-discipline. But Christians, whether easygoing or highstrung, derive inner strength from quiet waiting upon God. Martin Luther once claimed that he was so busy he couldn't get anything done unless he spent at least three hours a day in prayer. Too often we reverse the order. We get flustered and upset or we do things hastily because we fail to take the time to be alone with the Lord.

We can learn a lesson from that pastor. By waiting on the Lord, we can learn to be calm, cool, and collected in every situation. —R.W.D.

We must never take on more work
than we have time to pray about.

Friday

PSALM 62

My soul, wait silently for God alone,
for my expectation is from Him (Psalm 62:5).

I hate getting caught in slow-moving traffic on an interstate. It's especially frustrating when I want to get somewhere in a hurry. But what's really annoying is when I get hemmed in with a solid line of cars in both the right- and left-hand lanes, a huge semi just ahead of me, and another one behind. Sandwiched between two of these monsters, all I can do is read how much the carrier ahead of me pays in road taxes each year. I do not feel sympathetic.

I was in that kind of situation recently. As my patience ran low, my adrenalin ran high; and as my body and car idled, my brain went into action. This is a small drama of the Christian life, I thought. Sometimes in our walk with the Lord we get hemmed in by uncontrollable circumstances. We grind to a halt, move only occasionally, and then not very far. Impatience and anger compound the problem. If only we could see what's up ahead.

That must be how the psalmist felt when writing Psalm 62. But he reminded himself of his secure relationship with God and that the way would become clear.

In my Christian experience, as in interstate traffic, the "lanes" do open up eventually. We must choose not to fight life's traffic jams, but rather to see them as excellent opportunities to learn how to wait silently for God. He has never been known to disappoint those whose expectation is from Him. —D.J.D.

**Patience means awaiting God's time
without doubting God's love.**

Saturday

PSALM 37:1–11

Trust in the Lord, and do good; . . . wait patiently for Him
(Psalm 37:3, 7).

The Scriptures encourage us to rest in the Lord, and this reliance is to be accompanied by right thoughts and actions. Regardless of the circumstances stacked against us, we must believe that in time He will honor us for following His pattern for living. Patient perseverance should characterize the life of every believer trying to do God's will.

John Wooden, head basketball coach at UCLA for many years, made his teams play patiently. In his book *They Call Me Coach,* he said, "In game play, it has always been my philosophy that patience will win out. By that, I mean patience to follow our game plan. If we do believe in it, we will wear the opposition down and will get to them. If we break away from our style, however, and play their style, we're in trouble. And if we let our emotions command the game rather than our reason, we will not function effectively. I constantly caution our team, 'Play your game. . . . Eventually, if you play your game, stick to your style, class will tell in the end! This does not mean that we will always outscore our opponent, but it does ensure that we will not beat ourselves.'"

In Psalm 37, God is saying, in effect, "Do what's right and trust Me. Regardless of how badly you may seem to be losing, just do My will and leave the outcome to Me. I'll make sure that eventually you'll be the winner." Such a strategy will not only keep us from beating ourselves, it will lead to glorious victory. —M.R.D.II

**God seldom does great things in a hurry;
wait patiently for Him.**

283

Week 35

CHRIST'S BIRTH

In the beginning was the Word, and the Word was with God, and the Word was God. . . . And the Word became flesh and dwelt among us, and we beheld His glory (John 1:1, 14).

THEME

INCARNATION

Reverend Nico Smith and his wife, Ellen, are the only whites in the black township of Mamelodi near the South African city of Pretoria. Going to a community of 300,000 blacks was a "complete change in his life, a rejection, in fact, of everything that his life had been until then and everything fundamental in Afrikaner society and Afrikaner belief." Smith has begun to see life and people in a completely new way. As *Time* put it, "Nico Smith is almost one of them—not exactly, but almost."

The incarnation is about how Jesus became almost one of us. In one sense, He was like any other man—completely human. In another way, He was totally different—completely God. The birth of Jesus was not the first time God appeared as a human; the Old Testament records a number of times when God briefly appeared in some bodily form. Yet the Bethlehem birth was unique; God became a member of the human family and stayed around for thirty-three years.

In those thirty plus years, Jesus grew physically and mentally. He got hungry, tired, and thirsty. He slept and wept. He was tempted with typical human desires. He felt anguish. He showed concern. And His veins flowed with blood. Like every human, He died.

In His humanity Jesus was not just God with skin, but He wasn't just a person without sin either. He was like us, but different, and that made all the difference in the world. He could save us from ourselves, gather up the broken images, and make us like Himself.

Sunday

JOHN 1:14–18

And the Word became flesh and dwelt among us
(John 1:14).

Jesus is God in human form. In coming into our world, He revealed the heavenly Father to us. That's what John meant when he said that "the Word became flesh." We call this the doctrine of the incarnation.

F. W. Boreham applied this truth in his book *Faces in the Fire*. He wrote, "The Christian man must accompany the Christian message. The Word must be presented in its proper human setting. . . . The Word made flesh is thus pronounced with an accent and an eloquence which are simply irresistible. . . . The words of men become [filled] with passion and with power only when they are made flesh. And in the same way, the thoughts of God to men are only eloquent when they are so expressed."

To emphasize the importance of putting actions behind our words, Boreham quoted English writer George Eliot (pen name for Mary Ann Evans). Speaking of how people's lives convey the meaning of ideas, Eliot said, "Sometimes [words] are made flesh; they breathe upon us with warm breath, they touch us with soft responsive hands, they look at us with sad, sincere eyes, and they speak to us in appealing tones; they are clothed in a living human soul."

Likewise, if people are to "hear" the Word of God, they must "see" it demonstrated in our lives. Jesus said, "Let your light so shine before men, that they may see your good works and glorify your Father in heaven" (Matt. 5:16). Christians who live what they believe give flesh to the Word. —R.W.D.

We teach more with our life than with our lips.

Monday

HEBREWS 2:14–18

Therefore, in all things He had to be made like His brethren (Hebrews 2:17).

When Christ became a man, He showed His willingness to be tempted, tested, hated, and hurt. During His life on earth, He faced the same struggles we encounter. He had been sympathetic to man's weaknesses before He came, but by taking a human body He identified with us in a dramatic way. His incarnation revealed the extent to which He would go to pay for our sin and to be touched by the trials and infirmities that make life so difficult for us.

On a smaller scale, people try to empathize with the sufferings of others. John Griffin, a white man, darkened his skin in an effort to understand what it meant to be black in a predominantly white society. He told about his experiences in a book titled *Black Like Me.* More recently, a thirty-year-old woman, an industrial designer, masqueraded as an elderly woman once a week for three years to find out how it feels to be old in America. What she learned is heartbreaking. She was robbed, insulted, and frightened by a world that isn't easy on its elderly.

As touching as these examples are, they are nothing compared with Christ's coming into our world. No one else left so high a position to feel what mortal man feels. Jesus gave up heaven's glory and was tempted in all points as we are, yet He did not sin. He bore our sins on the cross so that He could be merciful to us.

We have One who cares. When we face temptations and trials, we can go to Jesus. He knows the feeling. —M.R.D.II

Earth has no sorrow that heaven cannot feel.

Tuesday

JOHN 1:1–14

In the beginning was the Word, and the Word was with God, and the Word was God (John 1:1).

At one time a wise and beloved Shah who cared greatly for his people and desired only the best for them ruled Persia. One day he disguised himself as a poor man and went to visit the public baths. The water for the baths was heated by a furnace in the cellar, and the Shah made his way to that dark place to sit with the man who tended the fire. The two men shared the coarse food, and the Shah befriended him in his loneliness. Day after day the ruler went to visit the man. The worker became attached to this stranger because he "came where he was" (Luke 10:33). The Shah expected the man to ask for a gift when he learned his true identity. Instead, he looked with love and wonder into his leader's face and said, "You left your palace and your glory to sit with me in this dark place, to eat my coarse food, and to care about what happens to me. On others you may bestow rich gifts, but to me you have given yourself."

As we think of what our Lord has done for us, we can echo that fire tender's sentiments. He stepped from heaven to earth, from the worship of angels to the mocking of cruel men, from glory to humiliation. To provide our salvation, Jesus came in human flesh, took upon Himself the form of a servant, and "became obedient to the point of death, even the death of the cross" (Phil. 2:8). Our great Creator became our Savior. He deserves our heartfelt worship and humble adoration.

—P.R.V.

God's highest Gift should awaken our deepest gratitude.

Wednesday

COLOSSIANS 1:15–19

He is the image of the invisible God,
the firstborn over all creation (Colossians 1:15).

A little boy looked into the sky and asked his mother, "Is God up there?" When she assured him that He was, the youngster replied, "Wouldn't it be nice if He would put His head out and let us see Him?"

What the boy didn't understand was that God has let us see Him— in the person of His Son. We don't have to guess what God is like. Nor do we have to wonder if He's alive. By sending Christ to earth as a man, the heavenly Father fully revealed Himself. Jesus was God "manifested in the flesh" (1 Tim. 3:16).

Christ made this point clear when He said to Philip, "He who has seen Me has seen the Father" (John 14:9). This is the good news we celebrate, especially at Christmas. God has shown us what He is like in the person of His Son. He left heaven's glory and came to earth to be born of a virgin. The baby that Mary cradled in a Bethlehem manger was the "image of the invisible God." All the attributes of the infinite God resided in Him. In fact, He was the One by whom "all things were created" and in whom "all things consist" (Col. 1:16–17).

Looking into the face of our Savior, we can see displayed the holiness, the grace, and the love of our eternal, heavenly Father. This realization should make us rejoice, for we are gazing at God, who stepped out of heaven and came to this earth. Jesus Christ is Immanuel, God with us! —P.R.V.

Bethlehem's manger was the first step
in God's love-journey to Calvary's cross.

Thursday

JOHN 1:14–18

"You shall see heaven open, and the angels of God ascending and descending upon the Son of Man" (John 1:51).

We have glamorized the birth of Jesus. Christmas card art often depicts an idyllic manger scene with halos of light surrounding the faces of Mary, Joseph, and the Christ-child. His birth, however, was like any normal human birth, except for its crude and unusual setting. Yet that lowly scene encompassed the wonder of the incarnation—the infinite God of the universe came from the heights of heaven to the depths of earth.

Referring to the words of Christ in John 1:51, Andrew Murray captured the dramatic contrast inherent in this amazing event. In *The Life and Light of Men,* he wrote: "The nature of our Lord Jesus is infinite in its extent. On one hand it touches the height of Godhead, on the other the depth of manhood. To use His own comparison [John 1:51], it resembles the mystic ladder, which in the dream of the wanderer [Jacob], linked the far distant depths of sky—where, more brilliant than sun or moon, the light of the Shekinah shone—with the moorland, strewn with huge boulders of stone, on which he lay. At one end is the title, Son of God; at the other, Son of Man."

Jesus is Son of God, in all His deity, and He became Son of Man, in full humanity. Yet He did not sin. Thus His death guarantees forgiveness and eternal life if we trust Him as our Savior. Because God descended from heaven to earth in Christ, we can ascend from earth to heaven through Christ. —D.C.E.

The Son of God became the Son of Man that He might change the sons of men into sons of God.

Friday

No one has seen God at any time. The only begotten Son . . .
has declared Him (John 1:18).

In an article in *Moody Monthly,* Frank M. Fairchild told of a beautiful fresco on the ceiling of a Roman palace. Painted by Guido Reni in 1614, it was one of the most impressive works of its day. But visitors couldn't fully appreciate the masterpiece because they had to crane their necks to see it. To solve the problem, palace officials placed a large mirror on the floor beneath the painting, enabling viewers to study its reflection and more fully appreciate its beauty.

Fairchild made this observation: "Jesus Christ does precisely that for us when we try to get some notion of God. . . . He interprets God to our dull hearts. In Him, God becomes visible and intelligible to us. We cannot by any amount of searching find out God. The more we try, the more we are bewildered. Then Jesus Christ appears. He is God stooping down to our level, and He enables our feeble thoughts to get some real hold on God Himself."

Christ came to reveal God to us. But He is more than a reflection of the Father. He is God in human flesh. Hebrews tells us that He is "the express image" of God (1:3). And Jesus Himself said, "He who has seen Me has seen the Father" (John 14:9).

As we meditate on the wonder of "the Word made flesh," we will say with the hymnwriter, "O come, let us adore Him, Christ, the Lord."
—R.W.D.

**Christ's birth brings the infinite God
within the finite reach of man.**

Saturday

JOHN 1:1–14

But as many as received Him, to them He gave the right
to become children of God (John 1:12).

As finite creatures, we sense that our earthly life and eternal destiny
are somehow bound up with our Creator. Most religions of the world
represent man's effort to reach up to God and become acceptable to
Him. In China, for example, devout pilgrims ascend a sacred mountain called Taishan. They climb seven thousand steps to its summit,
first passing through the "middle gate," then through "heaven's
southern gate." Finally they reach one of the most beautiful buildings in all of China—the Temple of the Azure Cloud. Here they
offer sacrifices, which the worshipers believe will gain God's favor.
Such effort represents great religious fervor—and futility, for it
brings devotees no closer to God than when they mounted the first
step.

By contrast, Christianity begins with the Creator of heaven and
earth reaching down to us. In His holiness He is beyond the highest
mountain peak, so far out of reach of sinners that only He Himself
could span the gulf. And that's exactly what He did. By the miracle of
the incarnation, He became flesh and offered Himself as a once-and-
for-all sacrifice for our sin. Then, after rising from the dead, He went
back to Glory. And He did it all for us. Our part is to confess that we
are sinners, to renounce all efforts to earn our salvation, and to trust
Him as our Savior.

Those still climbing endless steps of self-effort may as well give up.
They lead nowhere. Instead, take that all-important step of faith in the
Lord Jesus. It's the only step that leads to heaven. —D.J.D.

**Salvation is not something we *achieve*
but something we *receive*.**

Week 36

JOHN PREACHES

And [John] went into all the region around the Jordan, preaching a baptism of repentance for the remission of sins. . . . Then he said to the multitudes . . . "Bear fruits worthy of repentance" (Luke 3:3, 7–8).

THEME

REPENTANCE

Thomas Russell Ybarra defined a Christian as a person who does "repentance on a Sunday for what he did on Saturday and is going to do on Monday."

True biblical repentance is never that shortlived; it is a complete about-face. John challenged the Jews to prepare themselves for the coming Messiah by turning from their sins to holiness. This meant changing their minds and actions.

The sorry truth is that repentance has very little to do with crying our eyes out. Repentant people may be tearful, but tearful people are not always repentant. Repentance means turning around. It is a compass test; does a person know how to go south after he or she has been going north?

God is sometimes described as repenting of His plans, such as with Nineveh (Jonah 3:10 KJV), but this may be humanity's limited attempt to explain the actions of an all-knowing God. What is significant, even if from a human standpoint, is that God in His repentance makes a complete U-turn, and this is a perfect model for us to follow.

Never-on-Sunday sinning is not what the Changemaker had in mind. Change of heart means a change of life every day.

Sunday

LUKE 3:1–16

"The rough ways [shall be] made smooth"
(Luke 3:5).

Bad roads were getting worse in a Detroit suburb. Commuters and homeowners let their local government officials know they wanted action, not more talk about who was responsible—the city or the borough—for the repairs. They wanted the road fixed and the potholes filled. They didn't want to risk losing a tailpipe or a tire every time they ventured onto Lakeshore Drive. Though one of the most scenic drives in the city, it had become what one Detroiter called a "kidney-crunching, teeth-chattering, tire-popping experience that even bus drivers dreaded."

Luke 3 tells of another kind of rough road—"the way of the Lord"—that needed repair, not talk. In John the Baptist's day this "road" was in bad shape, for the moral and spiritual condition of the nation of Israel had deteriorated. John made it clear that if the people were going to be ready for the Messiah they had to "prepare the way" by getting rid of the road hazards of selfishness, greed, and violence. He also made it plain that they had to do more than just talk about changing their ways. He challenged His hearers to prove their faith by turning from their sins in genuine repentance.

Although John's message was directed to Israel, every Christian can profit from it. Unconfessed sins are the potholes of the Christian journey. To repair the road, we need only repent. —M.R.D.II

Repentance not only regrets sin, but also renounces it.

Monday

REVELATION 2:1–7

"Remember therefore from where you have fallen; repent and do the first works" (Revelation 2:5).

Repentance in the Christian life is a painful but necessary step we must take when we offend God or hurt others. Yet it is not a cleanup job that we accomplish. C. S. Lewis clarifies the issue when he says that repentance "is not something God demands of you before He will take you back. . . ; it is simply a description of what going back is like."

A Christian, writing anonymously in *Leadership* magazine, told of his ten-year bondage to lust, which included a regular diet of pornography. During this time, he conducted Christian conferences and seminars across the country. The agony of his inner conflict finally became unbearable. To his horror, he realized that such pleasures as a breathtaking sunset or the soft spray of an ocean breeze no longer excited him. His obsession with lust had dulled his appreciation of life's finest enjoyments and prevented the joy of fellowshipping with Jesus. Although he had been outwardly faithful to his wife, not having engaged in adultery, he had sinned against her, and their relationship had suffered. When he turned anew to God, he realized that a necessary step in breaking his lustful pattern was a long talk with his mate. The whole experience was painful and awkward, but the repentance was genuine. She forgave him, and love returned to their marriage.

Repentance, though painful, results in life's true pleasure—communion with God and spiritual oneness with fellow believers.

—D.J.D.

Repentance means not only a heart broken for sin but from sin.

Tuesday

REVELATION 3:14–22

"As many as I love, I rebuke and chasten.
Therefore be zealous and repent" (Revelation 3:19).

Pastor Louis Paul Lehman told of a humbling experience in a former church. A missionary who had come to present his work failed to impress Lehman. His appearance, presentation, and type of ministry all seemed to say, this person is a misfit. Months later, a newsletter came from the missionary that contained striking reports of conversions under his ministry. He was doing a solid work for God. Pastor Lehman realized he had misjudged the man. "When I read that letter," he said, "I went to my study and wept and repented."

In his booklet *A Call to Repentance,* Bob Stokes wrote, "Repentance is not only an act, it's an attitude. In other words, a repentant sinner carries the characteristic of repentance right through into his Christian experience." Larry Love put it like this: "Repentance is turning from all known sin in order to turn from all sin when it becomes known."

Christians should be the first to admit a wrong attitude or action when God's Spirit reveals it to them. Although it is difficult to humble ourselves, a repentant attitude reveals a vibrant faith, a humble heart, and a secure relationship with Christ. We cannot grow without it. According to Revelation 3, God loves His children so much that He rebukes and chastens them so they will know the full joy of their salvation. Repentance is not only for hardened sinners but also for deeply sensitive saints who want nothing to come between them and their Lord. Repentance is for everyone. —D.J.D.

A broken heart is the handiwork of God. —Bunyan

Wednesday

LUKE 13:1–5

"Repent, and believe in the gospel"
(Mark 1:15).

Ever wondered about people who say they believe in Jesus yet demonstrate no evidence of a change of heart? They show no remorse for wrongdoing, no longing for righteousness. They lack repentance.

Several years ago a prominent underworld figure attended a large evangelistic crusade. Realizing that the cause of evil would be weakened if this man would be converted, those conducting the meeting witnessed to him about Christ. One night they urged him to "open the door" of his heart and let Jesus in. The man supposedly accepted the Lord, but as the months passed his lifestyle remained the same. When confronted with this fact, the gangster said that no one had told him that in saying yes to Jesus he would be turning his back on his former life. He knew of Christian football players, Christian cowboys, Christian politicians—why not a Christian gangster? When they explained the need for repentance, the man wanted nothing more to do with Christianity.

The Greek word for repentance, *metanoia,* means "to change the mind." This involves thinking rightly about sin, self, and God. We recognize that we are condemned sinners before God and unable to save ourselves. We turn from our self-sufficiency to Christ and by faith receive Him as our Savior.

If we are willing to repent, God will empower us. But we need to know that turning to Christ means turning from sin. We can't have one without the other. —D.J.D.

**We do not repent in order to go to Christ;
we go to Christ in order to repent.**

Thursday

JOEL 2:12–17

So rend your heart, and not your garments
(Joel 2:13).

The Baouli people of West Africa describe repentance this way: "It hurts so much I want to quit it." Genuine repentance hurts our pride and wounds our ego. But it's a necessary and healing hurt.

John Calvin said, "Let everyone search himself and he will find that he labors under this evil—that he would rather rend his garment than his heart." Calvin was thinking of the time God brought His people Israel to repentance by sending a vast army of locusts to invade the land. The insects consumed all vegetation and stripped fruit trees and gardens bare. Man and animals languished under the effects of this widespread devastation. The prophet Joel seized the occasion to call Israel to repentance, to "rend your heart, and not your garments." According to the record, they heeded his warning and turned from their sin (Joel 3:18–19).

Sometimes we find ourselves hemmed in by economic or domestic pressures. And sometimes accidents or natural tragedies disrupt our lives. Through these events we recognize our need for God. It's as if He is saying, "Examine your life and conduct. Are you walking with Me, obeying My commands, putting Me first?"

God pleads with us to "rend our heart" when we sin so He can relieve our pain and show Himself as a gracious God, ready to forgive, slow to anger, and full of mercy. —D.J.D.

Repentance is sorrow for the deed, not for being caught.

Friday

LUKE 5:17–32

Do you see a man wise in his own eyes? There is more hope for a fool than for him (Proverbs 26:12).

In 1984, the House of Representatives disciplined two United States congressmen for immoral behavior. The first, a conservative known for his stand against abortion-on-demand and pornography, tearfully confessed his wrongdoing and voted with his colleagues for his own censure. Many newspeople, however, continued to criticize him. They focused on his prior hypocrisy, refusing to commend him for repenting and turning from his immorality. The second politician, a liberal who openly favored abortion and pornography, defiantly maintained he had done nothing wrong and admitted he was a homosexual. Many newspeople who condemned the first man were far less critical of the second. Apparently they were more comfortable with an open, calloused attitude toward immorality than an open and genuine sorrow for sin.

This incident points out our greatest sin—the refusal to acknowledge our transgressions. The Lord Jesus reached down to the most despised people of His day—publicans and harlots—and forgave them when they repented. But He condemned self-righteous people and resisted all who didn't face up to their sin. Refusing to acknowledge sin is a sure ticket to hell!

Insisting we don't need His forgiveness is life's greatest sin. God can forgive us no matter what we do, but we must repent and turn to Jesus. —H.V.L.

Forgiveness flourishes in the soil of confession.

Saturday

ROMANS 6:11–23

He who covers his sins will not prosper, but whoever confesses and forsakes them will have mercy (Proverbs 28:13).

I don't know where it all comes from. Out of the nooks and crannies of the earth comes the strangest assortment of boards, broken ladders, bottles, dirt-bike parts, old tires, baseball bats, buckets, assorted rakes, shovels, and garden hoses—and they all assemble in my garage. The space where we put the car shrinks until anyone who can squeeze it in deserves a world class driver's medal. So every spring and fall, or whenever necessary, I put on my old clothes, gather some barrels, roll up my sleeves, recruit one of my sons, and give the garage a good cleaning. The satisfaction that follows is reward enough for all the effort.

Occasionally our hearts and minds also become cluttered with junk that we need to get rid of. Petty hurts and grudges pile up. Little sins collect in the corners. Broken promises need repair. Resentments occupy more and more of our life-space, leaving little room for thoughts about God and how we can please Him. We neglect prayer and lose the Bible somewhere in the mess. Our heart's garage needs a good cleaning.

When our lives become cluttered with worldliness through spiritual neglect, the Holy Spirit will help us get rid of the junk and clean the dirt. When we acknowledge our sins, confess them to God, and repent, we'll find that a thorough cleaning will give new joy to our Christian life. —D.C.E.

When our Christian life becomes a drag,
worldly weights are probably to blame.

Week 37

SATAN TEMPTS JESUS

Then Jesus, being filled with the Holy Spirit, returned from the Jordan and was led by the Spirit into the wilderness, being tempted for forty days by the devil (Luke 4:1–2).

THEME

TEMPTATION

"I see the devil's hook and yet cannot help nibbling at his bait," bemoaned Moses Adams, the eighteenth-century American humorist.

The biggest fish Satan could hook would be God Himself. In the wilderness temptation, the Spirit led Jesus to Satan; God did not fear the wiles of the master trickster.

To the Jews of the first century, the three temptations had a powerful message. Although God had promised to meet their needs, protect their lives, and give them hope for tomorrow, Israel of old continually worried about groceries, safety, and the future. In resisting Satan's offers of food, protection, and power, Jesus proved that God could provide these three things and more.

We do not easily grasp how God Incarnate could be tempted in all the same ways as we are, but real men have real temptations. We can believe in Christ's sinless perfection, but our minds invariably sanitize His temptations. Though Christ totally resisted sin, He was not tempted with just lily-white dalliances. Whatever our attempts to whitewash Christ's humanity, the perfect God-man, nevertheless, truly knows temptation. Only such a Person could provide a salvation that meets people's deepest needs.

Satan may have a digitized fish-finder and chartreuse lures, but Christ has seen all his devices. He understands and sympathizes with us, and He provides us with food that satisfies and gives us strength to resist Satan's shiny bait.

Sunday

LUKE 4:1–13

**Then Jesus was led up by the Spirit into the wilderness
to be tempted by the devil (Matthew 4:1).**

Before I was old enough to get a driver's license, I had a haunting fear of getting behind the wheel of a car. When I thought about driving with an open stretch of road before me, I was afraid I'd be overwhelmed by an obsession to go as fast as the car would go. I couldn't imagine having the self-control to drive no faster than road conditions and the speed limit would allow. When I turned sixteen, though, I learned that I could control the accelerator instead of being controlled by it. Just because I was *able* to press the pedal to the floor didn't mean I *had* to do so.

Many times I've heard people try to justify sin by claiming that a sudden, unusual, and irresistible temptation had confronted them. And sometimes we reason that a certain questionable action might actually be all right because the opportunity came along at just the right time and provided just what we thought we needed.

One of the lessons we learn from the temptation of Jesus is that God will always provide a way of escape from temptation or He will give us the strength to resist it. He expects us to be discerning and to be conscious of the meaning of temptation. Beyond that, He wants us to know that we can rely on His Spirit and His Word, the way Jesus did, and to resist temptation rather than be ruined by it. —M.R.D.II

Every temptation is an opportunity to get nearer to God.

Monday

MATTHEW 4:1–11

"I will strengthen you; yes, I will help you,
I will uphold you" (Isaiah 41:10).

On the day before my mother died in 1976, my brother and I were called to her bedside. Though too weak for extended conversation, she quoted two verses—Isaiah 41:10 and John 10:29—not simply to console us, but to reinforce her own faith. She held fast to what God had said; and what God said held her fast.

The Word of God has tremendous holding power. When tempted in the wilderness, our Lord overcame the enemy's suggestions by quoting Scripture. He did this to strengthen Himself, not to intimidate Satan. Though sinless, Jesus was truly human, and the temptation was real. Sometimes we allow His deity to overshadow this event and assume that the Savior casually brushed Satan aside with a few Scripture verses. But the Bible leaves no doubt that He was "tempted as we are, yet without sin" (Heb. 4:15). Therefore, the Word held Him steady. Jesus did not quote verses to Satan because they contained some magical power. Rather, He called them to mind to guide and reinforce Himself so that He would remain true to God's will. Because He kept His life under the control of the Word, Satan could not deter Him from doing His Father's will.

Whenever we are tested—whether it's a severe temptation, an overwhelming fear, or the specter of death itself—we can rest with confidence on God's sure and abiding Word. Down through the centuries countless saints have been held by its power, and it is as strong as ever. —D.J.D.

**The strongest weapon in Satan's arsenal is no match
for the sword of the Spirit, the Word of God.**

Tuesday

MARK 14:32–50

"Watch and pray, lest you enter into temptation"
(Mark 14:38).

When we recognize the ugliness of temptations, we will be better able to resist them. Someone wrote, "If only I could see my temptations as I see other people's, they wouldn't be a bit hard to fight. Other people's temptations look so ugly and foolish. But my own temptations come with a rosy light about them so that I don't see how hateful they are until afterward. There are two ways to see temptations in their true colors. One is to pray about them and thus bring them into the clear light of God's presence. The other is to say, 'How would this look if someone else yielded to it?'" To the one being tempted, enticement to sin may be appealing. But if we yield, we start down a path of self-destruction.

In Matthew 4, the first temptation Satan presented to Christ seemed harmless. He tempted Jesus to satisfy His hunger. Then he posed another concerning God's protection. In the third, he openly requested Christ to worship him. But the Savior saw Satan's true intent—to divert Him from going to Calvary and thus prevent Him from paying sin's penalty. Christ met every appeal by quoting the Scriptures. Jesus was saying to Satan, "I am living under the authority of My Father and His Word."

If we know God's Word, which is the sword of the Spirit, and understand how to wield it, we too can be victorious over Satan. To resist temptation, we must be strong in the Lord, filled with His Spirit, and quick to recognize the ugliness of sin. —R.W.D.

If you want to master temptation, let Christ master you.

Wednesday

1 CORINTHIANS 10:1–13

God is faithful, who . . . with the temptation will also make the way of escape (1 Corinthians 10:13).

In 1346, during the Hundred Years' War, the English army of King Edward III met a French battalion at Crecy, France. The King's son, Prince Edward, led one vital division of the British force while Edward III stood nearby with a strong band of soldiers, ready to send relief if needed. Soon after the battle started, the prince thought he was in danger, so he sent for help. But the king didn't come. Young Edward sent another message, pleading for immediate assistance. His father responded by telling the courier, "Go tell my son that I am not so inexperienced a commander as not to know when help is needed, nor so careless a father as not to send it."

This story illustrates the heavenly Father's relationship with believers as we battle temptation and sin. Often we cry out for help, but it seems that God sends no relief. Yet at no time does He withdraw His eye from our precarious position. He never allows us to be tempted beyond what we are able to bear, and when He sees that we are about to be overcome He rushes to our aid or provides a way to escape. So we need not get frantic—our Father is aware of our situation. In 1 Corinthians 1:9 the apostle Paul said, "God is faithful." Commenting on this, Ambrose Serle noted, "He is wise to foresee and provide for all my dangers. He is faithful to perfect and perform all His promises."

No matter how hot the conflict, the Lord is ready to intervene at the right moment. He is always standing by. —P.R.V.

When God sends us, He also goes with us.

Thursday

HEBREWS 2:9–18

For in that He Himself has suffered, being tempted, He is able to aid those who are tempted (Hebrews 2:18).

We had everything set for the first bass fishing expedition of the year. We had exotic new lures that we knew would be irresistible to those big six-pounders lurking beneath the surface of our favorite fishing lake. We would tempt them with Sassy Shads, brightly colored new Hula Poppers, buzz baits, a "killer" red flatfish with a black stripe, and a white double spinner with long bright streamers. And, if all else failed, we had some fresh Canadian crawlers. Out at dawn, we hit all the best spots with our assortment of delectable temptations. But nothing happened. We worked the shore. We cast along the weeds. We tried every lure in the tackle box—even the crawlers. Finally we gave up. Heading back to the cabin, we concluded, "The fish just aren't hungry."

Satan has a whole "tacklebox" of alluring devices he uses to tempt us. Some are gaudy and exotic, easy to spot—yet oh, so tempting. Others whet our appetites in quiet and subtle ways, appearing harmless until the hook is set. Whatever the temptation, we can best resist if we do not let our thoughts dwell on evil but on things that are true, noble, just, pure, and lovely (Phil. 4:8). With mental discipline and the help of the Holy Spirit, we can keep our hearts full of goodness. Then, in frustration, Satan will have to say, "They just aren't hungry."

—D.C.E.

**Every step away from the devil
leads us one step closer to God.**

Friday

No temptation has overtaken you except such as is common to man; but God is faithful (1 Corinthians 10:13).

Concerned about his personal life, Ed went to his pastor for help. After listening to the young man's mild list of supposed sins, the wise preacher felt that he had not been completely honest. "Are you sure that's all?" the preacher asked. "Yes, pastor," Ed said. "Are you positive you haven't been entertaining any impure thoughts lately?" the pastor continued. "Oh, no," Ed replied, "but they've sure been entertaining me."

Temptation may be defined as a desire for sinful pleasure. If it didn't offer pleasure, it would be easy to resist. Perhaps that's why we understand the truth behind the cartoon in which a man says, "I don't mind fleeing temptation—as long as I can leave a forwarding address." And, if we're honest, we admit that sin often takes place first in our mind. For many people, illicit sexual thoughts provide pleasure.

Temptation is not sin. For it to develop into sin, we have to welcome it, dwell on it, and enjoy it. For example, the temptation to get back at someone who has hurt us is wrong only when we begin to think about ways to harm that person and get revenge. Paul said that every thought must be brought "into captivity to the obedience of Christ" (2 Cor. 10:5).

When we allow wrong thoughts into our minds, we must confess them as sin, ask God to help us, and then fill our minds with good and pure thoughts. When we submit to God and resist the devil, we can say no to tempting thoughts. —D.C.E.

Character is shaped by what the mind takes in.

Saturday

**My brethren, count it all joy
when you fall into various trials (James 1:2).**

Temptations and trials are two different experiences. Though they often occur at the same time, there is a fine line between them. In the New Testament a single Greek word covers both situations. James 1:2 tells us to rejoice when we fall into various trials, but in Matthew 26:41 Jesus tells His disciples to pray that they enter not into temptation. The first is an occasion for good, the second a danger to avoid.

In a sermon entitled "Faith Tested and Crowned," Alexander MacLaren distinguished between being tempted and being tested or tried. He said that "the former word conveys the idea of appealing to the worst part of man, with the wish that he may yield and do the wrong. The latter means an appeal to the better part of man, with the desire that he should stand. Temptation says, 'Do this pleasant thing; do not be hindered by the fact that it is wrong.' Trial or proving says, 'Do this right and noble thing; do not be hindered by the fact that it is painful.' The one is a sweet, beguiling melody, breathing soft indulgence and relaxation over the soul; the other is a pealing trumpet-call to high achievements."

Every hardship holds the potential to be a temptation and a trial. By resisting all suggestions we know are wrong and accepting all circumstances as opportunities for growth, we cooperate with the Holy Spirit in His sanctifying work in us. We move toward that desired goal of being "perfect and complete, lacking nothing" (James 1:4). —D.J.D.

**Satan tempts us to bring out the worst in us;
God tests us to bring out the best in us.**

Week 38

SERMON ON THE MOUNT

And seeing the multitudes, He went up on a mountain, and when He was seated His disciples came to Him. Then He opened His mouth and taught them (Matthew 5:1–2).

THEME

HAPPINESS

The pursuit of happiness has always been the American dream, but Ashley Montagu, author of *The American Way of Life,* sees it differently. "The moments of happiness we enjoy take us by surprise. It is not that we seize them, but that they seize us."

Under the thumb of Rome, the Jews were trigger-happy. They wanted the Messiah to seize happiness, to bring back the glory days of David and Solomon. Instead, Jesus spoke in riddles about happiness. He talked about humility, mourning, meekness, righteousness, mercy, purity, peacemaking, and suffering—hardly topics for a national or a personal joyride. They sounded more like sadness than gladness, but Jesus had a different perspective.

Jesus implied that certain qualities, as they become a part of our lives, have their own built-in reward. Yet a person should not become humble to become happy; that is a path to pride rather than to joy. The beatitudes are backhanded blessings; joy surprises people.

James, perhaps remembering some of his half-brother Jesus' words about happiness, proclaimed that trials produce happiness and the endurer will receive a crown of life (1:12). The crown probably pictured a quality of life that enveloped the whole body rather than a wreath to be worn on the head.

Cultivating Christ's life within us has an inherent bonus—a qualitative existence both now and in the future. As Paul put it, godliness has promise in this life and in the one to come (1 Tim. 4:8). Happiness seizes us here, now, and hereafter as His life becomes ours.

Sunday

LUKE 15:11–24

"Blessed are the poor in spirit, for theirs is the kingdom of heaven" (Matthew 5:3).

An artist searching for a man to model as the prodigal son saw a beggar in the street and asked him to come to his studio and pose for him, promising to pay him. At the appointed time the man appeared, neatly shaven and all dressed up. "Who are you?" asked the artist. "I am the beggar," answered the man. "I thought I'd get cleaned up before I got painted." "I can't use you as you are now," said the artist, and dismissed him.

All who come to Jesus for salvation must come just as they are. Simple trust in Christ—with no claim of their own merits—that's what God is looking for. This attitude is also a key to growth in grace and a life of useful service. After we are saved, we may begin to think that we must clean ourselves up in order to prove ourselves worthy. Although we must "work out" our own salvation, pride and conceit blind us to the truth that it is God who works in us "both to will and to do for His good pleasure" (Phil. 2:12–13). Paul put it like this: "He who glories, let him glory in the LORD" (1 Cor. 1:31). Our part is to yield to His working in us.

Continued spiritual progress requires that we honestly recognize our continual spiritual poverty. Although we are saved once and for all, we must maintain that basic sense of need that prompted our initial response to Jesus in order for God's Spirit to remain in control. God can use only those who rely on Him and maintain a prodigal posture throughout all of life. —D.J.D.

To be rich in God is better than to be rich in goods.

Monday

"Blessed are those who mourn,
for they shall be comforted" (Matthew 5:4).

It isn't good to brood about our sins nor to lament constantly over our shortcomings. But neither should we take them too lightly. To disobey the moral law of a holy God is a serious thing. Although as Christians we bask in the warm glow of divine forgiveness, we must never minimize the awful reality of sin.

A young pastor visited Dundee, Scotland, shortly after Robert Murray McCheyne died at age thirty. Many people had come to Christ because of McCheyne's ministry, and the visitor wanted to know the secret of his great influence. The old sexton of McCheyne's church led the preacher into the rectory and showed him some of McCheyne's books lying on a table. Then he motioned to the chair the evangelist had used, and said, "Sit down and put your elbows on the table." The visitor obeyed. "Now put your head in your hands." He complied. "Now let the tears flow; that's what McCheyne did." Next he led him into the church and said, "Put your elbows on the pulpit." The visitor did. "Now put your face in your hands." He obeyed. "Now let the tears flow; that's what McCheyne used to do."

Robert Murray McCheyne cried freely over his sins and over those of his people. By contrast, our emotions are often hardened toward sin. We need to be more sensitive to the convicting voice of God's Spirit and more determined to live a separated life. We may rejoice in God's forgiveness, but we should never be afraid to mourn for our sins.

—D.C.E.

Calvary proves that sin troubles God—does it trouble you?

Tuesday

MATTHEW 5:1–12

**"Blessed are the meek,
for they shall inherit the earth" (Matthew 5:5).**

According to Bill Farmer's newspaper column, J. Upton Dickson was a fun-loving fellow who said he was writing a book entitled *Cower Power*. He also founded a group for submissive people and called it DOORMATS (Dependent Organization Of Really Meek And Timid Souls—if there are no objections). Their motto was: "The meek shall inherit the earth—if that's okay with everybody." Their symbol was the yellow traffic light.

Mr. Dickson sounds like he'd be a lot of fun. What disturbs me about all of this, though, is that many people assume that such humorous ideas represent the true quality of meekness set forth in Matthew 5:5. Many, even in the church, think that to be meek is to be weak. But the opposite is true. What the Bible is talking about is a powerful virtue. The slogan "strong enough to be gentle" comes close to defining it. True meekness is best seen in Christ. He was submissive, never resisting or disputing the will of God. His absolute trust in the Father enabled Him to show compassion, courage, and self-sacrifice even in the most hostile situations.

When we are meek, we will bear insults without lashing out in resentment or retaliation. We'll thank God in every circumstance, while using every circumstance, good or bad, as an occasion to submit to Him. Meekness would be weakness if it meant yielding to sin. But because it stems from goodness and godliness, it is a great strength.

—M.R.D.II

Meekness is strength harnessed for service.

Wednesday

MATTHEW 5:1–12

"Blessed are those who hunger and thirst for righteousness, for they shall be filled" (Matthew 5:6).

If we make holiness our goal, we'll attain happiness; if we make happiness our goal, we'll search a lifetime and never find it. Jesus implies this in the Sermon on the Mount. He said that the way to blessedness is through poverty of spirit, purity of heart, and a longing for righteousness. But He also stated that this path may bring persecution (vv. 10–12).

Some people think they can achieve happiness by getting rid of restrictions. Eliminating rules and regulations, they reason, would remove the frustration of having to decide between right and wrong, thereby avoiding separation in human relationships. One man who follows this philosophy said, "It is more important to me to enjoy my life and to be happy than it is to be right. Being right and suffering is no fun. This has been forcefully and clearly revealed to me in my relationship with my seven-year-old. Time and time again I see that [saying he's wrong] . . . only creates suffering and separation between us."

When we apply this line of reasoning to absolute standards of morality, we are in deep trouble. It denies the reality of sin in our hearts as the source of all our woes and forgets that all lasting joy is rooted in separation—separation *from* evil and *unto* God. —D.J.D.

Nothing but sin can take away the Christian's joy.

Thursday

MATTHEW 5:1–12

"Blessed are the merciful,
for they shall obtain mercy" (Matthew 5:7).

In the Sermon on the Mount, the Lord Jesus teaches us to combine idealism with realism. He shows us how to keep from getting so wrapped up in life as it is that we don't see life as it should be. On the other hand, He teaches us to avoid making the equally destructive mistake of becoming so attached to our ideals that we make impossible demands on those around us.

Columnist Sidney J. Harris wrote about the negative effects of impractical idealism. He described an author who had so much to give in his books, but so little to offer in real life. When Harris first read this writer's works, he thought they were "like a breath of fresh air in a fetid chamber. . . . He was big on Humanity, with a capital H, on family ties and folkways and children and animals and flowers. . . ." But, as Harris laments, it was not an idealism borne out in the author's own life. At home the man was a tyrant to his wife and a terror to his children. He had an unrealistic ideal of what others should be, and he could not tolerate their imperfections.

Christ instructs us to maintain a balance. His own example shows us how to respond in truth and love to those who are imperfect. He teaches us to be right but never to exclude mercy. If we follow Christ's example, we will hold to the highest ideals, but we'll always be in touch with the real world because our hearts are filled with love.

—M.R.D.II

A righteous heart makes room for mercy.

Friday

1 PETER 1:13–22

**"Blessed are the pure in heart,
for they shall see God" (Matthew 5:8).**

A boy who had just listened to a long sermon walked out of church with a big frown on his face. His father had pulled his ear during the service to keep him from fidgeting. "What's the matter, Johnny?" asked one of the deacons. "You look so sad." The frustrated young fellow responded quickly, "I am. It's hard to be happy and holy at the same time."

This boy was probably expressing the feelings of many young Christians, and perhaps many adults as well. They have the idea that if they are to be good, they can't possibly be happy. The nineteenth-century South African minister Andrew Murray corrected that misconception. He said, "Holiness is essential to true happiness; happiness is essential to true holiness. If you would have joy, the fullness of joy, an abiding joy which nothing can take away, be holy as God is holy. Holiness is blessedness. . . . If we would live lives of joy, assuring God and man and ourselves that our Lord is everything, is more than all to us, oh, let us be holy! . . . If you would be a holy Christian, you must be a happy Christian. Jesus was anointed by God with 'the oil of gladness,' that He might give us the 'oil of joy.' In all our efforts after holiness, the wheels will move heavily if there be not the oil of joy."

The joy of Christ should ring through our souls in our most holy moments. We're on the road to spiritual maturity when we've learned that happiness and holiness are not enemies, but friends. —D.C.E.

The holiest man is the happiest man.

Saturday

PSALM 37:1–11

"Blessed are the peacemakers,
for they shall be called sons of God" (Matthew 5:9).

As citizens of the heavenly kingdom ruled by the Prince of Peace, believers should do everything within their power to maintain a life of peace—especially in the family. This is not always easy, however. The fragile thread of trust and serenity within the home breaks easily, resulting in strife and conflict. To prevent this from happening, we must respect confidences, build loving relationships, and seek the good of others. We must be peacemakers.

In *The Heavenly Octave,* his classic work on the Beatitudes, F. W. Boreham wrote, "The ideal peacemaker is the man who prevents the peace from being broken. To prevent a battle is the best way of winning a battle. I once said to a Jewish rabbi, 'I have heard that at a Jewish wedding a glass is broken as part of the symbolism of the ceremony. Is that a fact?' 'Of course it is,' he replied. 'We hold aloft a glass, let it fall and be shattered to atoms, and then, pointing to its fragments, we exhort the young people to guard jealously the sacred relationship into which they have entered, since once it is fractured, it can never be restored.'"

Christ said, "Blessed are the peacemakers." This applies to us if we love peace and quickly try to resolve problems before permanent damage is done. We must also examine our own behavior honestly to make certain that we are not the cause of hostility. A peacemaker knows how to achieve peace through prevention. —D.C.E.

Never invite trouble; it always accepts.

Week 39

DISCIPLES LEARN TO PRAY

"And I say to you, ask, and it will be given to you; seek, and you will find; knock, and it will be opened to you" (Luke 11:9).

THEME

ACCESS TO GOD

In January, 1978, three of Roger and Patsy Hutson's children fell through the ice of a pond and drowned. Roger, a truck driver, recalled the agony: "I laid my head on the steering wheel and sobbed aloud because of the loneliness that filled my whole being . . . and because I had no one who cared. Then, in the emptiness, I became aware of the presence of someone else, someone who wanted to listen to me. . . . Jesus was in my cab, listening to me."

Jesus taught His disciples that God will respond to the needs of His children. The disciples could talk to God directly; and when they knocked, He would open the door. God was not ill with sleeping sickness; He cared about the people and the world He had created.

The prayers of Abraham, Moses, David, Hezekiah, and others fill the Old Testament. God has always been there to listen. But the New Testament adds a new dimension to prayer. It emphasizes our relationship with all three members of the Godhead.

God does not have an answering machine, but Jesus screens all His calls; no one talks to the Father without going through the Son first. The Holy Spirit, like a trusted friend, whispers in our ears just the right words. As we grow in our relationship with Jesus Christ, we learn God's direct number and dial with confidence. As we rely on the Holy Spirit and make His words ours, we stop stuttering and boldly tell God the intimate details of our lives.

Sunday

LUKE 11:1–13

"When you pray, say: 'Our Father . . .'"
(Luke 11:2).

Dr. Robert A. Cook, president of The King's College, told an audience at Moody Bible Institute that he had talked with Vice President George Bush the previous day. Two hours after that, he spoke briefly with President Ronald Reagan. Then, smiling broadly, Cook told us, "But that's nothing. Today I talked with God."

Prayer takes on new power and fervency when we become conscious of God's greatness and glory. When saints of past ages caught a glimpse of the Almighty, they were awestruck. Job, who had complained bitterly about his misfortune and had made some self-righteous statements, finally met the Lord and cried out, "I have heard of You by the hearing of the ear, but now my eye sees You. Therefore I abhor myself, and repent in dust and ashes" (Job 42:5–6). Isaiah saw a vision of God and exclaimed, "Woe is me, for I am undone!" (Isa. 6:5). Ezekiel observed the glory of the Lord and declared, "So when I saw it, I fell on my face" (Ezek. 1:28). The apostle John, after seeing a vision of the glorified Son of God, said, "I fell at His feet as dead" (Rev. 1:17).

To all of these men, the vision of God's greatness and glory brought an overwhelming sense of their weakness and depravity. Yet God invites us to talk to Him, and He wants us to address Him as "Our Father." —H.V.L.

Our highest privilege is to talk to God.

Monday

LUKE 5:12–16

"And when you have shut your door, pray to your Father" (Matthew 6:6).

In a letter to friends, hymnwriter Wendell P. Loveless told about a visitor to the United States who wanted to make a telephone call. He entered a phone booth, but found it to be different from those in his own country. It was beginning to get dark, so he had difficulty finding the number in the directory. He noticed a light on the ceiling, but he didn't know how to turn it on. As he tried again to find the number in the fading twilight, a passerby noted his plight and said, "If you want to turn the light on, you have to shut the door." To the visitor's amazement and satisfaction, when he closed the door, the booth was filled with light. He soon located the number and completed the call.

When we draw aside in a quiet place to pray, we must block out our busy world and open our hearts to the Father. He then will illuminate our darkened world of disappointments and trials. We will enter into communion with God, sense His presence, and be assured of His provision for us. Our Lord often went to be alone with the heavenly Father. Sometimes it was after a busy day of preaching and healing, as in Luke 5. At other times, it was before making a major decision (Luke 6:12).

We too can have the confidence that "if we ask anything according to His will, He hears us" (1 John 5:14). But we must remember that to "turn on the light," we must first "shut the door" by getting alone with God. —R.W.D.

One of the great secrets of prayer is prayer in secret.

Tuesday

EPHESIANS 3:13–21

**[He] is able to do exceedingly abundantly
above all that we ask or think (Ephesians 3:20).**

At the time of his death in 1956, Jim Elliot was trying to reach the Auca Indians of South America for Christ. Just three years earlier, after watching an Indian die in a jungle hut, he had affirmed his willingness to serve God and die if necessary among these people. Then he added this petition: "Lord, let me live until I have declared Thy works to this generation." Jim Elliot didn't expect God to answer his prayer by letting him be speared to death before he was thirty years old. But neither did he have any idea that within three years his name would be known all over the world and that his journals would challenge many to give themselves to the Lord's service. He's been in heaven for more than thirty years, but he is still "speaking" to thousands of people.

God loves us deeply and listens to our prayers, but He doesn't always give us exactly what we ask. Since He "is able to do exceedingly abundantly above all that we ask or think," we can be sure that if He doesn't fulfill all our requests it's because He wants to give us something better.

When we don't receive everything we ask for, we need not be discouraged. God loves us and delights in giving us what we desire. But He also knows the end from the beginning, and sometimes He says no in order to give us something better. When we reach heaven, we will find that He did indeed answer our petitions "exceedingly abundantly above" all our fondest hopes and dreams. —H.V.L.

God always gives us what we ask for—or something better.

Wednesday

PHILIPPIANS 4:1–7

**By prayer and supplication, with thanksgiving,
let your requests be made known to God (Philippians 4:6).**

A friend of mine took his small son with him one day to run some errands. When lunchtime arrived, the two of them went to a familiar diner for a sandwich. The father sat down on one of the stools at the counter and lifted the boy up to the seat beside him. They ordered lunch, and when the waiter brought the food the father said, "Son, we'll just have a silent prayer." Dad got through praying first and waited for his son to finish his prayer, but he just sat with his head bowed for an unusually long time. When he finally looked up, his father asked him, "What in the world were you praying about all that time?" "How do I know?" the child replied. "It was a silent prayer."

A lot of our praying is like that, whether silent or aloud. We don't say anything to the Lord. We call words to mind, but they are repetitious or insincere. What the Lord needs to hear from us is earnest, heartfelt prayer—prompted by the Holy Spirit and offered in the name of the Lord Jesus. The result, according to Paul, is "the peace of God, which surpasses all understanding," that "will guard [our] hearts and minds through Christ Jesus" (Phil. 4:7).

We need to take prayer seriously. Closing our eyes, bowing our heads, and repeating nice-sounding words is insufficient. Our requests must be in line with God's Word, and they must come from sincere hearts. —P.R.V.

True prayer does not require eloquence but earnestness.

Thursday

**"I have prayed for you, that
your faith should not fail" (Luke 22:32).**

While very ill, John Knox, the founder of the Presbyterian Church in Scotland, called to his wife and said, "Read me that Scripture where I first cast my anchor." After he listened to the beautiful prayer of Jesus recorded in John 17, he seemed to forget his weakness. He began to pray, interceding earnestly for his fellowmen. He prayed for the ungodly who had thus far rejected the gospel. He pleaded in behalf of people who had been recently converted. And he requested protection for the Lord's servants facing persecution. As Knox prayed, his spirit went Home to be with the Lord. The man of whom Queen Mary had said, "I fear his prayers more than I do the armies of my enemies," ministered through prayer until the moment of his death.

Prayer is the working force of the Christian's life. Although we normally think of it as an element of worship, it is also vital in our service for God. By word and through example the Lord Jesus taught us that prayer is just as much a ministry as preaching, teaching, witnessing, and doing kind deeds in His name. The Savior did just as much on Peter's behalf by praying for him as He did by exhorting him. We may be assured that we are never useless as long as we can pray.

Prayer is our chief duty. If we believe this, we'll spend more time praying. When we are in circumstances that make it impossible for us to do much of anything else, we can still pray. We'll be exercising the greatest of all ministries. —H.V.L.

God's soldiers fight best on their knees.

Friday

1 JOHN 3:19–24

And whatever we ask we receive from Him, because we . . .
do those things that are pleasing in His sight (1 John 3:22).

While Josh McDowell was attending seminary in California, his father
went Home to be with the Lord. His mother had died years earlier, but
Josh was unsure of her salvation. He became depressed, thinking that
she might be lost. Then he became obsessed. Though it seemed like an
impossible request, he prayed, "Lord, somehow give me the answer so
I can get back to normal. I've just got to know."

Two days later, Josh drove out to the ocean. He walked to the end of
a pier to be alone. An old woman sitting in a lawn chair, fishing,
started talking to him. "Where's your home originally?" she asked.
"Michigan—Union City," Josh replied. "Nobody's heard of it. I tell
people it's a suburb of—" "Battle Creek," interrupted the woman. "I
had a cousin from there. Did you know the McDowell family?" Stunned,
Josh responded, "Yes, I'm Josh McDowell!" "I can't believe it," said the
woman. "I'm a cousin to your mother." "Do you remember anything
at all about my mother's spiritual life?" asked Josh. "Why sure. Your
mom and I were just girls—teenagers—when a tent revival came to
town. It was the fourth night—we both went forward to accept Christ."
"Praise God!" shouted Josh, startling the surrounding fishermen.

If we are obedient to God, He delights to give us what we ask when
it is in His will. We should never underestimate God's desire to
respond to our prayers. A surprise answer may be just around the
corner. —D.J.D.

When we get definite with God, He'll get definite with us.

Saturday

1 JOHN 3:7–18

My little children, let us not love in word
or in tongue, but in deed and in truth (1 John 3:18).

A father, leading his family in their devotional time, prayed about the needs of the poor widow across the street. He listed the things she needed, and he proceeded to tell the Lord just how to send them. Tears of sympathy rolled down his wife's cheeks. But one member of the family—the couple's son—wasn't praying. He was thinking. When the father said "Amen," the son walked over to him with his hand held out. "Dad," he said, "give me your wallet and I'll go over and answer your prayer myself."

That youngster knew that prayer and practice go together. Our conversation with God must be followed by action. When we pray for the Lord to "send out laborers into His harvest," we must make ourselves available. When we pray for the salvation of friends, we must be willing witnesses. When we pray, "Even so, come, Lord Jesus," this purifying hope should make us ethical in our business, good stewards with our budgets, and Christ-honoring in our lifestyle.

John explained this concept in his first epistle. He said we shouldn't restrict our love to words; we must demonstrate it with our deeds. And later he said that "whatever we ask we receive from Him because we . . . do those things that are pleasing in His sight" (3:22). The genuineness of our prayers will be evident in our willingness to practice what we pray. —P.R.V.

Our good deeds are often the best answers to our prayers.

Week 40

JESUS CALMS THE STORM

Then He arose and rebuked the wind, and said to the sea, "Peace, be still!" And the wind ceased and there was a great calm (Mark 4:39).

THEME

PEACE

Breton fishermen on the coast of France have a brief prayer that humbly acknowledges God's control of nature and life: "God, your sea is so great and my boat is so small." In recognizing that the sea belongs to God, the fishermen see God as the only source of safety for their boats.

In calming the Sea of Galilee, Jesus taught the disciples not only about His power over nature but also about external and internal peace. The lesson about external peace was the easier of the two; He stopped the storm. Dealing with the storm inside the disciples was more difficult; fear had replaced the disciples' faith.

Trust and tranquility are twins in the spiritual life. Isaiah said that perfect peace comes from complete trust (26:3). Much of the Old Testament is about peace—how to lose it and how to find it. To the nation of Israel, surrounded by hostile neighbors, Isaiah promised a Prince of Peace (9:6).

The New Testament explains why peace is associated with this Prince; it is part of His character (Col. 3:15). In contrast, we humans, often scared of our shadows, churn with anxiety.

If we criticize Jesus for taking a nap in the stern of a boat on rough Galilee, we are like the disciples and miss the point. Of course it is easy for Him to sleep through a storm; He is all-powerful. But if that is so, we should not play captain of the ship.

Sunday

MATTHEW 8:23–27

"Why are you fearful, O you of little faith?"
(Matthew 8:26).

No Christian is immune from the storms of life. The transforming power of God's grace does not come with a guarantee that we will be free from difficulty and trial. Yet we are assured of God's abiding presence and mighty power to calm our fears and hold us secure in times of trouble.

One night an unexpected storm swept over a passenger ship sailing from England to New York, tossing the ship violently and awakening everyone on board, including the captain's eight-year-old daughter. "What's the matter?" the frightened child cried. After her mother explained about the storm, she asked, "Is Father on deck?" Assured that he was, the little girl snuggled back into her bed and in a few moments was sound asleep. Although the winds still blew and the waves still rolled, she had peace because her father was at the helm.

Although the squalls of life strike us, we are assured of our Father's presence. He controls our lives and upholds us with His right hand. We may not dodge the storm, and the winds may still blow, but the Master of wind and wave is on board. And if we trust Him, He will either calm the waves or quiet our hearts. —P.R.V.

**We need not nervously pace the deck
if the Captain of our salvation is at the helm.**

Monday

2 CORINTHIANS 4:7–18

"I have been crucified with Christ; it is no longer I who live, but Christ lives in me" (Galatians 2:20).

The frigid waters around Greenland contain countless icebergs, some little and some gigantic. Sometimes the small ice floes move in one direction while their massive counterparts flow in another. The explanation is simple. Surface winds drive the little ones, whereas deep ocean currents carry the huge masses.

When we face trials and tragedies, our lives are subject to two forces—surface winds and ocean currents. The winds represent everything changeable, unpredictable, and distressing. But operating simultaneously with these gusts and gales is another force that's even more powerful. It is the sure movement of God's wise and sovereign purposes, the deep flow of His unchanging love. The secret of victory is to be certain that we are in touch with that unseen current. Asaph, buffeted by thoughts of the prosperity of the wicked, went into the sanctuary to be alone with God. Only then did he gain the divine perspective (Psalm 73:17). Job faced his calamities by affirming, "Though He slay me, yet will I trust Him" (Job 13:15). And the apostle Paul, realizing that he had been "crucified with Christ," was convinced that the Lord Jesus was living in him. He could therefore say, "We are hard pressed on every side, yet not crushed" (2 Cor. 4:8).

Although the surface winds of trial become severe, we need not be alarmed. If we trust the Lord, the deep currents of His love and wisdom will carry us peacefully along. —D.J.D.

Better the storm with Christ than smooth waters without Him.

Tuesday

PSALM 107:21–30

**Then they cry out to the LORD . . . , and
He brings them out of their distresses (Psalm 107:28).**

Through binoculars, I watched the twelve-meter yachts Liberty and Australia II compete off the coast of Rhode Island for the prestigious America's Cup championship. Although basically the same size, there was a marked difference between the two boats. The heavier Liberty sailed best under winds of fifteen to twenty knots, but the Australia II, with her innovative superkeel, performed better in winds between seven and twelve knots. Yet, no matter what race conditions the crews faced, they took full advantage of the available wind and competed with great skill.

Christians are a lot like those two boats. Some require the strong winds of adversity to develop their character; others make the best progress when the sailing is not too rough. In either case, we need to learn to adapt ourselves to God's conditions. The heavenly Father knows whether our "vessel and keel" are made for heavy winds or light. And He is in control. The psalmist said, "He commands and raises the stormy wind" (Psalm 107:25), and "He calms the storm" (v. 29). This applies to His control over our trials as well as the physical elements.

Unlike the contestants in the America's Cup match, Christians don't have meteorologists to forecast life's wind speed and direction. But we have peace in God's assurance that He will guide us, in calm or stormy weather, safely to our harbor (v. 30). —P.R.V.

We cannot direct the wind, but we can adjust our sails.

Wednesday

HEBREWS 6:9–20

**This hope we have as an anchor of the soul
(Hebrews 6:19).**

A newsboy, thinly clad and drenched by the soaking rain, stood shivering in a doorway one cold day in November. To get a little warmth, he would hold one bare foot against his leg for a moment and then the other. Every few minutes he would cry out, "Morning paper! Morning paper!" A man who was well protected by his coat and umbrella stopped to buy the early edition. Noting the boy's discomfort, he said, "This kind of weather is pretty hard on you, isn't it?" Looking up with a smile, the youngster replied, "I don't mind too much, Mister. The sun will shine again."

Chilling winds of adversity and gray skies of a sinful environment easily discourage us. But we can count on better days because we know God is working in our lives. This hope is called an "anchor of the soul," and the Bible says that it abides (1 Cor. 13:13) and does not disappoint (Rom. 5:5). It promises righteousness (Gal. 5:5), eternal life (Titus 1:2), and the return of Jesus (Titus 2:13). It is a "living hope," founded on the resurrection of Jesus from the dead (1 Pet. 1:3).

When circumstances get out of control and pressures threaten to overwhelm us, we know that Jesus died for us, is working in us, and will never leave us. We can hold fast to God's promises and patiently endure. The "anchor of hope" will hold us firm. —D.J.D.

It is always darkest just before dawn.

Thursday

ACTS 27:9–25

"Behold, God is my salvation,
I will trust and not be afraid" (Isaiah 12:2).

An old seaman said, "In fierce storms we can do but one thing. There is only one way [to survive]; we must put the ship in a certain position and keep her there." Commenting on this idea, Richard Fuller wrote, "This, Christian, is what you must do. Sometimes, like Paul, you can see neither sun nor stars, and no small tempest lies on you. Reason cannot help you. Past experiences give you no light. Only a single course is left. You must put your soul in one position and keep it there. You must stay upon the Lord; and, come what may— winds, waves, cross seas, thunder, lightning, frowning rocks, roaring breakers—no matter what, you must lash yourself to the helm and hold fast your confidence in God's faithfulness and His everlasting love in Christ Jesus."

In the storms of life, we must place our trust in the Lord and cling firmly to the sure promises of His Word. Our confidence in God should be so steadfast that no matter how severe the trial, with Job we can resolutely affirm, "Though He slay me, yet will I trust Him" (Job 13:15). And to those who trust Him, He gives His "perfect peace" (Isa. 26:3).

With the psalmist we can say, "Be merciful to me, O God, be merciful to me! For my soul trusts in You; and in the shadow of Your wings I will make my refuge, until these calamities have passed by" (Psalm 57:1). —R.W.D.

**We realize the strength of the Anchor
when we feel the stress of the storm.**

Friday

As for God, His way is perfect;
the word of the LORD is proven (Psalm 18:30).

The search for genuine happiness goes on and on. New books, promising an end to heartache and strife, continually put forth new philosophies, fresh ideas, and startling discoveries. They burst on the popular scene like gigantic fireworks, burn brightly for a while, capture a popular following, and then fade away, leaving only a few diehards behind.

In his *Journal,* Henry D. Thoreau, the nineteenth-century American writer, said, "This is man: a writer of books, a putter-down of words, a painter of pictures, a maker of ten thousand philosophies. He grows passionate over ideas, he hurls scorn and mockery at another's work, he finds the one way, the true way, for himself, and calls all the others false—yet in the billion books upon the shelves there is not one that can tell him how to draw a single fleeting breath in peace and comfort. He makes histories of the universe, he directs the destiny of nations, but he does not know his own history, and he cannot direct his own destiny with dignity or wisdom for ten consecutive minutes."

Thoreau was right in saying that our best-written books and most carefully constructed philosophies fail to bring peace. We would face certain despair if all we had was our own wisdom. But one book is different—God's Word. Out of "the billion books upon the shelves," only the Bible shows the way to peace, freedom, and happiness. It points us to Jesus Christ, and He alone reveals the true way. —D.C.E.

**There is a vast difference between
the books men make and the Book that makes men.**

Saturday

JOHN 14:27–15:7

**"Peace I leave with you, My peace I give to you. . . .
Let not your heart be troubled" (John 14:27).**

When Australian pastor H. B. Macartney visited Hudson Taylor in China, he was amazed at the missionary's serenity in spite of his many burdens and busy schedule. Macartney finally mustered up the courage to say, "You are occupied with millions, I with tens. Your letters are pressingly important, mine of comparatively little value. Yet I am worried and distressed while you are always calm. Tell me, what makes the difference?" Taylor replied, "I could not possibly get through the work I have to do without the peace of God which passes all understanding keeping my heart and mind." Macartney later wrote, "He was in God all the time, and God was in him. It was the true abiding spoken of in John 15."

When life becomes more like Macartney's than Taylor's, when we become tense, troubled, anxious, and fearful, and when we desire the peace Jesus promised, we must learn to abide in Christ as Hudson Taylor did. Abiding in Christ means to be in touch with Him continually so that the composure He experienced while on earth rules our lives. We need not agonize or plead or try to work up a certain feeling. The path to abiding in Him is that of confessing and rejecting all known sin, surrendering completely, and looking trustfully to the Lord Jesus for strength. It's continual dependence on Him.

We can enjoy the serenity of a peace-filled life if we will learn to abide in Christ. —H.V.L.

Peace floods the soul when Christ rules the heart.

Week 41

A SAMARITAN HELPS

"So which of these three do you think was neighbor to him who fell among the thieves?" And he said, "He who showed mercy on him" (Luke 10:36–37).

THEME

MERCY

As Wordsworth put it, "The best portion of a good man's life is his little, nameless, unremembered acts of kindness and of love."

To a wily, Jewish lawyer Jesus unfolded a three-act play about a good man. In a surprise ending, the story revealed an unexpected white knight—not a priest or Levite but a hated Samaritan. Knowing that Jesus had trapped him, the legal expert admitted that the expected villain had become a hero because he showed mercy, not because he followed the letter of the law.

The priest and the Levite who passed by the injured man were not really the muscle men of God's Word; they were spiritual weaklings. They had somehow missed all the Old Testament verses about God's great mercy; they had skipped Micah's claim that good people love mercy (6:8).

Like the two religious men of Jesus' parable, we sometimes forget that pure religion is looking after those who can never repay us, such as orphans and widows (James 1:27). Our obtuseness comes from not appreciating the great mercy God showed in loving us.

Paul argued that those who understand God's mercy overcome the evil of this world with good (Romans 12:1–21). Our nameless acts of compassion do not go unremembered by Him.

Sunday

Luke 10:25–37

"Execute true justice, show mercy and
compassion everyone to his brother" (Zechariah 7:9).

The Good Samaritan in Jesus' parable set a worthy example. He stopped to help a Jewish man, even though he knew that Jews despised Samaritans and that most of his fellow Samaritans hated Jews. He acted sacrificially—his deed cost him time and money. And he took a risk by stopping on that Jericho road—he too could have been attacked by a band of robbers.

A friend recently came upon a dangerous situation along the freeway. He saw a truck swerve to miss a reckless driver and then crash into a guardrail. As he approached the scene, he noticed gas leaking from the truck's fuel tank. Fearing an explosion, he screeched to a stop, jumped out of his vehicle, and pulled the dazed driver out of his cab. He was a modern-day Good Samaritan. He too took a risk to help a "neighbor."

If we take seriously Jesus' teaching in Luke 10:25–37, we will sacrifice our time and money to help all kinds of people. We may not have the opportunity to do something dramatic, as my friend did, but we can offer kindness to a discouraged divorcee, a person dying with AIDS, or a misunderstood teenager. Showing mercy to others is a way to express our gratitude to God for His salvation. When we reach out to others, we show our desire to obey Jesus' command to love God above all and our neighbors as ourselves. Getting involved, even when it means taking a risk, is a good risk. —H.V.L.

**How much we are willing to sacrifice
is the measure of our love.**

Monday

"Your Father who sees in secret
will Himself reward you openly" (Matthew 6:4).

Have you ever gone out of your way to do something for someone and had it go unnoticed? Almost killed you, didn't it? Perhaps I'd better not speak for you, but I've had the problem. At times I've wondered if doing good to others is worth the effort, especially when I don't receive a thank you in return. And yet, serving without looking for reward is what walking with God is all about. As Christians, we should not display a "cash and carry" attitude that expects immediate appreciation for the good we do. God wants us to remember that someday He Himself will richly reward us.

A newspaper article reminded me of the kind of "delayed returns" we should be living for. A car dealer went out of his way to give a foreign student an honest deal on a new automobile. Fifteen years later, the young man became the sole purchasing agent for the Iranian Contractors Association. He showed his gratitude to the car dealer by placing a multimillion-dollar order with that dealer for 750 heavy dump trucks and 350 pickups. "It's unbelievable!" exclaimed the businessman. The good he had done was rewarded years later beyond his wildest imagination.

Just as that salesman's reward came later, so too God will commend us in Heaven. If we do good to others for the immediate thanks we receive, we already have our reward. But if we do it for God, the future return will be as sure and generous as He is. —M.R.D.II

**There is no reward from God to those who seek it from men.
—Spurgeon**

Tuesday

PROVERBS 11:17–25

The merciful man does good for his own soul
(Proverbs 11:17).

R. Lee Sharpe once went with his father to a blacksmith shop to get a rake fixed. When the job was finished, his father asked what the charge would be. The smithy replied, "Oh, there is no charge. I'm happy to do it for you!" But Sharpe's father did not feel right about accepting charity, so he persisted in trying to give at least a token payment. Over and over the blacksmith refused to accept any money until his patience was about to run out. Finally he exclaimed to his friend, "Ed, can't you let a man do something now and then just to stretch his soul?" Commenting on that boyhood experience, Sharpe later wrote, "I'll never forget that great man's reply. That short but big sermon from the lips of a humble, lovable blacksmith has caused me to find, again and again, the great joy and quiet happiness that comes from a little stretching of the soul."

Proverbs 11 speaks about enlarging one's soul as it relates to mercy. W. F. Adeney, writing in *The Pulpit Commentary,* said, "The merciful man is blessed in the very exercise of mercy. . . . By a singular law of nature the exercise of mercy begins in the pain of self-sacrifice, but it soon bears fruit in inward peace and gladness. . . . [Showing mercy] is elevating and ennobling."

Although Proverbs 11:17 refers to the "merciful man," all who are loving and generous experience the benefits he enjoys. Doing good carries its own blessed reward. It's a wonderful way of stretching our souls. —R.W.D.

Those who are good to others are good to themselves.

Wednesday

1 THESSALONIANS 1

**You became examples to all in Macedonia
and Achaia who believe (1 Thessalonians 1:7).**

The best "preaching" is often expressed in actions rather than in words. When we do right without saying anything, we can have far greater impact for good than when we tell others what they should do without doing it ourselves. Indeed, we might do better to skip the "preaching" altogether if there is no "practicing."

Many parents overlook this as they instruct their children. They talk about God, explain salvation through Jesus, and expect good works—but it all ends there because their own example fails to match the expectations they have for their children. In other Christian homes, however, mothers and fathers make sure their walk supports their talk. Their exemplary living provides clear and consistent guidelines. Wise parents do not neglect verbal instruction, but they balance it with a worthy example.

We usually think of preachers as those who speak from the pulpit, but the truth is that we all are "preaching" every day. Our conduct at home, the way we handle business matters, our response to difficulties, our reaction to temptation—everything people observe about us is "preaching." Someone said, "What you do speaks so loudly that I can't hear what you say."

The actions of the Good Samaritan spoke so loudly that people still hear them today. Without demanding or expecting anything for himself, He showed mercy to an injured man. As he did, we must make sure that all of our actions are in harmony with God's revealed will. Whether we realize it or not, our walking does our talking. —R.W.D.

Every Christian should be a walking sermon.

Thursday

HEBREWS 10:19–25

**And let us consider one another in order
to stir up love and good works (Hebrews 10:24).**

As we rounded a curve, the beams from my headlights suddenly shone on a woman desperately waving her arms. I did not want to stop. It was late and very cold. My wife and I were exhausted from ministering all day in a small church where I was student pastor, our small son was asleep on the back seat, and I had to be in class at 8:30 the next morning. "Somebody else will come along," I said to my wife, rationalizing to myself that the woman might be trying to lure us into a trap. But my conscience made me stop. And it's a good thing we did. In the woman's car we found four unconscious children, overcome by fumes from a faulty muffler. Quickly we loaded them into our car and headed for a nearby hospital, where they soon recovered after prompt treatment.

I don't advocate stopping along the highway for just anyone. Yet so many pressing needs go unmet. For instance, an elderly couple, no longer able to drive, haven't been to church for several months because no one has offered to take them. And a widow with multiple sclerosis wishes that somebody would take her grocery shopping and help her get to church on Sunday. "Why isn't somebody meeting these needs?" I wondered. Then I remembered my own initial response that night along the highway: Somebody else will come along.

Hebrews 10:24 holds the solution to this problem. As Christians, we can stir up fellow believers to love and good deeds by setting a good example. We can be that "somebody else." —H.V.L.

**When it comes to doing things for others,
some people stop at nothing.**

Friday

LUKE 14:7–14

"Invite the poor . . . and you will be blessed,
because they cannot repay you" (Luke 14:13–14).

An essential element in Christian love is unselfishness. When we give no thought to personal reward, when we do good things for people simply because we want to help them and honor our Lord—that's when we demonstrate Christlike love.

Christian philanthropist Fred Smith tells how his daughter and her husband befriended an ex-convict and the woman with whom he was living. Rick gave the man a job. Brenda spent time with the woman, bought things for her, and witnessed to her about Christ. Together they convinced the couple that getting married was the right thing to do. They even asked a minister to perform the ceremony and offered to open their home for the occasion. But a few days later, Rick found a note from the man saying that they were leaving town to get away from a hired assassin. Later, Mr. Smith asked his daughter how she felt about spending so much time, energy, and money on these people, only to have the relationship end so suddenly. Tears welled up in her eyes. "No matter where they are or how long they live," she said, "they'll always know that somebody cared." Brenda and Rick had loved unselfishly, and for them that was reward enough.

We can easily fall into the trap of giving just to receive something in return, but that kind of caring does not honor God. Yet showing Christian love has an encouraging paradox. When we do good deeds with a selfless motive, we lay up heavenly rewards. —H.V.L.

A selfish heart loves for what it can get;
a Christian heart loves for what it can give.

Saturday

EXODUS 18:13–27

"Both you and these people who are with you will surely wear yourselves out" (Exodus 18:18).

Over the years, social service jobs have drawn concerned young people into careers of helping others. In time, many of them become what some psychologists call "burned-out Samaritans." After listening to so many people's problems and trying to help, they get to the place where they can't take any more. This happens to doctors, ministers, social workers, psychiatrists, and policemen. To save themselves emotionally, they must either quit, stop caring, or readjust.

As Christians, we too are subject to burn-out because helping others is part of our calling. We may feel overwhelmed by the complexity, intensity, and sheer volume of human need. We discover that we can't keep burying ourselves in all the pain without paying the price. We too have to quit, stop caring, or readjust. If we stop trying to help others, we break our fellowship with Christ. If we become unfeeling, we fall far short of His example. But we can readjust by making changes that will ease our burden. Like Moses who heeded the good counsel of his father-in-law Jethro and began delegating responsibility, we must recognize our human limitations and learn to act wisely.

Some believers assume that the more godly we are, the more we will keep pushing until we just "wear out for the Lord." And some devout Christians do just that. But according to the Bible, it's wiser to adjust our service. Then we won't become burned-out Samaritans.

—M.R.D.II

A willing heart must always be kept under the control of a wise head.

Week 42

JESUS FEEDS MULTITUDES

And Jesus took the [five] loaves, and when He had given thanks He distributed them to the disciples, and the disciples to those sitting down; and likewise of the [two small] fish, as much as they wanted (John 6:11).

THEME

STEWARDSHIP

"A small circle of usefulness is not to be despised," observed Hudson Taylor, the pioneer missionary to China.

When Jesus depicted usefulness, He often startled His listeners. He used a boy's picnic pak to make more than five thousand fish sandwiches for a supper on the grass. We know nothing about the boy except that he shared what he had.

In contrast, the disciples worried about how much it would cost for this unplanned shindig—eight months of salary. The crowd was not exactly a grateful group; Jesus was nothing more to them than a fish-in-every-pot politician. The disciples and crowd both missed the point; perhaps the boy understood. A barley loaf in Jesus' hand became life-giving bread because it pointed to the Bread of Life; only He could take the insignificant and make it important.

In the Old Testament, God did not give Israel water from the rock to promote the use of mineral water; He took common water and gave it uncommon symbolism. Every drop should have reminded Israel of the everlasting Water of Life.

To paraphrase Paul's words, we are nothing but old jelly jars; yet He takes what we have and who we are and reveals Himself through us (2 Cor. 4:7–12). When we are faithful in giving Him what we have, He increases our circle of usefulness. He takes all things great and small and makes them wise and wonderful.

Sunday

JOHN 6:1–14

**"There is a lad here who has five barley loaves
and two small fish" (John 6:9).**

About halfway through a rehearsal conducted by Sir Michael Costa, with trumpets blaring, drums rolling, and violins singing their rich melody, the piccolo player muttered to himself, "What good am I doing? I might just as well not be playing. Nobody can hear me anyway." So he kept the instrument to his mouth, but he made no sound. Within moments, the conductor cried, "Stop! Stop! Where's the piccolo?" The most important person of all missed the piccolo's seemingly unimportant contribution.

At certain times in life we all feel insignificant and useless. Surrounded by people with greater talent than ours, we are tempted in our weak moments just to settle back and "let George do it." We reason that what we have to offer won't make much difference anyway. We forget that Jesus used five loaves and two small fish to feed a multitude. Like that young boy on the mountainside, each of us has something important to offer, and we are foolish to hold back because we discount the value of our contribution.

Whether our talent is great or small, the performance isn't complete until we do our best with what we have. —R.W.D.

**In God's eyes it is a great thing
to do a little thing well.**

Monday

LUKE 19:11–27

"Because you were faithful in a very little, have authority over ten cities" (Luke 19:17).

One stormy night an elderly couple entered the lobby of a small hotel and asked for a room. The hotel was filled, but the clerk said, "I can't send a nice couple like you out in the rain at one o'clock in the morning. Would you be willing to sleep in my room?" The couple hesitated, but the clerk insisted. The next morning when the man paid his bill, he said, "You're the kind of manager who should be the boss of the best hotel in the United States. Maybe someday I'll build one for you." The clerk smiled, amused by the older man's joke. A few years passed and the clerk received a letter from the elderly man. He recalled that stormy night and asked the clerk to come to New York for a visit. A round-trip ticket was enclosed. When the clerk arrived, his host took him to the corner of 5th Avenue and 34th Street, where a magnificent new building stood. "That," explained the man, "is the hotel I have just built for you to manage." "You must be joking," said the clerk. "I most assuredly am not," he replied. "Who—who are you?" stammered the other. "My name is William Waldorf Astor." That hotel was the original Waldorf-Astoria, and the young clerk who became its first manager was George C. Boldt.

In heaven there will be "many mansions" to manage. So we should never underestimate the importance of what we are doing now for Jesus' sake, for He sees it all. Faithful service here on earth prepares us for great things in Glory. —D.J.D.

**God's requirement is faithfulness;
our reward is fruitfulness.**

Tuesday

2 TIMOTHY 4:1–8

But you be watchful in all things, endure afflictions, . . . fulfill your ministry (2 Timothy 4:5).

Sometimes we are not satisfied with the responsibilities God has given us, thinking we are fitted for a larger ministry. Looking enviously at the size or scope of another believer's calling, we think less of our own work and begin to neglect it.

In his book *Be Faithful,* Warren W. Wiersbe told how C. H. Spurgeon, the famous Baptist preacher, handled that problem. "A young preacher once complained to Spurgeon that he did not have as big a church as he deserved. 'How many do you preach to?' Spurgeon asked. 'Oh, about a hundred,' the man replied. Solemnly, Spurgeon said, 'That will be enough to give account for on the day of judgment.'"

The truth of Spurgeon's statement is borne out in Paul's reminder to "fulfill your ministry." The apostle was telling his young friend in the faith to do all that God had called him to do. But this did not mean that Timothy was to do the same things as Paul. Nor did it mean that he would accomplish as much as the apostle would. Rather, it meant that whether Timothy's task was large or small, in the limelight or behind the scenes, he was to fulfill his ministry in a diligent and commendable manner. —D.C.E.

**We are to do what we can,
where we are, with what we have.**

Wednesday

JOHN 6:1–12

"For who has despised the day of small things?"
(Zechariah 4:10).

When a young boy offered his bread and two tiny fish to Jesus, the Lord blessed his small lunch and it became a bountiful provision for many hungry people. God does the same when we offer Him our insignificant actions. He takes what little we have and uses it mightily for His glory.

One night in London two Christian men were trying to decide whether to cancel a missionary society meeting because the weather was so bad. "Is it worthwhile to hold this service?" one man asked. "Perhaps not," the other answered, "but I don't like to shirk my responsibility. Besides, the meeting has been announced, and someone might come." So, as thunder rumbled and torrents of rain poured down, they started the service, even though only one person had showed up. A man who was walking past the brightly lighted chapel stepped inside to take refuge from the storm and doubled the size of the audience. As he sat down to dry off, he heard the speaker make a powerful plea for workers among the Indians in North America. After the service, one of the leaders remarked to the other, "Time thrown away tonight." But he was wrong. The passerby had heard God's call and yielded his life to Him. Within a month he had sold his business and was preparing himself to work among the Indians in British Columbia, where he would stay for thirty-five years.

The title of a gospel song is true: "Little Is Much When God Is In It." When we link our faith with God's omnipotence, we can expect results. —P.R.V.

> Don't despise little things; a lantern can do
> what the sun never can—shine at night.

Thursday

ROMANS 16:1–16

Greet Apelles, approved in Christ. Greet those
who are of the household of Aristobulus (Romans 16:10).

Few have ever heard of Apelles or of the unnamed Christians in the
house of Aristobulus: Yet these people were important enough to the
growth of the church at Rome for Paul to mention them. This tells us
that in the service of Christ, the efforts of the "little guys" are as
important as the "all stars."

In a 1984 article for the *Detroit News,* Ernie Harwell, radio an-
nouncer for the Detroit Tigers, wrote, "When the Tigers got off to
their roaring 35-5 start this season, the experts began writing and
talking about the 1927 New York Yankees, a team rated by most as the
outstanding aggregation in the history of baseball. Those Yankees
were graced with bigger-than-life heroes. Babe Ruth, Lou Gehrig, Earl
Combs, Herb Pennock, and Waite Hoyt from that team are in baseball's Hall of Fame. But what about their teammates? What about Joe
Giard, Mike Gazella, Ray Morehart, John Grabowski, and Pat Collins?
Not only did they miss the Hall of Fame, they're not even household
words." Harwell then commented, "We all remember the greats, but
the little guys also have their roles. It might be the role of a utility
man, a pinch hitter, or maybe even a substitute who is just a holler
guy—the kind who keeps up the spirits on the team. . . . It also takes
those little-known guys to win a pennant."

Although we may play only a minor role in our church, we must
stay with it. Our contribution is vitally important to the church's
spiritual success—even if we're not a Hall-of-Famer. —D.C.E.

**It is a great waste to do nothing
because we think we can only do a little.**

Friday

I would rather be a doorkeeper in the house of my God
than dwell in the tents of wickedness (Psalm 84:10).

Serving the Lord, even in some lowly way, is a great privilege. The writer of Psalm 84 was keenly aware of this. He was probably a Levite who normally performed duties at the temple. But at the time he wrote these words, he couldn't be there. Maybe he was sick; maybe he even had leprosy. Whatever the reason, he wanted to be at the temple so much that he envied the birds who lived there (v. 3). He thought of the pilgrims traveling to the temple for worship, praise, and fellowship. In poetic language he pictured them as finding bubbling springs in desert places (vv. 5–7). He prayed God's blessing on the king and then declared that he would rather serve in the humblest of all tasks at the house of God than to sit in the place of a chief person among the wicked (vv. 9–10). When he spoke of being a "doorkeeper," he used a term that probably referred to a person at the threshold of the temple assigned to pick up the refuse thrown away by careless people.

Through years of working with others in the Lord's service, I have come to appreciate deeply those who consider it a privilege to serve God no matter how unglamorous their task. If they have mechanical skills, they repair the church bus. Others go out of their way to give an elderly couple a ride to church. Some call on absentees. Others volunteer whenever work needs to be done. These dedicated people do these things willingly as to the Lord. They view lowly service as a high honor. —H.V.L.

**God often entrusts us with a little
to see what we will do with a lot.**

Saturday

1 CORINTHIANS 12:12–31

But now God has set the members, each one of them, in the body just as He pleased (1 Corinthians 12:18).

The name of the extinct dodo bird has long been used to speak of someone who is foolish, stupid, and worthless. Larger than a turkey, this ash-gray bird had a fat and lumpy fifty-pound body and a ridiculous tuft of curly feathers for a tail. Its stubby wings sported no more than three or four black feathers. It had a hooked beak, large legs, and heavy feet. The dodo lived in obscurity on three islands in the Indian Ocean until settlers came along and wiped out the defenseless creatures. These ugly birds seemed destined for ridicule. Their discoverer wrote of them in his journal, "We called these birds walghvogels [disgusting birds] for the reason that the more and longer they are cooked, the less soft and more unpalatable their flesh becomes."

But then came a surprising discovery. In 1977 scientists learned that the beautiful calvaria tree, which grows on the dodo's native island, depended on the bird for its survival. The tree's seeds had such thick hulls that they could sprout only after being run through the rigors of the dodo's digestive system. Just in the nick of time, some turkeys were imported to take the dodo's place and perpetuate the thirteen dying calvaria trees that remained.

In the church, as in nature, the Lord doesn't make worthless things. Every one of us is an important part of the body. Some of us might not look like much, but God has placed us "just as He pleased." Each has a purpose, and in Christ that purpose is eternal. —M.R.D.II

**Those who appear small in our sight
are often giants in God's sight.**

Week 43

TRIUMPHAL ENTRY

Now as He drew near, He saw the city and wept over it, saying, "If you had known . . . the things that make for your peace! But now they are hidden from your eyes (Luke 19:41–42).

THEME

TEMPORAL VALUES

In the 1662 English Prayer Book, the devout proclaim, "O God . . . may [we] so pass through things temporal, that we finally lose not the things eternal."

With only the temporal in mind, the Jerusalem crowds triumphantly welcomed Jesus. They wanted a deliverer, someone who could rout the Romans. Having seen His miracles, they were convinced of His might, but they never really saw the Man behind the miracles. Jesus wept over their shortsightedness (Luke 19:41–44).

Perhaps the two Emmaus disciples were in that crowd, for they confessed to Jesus, their unidentified Companion on the road, that they had hoped the Nazarene would deliver Israel (Luke 24:21). Jesus corrected their value system by giving them an eternal perspective. He called them foolish for not realizing that suffering always precedes glory, just as the Old Testament had revealed.

Isaiah described Jesus as an innocent lamb at a slaughterhouse and as a war hero at a spoil-dividing summit (53:7, 12). The horror of death on the cross came before the honor of victory.

Like the Jerusalem throngs, we often focus on the immediate; we need to lay aside the magnifying glass, climb the mountain, pick up the binoculars, and search the horizon.

Sunday

JOHN 12:12–19

Then the multitudes . . . cried out, . . . "Blessed is He who comes in the name of the Lord!" (Matthew 21:9).

It's Sunday morning, time for the electronic church in America. Thousands lounge in their living rooms watching television. Almost every channel carries a religious program. Some preachers proclaim a clear-cut gospel message. Others, however, pace before an enraptured audience, telling them that Jesus will heal all their diseases and make them rich. "He wants you well! Poverty is of the devil!" shouts the preacher. And the swelling of applause picks up where he leaves off. People love the "gospel" of prosperity and deliverance from sickness.

Now turn back the calendar to a Sunday morning around 33 A.D. The city is Jerusalem. There's no TV, but there is a preacher who stirs the hopes of an excited crowd. For three years He's been going about Judea and Galilee, healing the sick, feeding the hungry, and even raising the dead. Now He rides into Jerusalem on a colt, gladly receiving the acclaim of the crowd. But those who shout "Hosanna!" are accepting Him for what they think He will give them, not for who He is and what He came to do. They want an earthly Messiah who will provide for their material welfare, not a suffering Messiah whose death on the cross will expose their sin, provide forgiveness, and call for a life commitment.

Jesus didn't promise release from all the suffering in the world. But He did offer forgiveness, peace, eternal life, and a cross. Anything less than taking up that cross in serving Him is shallow allegiance.

—D.J.D.

The word *easy* appears only once in the New Testament, and then in connection with *yoke*.

Monday

MATTHEW 21:1–11

A great multitude . . . cried out: "Hosanna! 'Blessed is He who comes in the name of the Lord!'" (John 12:12–13).

Sometimes I wonder how many of those who enthusiastically cried, "Hosanna!" on Palm Sunday were shouting, "Crucify Him! Crucify Him!" a few days later. People must have been disappointed, even resentful, that Christ didn't overthrow the Romans and set up an earthly kingdom. He had had a golden opportunity to rally support as He rode into Jerusalem. In contrast to His earlier actions, He didn't try to dampen this jubilant demonstration. Yet neither did he capitalize on the fervor of the crowd and issue a call to arms. Those who longed only for release from foreign domination were disillusioned. The Messiah had not fulfilled their expectations.

Jesus' contemporaries failed to recognize that before He could assert His outward sovereignty, He had to rule the inner citadel of their hearts. The Jews' greatest need was not freedom from Caesar's legions but release from the chains of their own sin. Jesus would rule in power and glory one day, but first He had to pay sin's penalty on the cross. The key to His kingdom was not revolution but repentance.

Through the centuries the issue has not changed. If we follow Christ only because we think He'll shield us from life's hardships, heal all our sicknesses, and guarantee prosperity, we're headed for disillusionment. But if we renounce sin, take up our cross, and live for Him because He is our God, our Creator, and our Redeemer, we will never be disappointed in Him. —D.J.D.

Putting Christ first brings satisfaction that lasts.

Tuesday

Although the fig tree shall not blossom . . .
yet I will rejoice in the Lord (Habakkuk 3:17–18 KJV).

Those who center their lives on spiritual values rather than material things are best equipped to endure the adversities of life and to profit from them. In fact, they can even rejoice in them.

In *450 Stories for Life,* Gust Anderson tells about visiting a church in a farming community of eastern Alberta, Canada, where there had been eight years of drought. The farmers were deep in debt, and their economic situation looked hopeless. In spite of their poverty, however, many of them continued to meet together to worship and praise God. Anderson was especially impressed by the testimony of one of these farmers. Dressed in overalls and an old coat—the best clothes he had—the man stood up and quoted Habakkuk 3:17–18. "Although the fig tree shall not blossom, neither shall fruit be in the vines; the labor of the olive shall fail, and the fields shall yield no meat; the flock shall be cut off from the fold, and there shall be no herd in the stalls; yet I will rejoice in the Lord, I will joy in the God of my salvation." Anderson thought, that dear saint has found the secret of real joy.

It isn't wrong to find pleasure in the good things money can buy, but we should never rely on them for happiness. If our fulfillment depends on material possessions, we are crushed when we lose them. But if our joy is found in the Lord, nothing can disrupt it, not even economic distress. Those who know and trust the Lord can rejoice—even in poverty. —R.W.D.

Happiness depends on happenings; joy depends on Jesus!

Wednesday

1 JOHN 2:12–17

Do not love the world or the things in the world
(1 John 2:15).

A man visiting a distant city made no comment when his friends showed him one of the city's most impressive buildings. Disappointed at his silence, one of the friends finally asked, "Don't you think it's beautiful?" "No, not really," he responded. "I've been to Rome, you see."

Because he had seen the magnificent structures of Rome's glorious past, the building his friends showed him did not impress him. It suffered tragically by comparison.

C. H. Spurgeon, commenting on that story, said, "O believer, if the world tempts you with its rare sights and curious prospects, you may well scorn them, having been by contemplation in heaven, and being able by faith to see infinitely better delights every hour of the day."

Believers who through faith in God's Word have had a foretaste of heaven and have considered their glorious spiritual blessings in Christ Jesus are not attracted by the enchantments of this world. They're not impressed by its empty baubles. They're not enamored with its allurements. Recognizing that which has genuine worth and lasting value, they respond to the earthly and temporal by saying, "Take the world, but give me Jesus." —R.W.D.

The world cannot distract us when Christ attracts us.

Thursday

LUKE 24:44–53

**If then you were raised with Christ,
seek those things which are above (Colossians 3:1).**

Christians are a "heavenly" people. That's what Paul meant when he told the Ephesians that God has "raised us up together, and made us sit together in the heavenly places in Christ Jesus" (Eph. 2:6). We live on earth, but "our citizenship is in heaven" (Phil. 3:20). We should therefore "seek those things which are above," and store up treasures in heaven.

We see a graphic difference between an earthly minded person and a heavenly minded person when we look at two Middle Eastern tombs. The first is the burial place of King Tut in Egypt. Inside, precious metal and blue porcelain cover the walls. The mummy of the king is enclosed in a beautifully inscribed, gold-covered sarcophagus. Although King Tut apparently believed in an afterlife, he thought of it in terms of this world's possessions, which he wanted to take with him.

The other tomb, in Palestine, is a simple rock-hewn cave believed by many to be Jesus' burial site. Inside, there is no gold, no earthly treasure, and no body. Jesus had no reason to store up this world's treasures. His goal was to fulfill all righteousness by doing His Father's will. His was a spiritual kingdom of truth and love.

The treasures we store up on earth will all stay behind when this life ends. But the treasures we store up in heaven we'll have for eternity. When we seek to be Christlike in thought, word, and deed, we will live like "heavenly" people. —P.R.V.

Wise are those who gear their goals to heavenly gains.

Friday

**"For where your treasure is,
there your heart will be also" (Matthew 6:21).**

Junior wanted a dump truck, and he let everyone in the store know it. When his mother said no, the little boy threw a temper tantrum. He howled louder and louder until the embarrassed mother bought the toy. As I watched, I thought of what my mother told me when I was young. "Don't hang your heart on things!" she said. At times I rebelled against that idea, but today I'm deeply grateful for her advice. And I think it should be displayed as a motto in every home.

The apostle Paul warned that the earth and all "the works that are in it will be burned up" (2 Peter 3:10). With this truth in mind, he went on to say, "Therefore, since all these things will be dissolved, what manner of persons ought you to be in holy conduct and godliness. . . ?" (v. 11). Because material things are transient, we ought to set our affection on "things above" (Col. 3:2).

In a day when we're bombarded as never before by appeals to buy and have, it's difficult, even for believers, to stand firm against an excessive desire for things. Beautiful full-color spreads in magazines, scintillating radio commercials, and persuasive television ads combine to make us feel that we can't get along without certain products.

We need to guard ourselves against the tendency to want more and more material possessions. They can become heart hang-ups that draw us away from the Lord. Material values pass away; spiritual values last forever. —R.W.D.

**Hold lightly to the things of earth
but tightly to the things of heaven.**

Saturday

DEUTERONOMY 6:1–5

"You shall love the Lord your God with all your heart"
(Deuteronomy 6:5).

Many people come to a sad end because they worship wrong gods. Some are wicked, having made a god out of sensual pleasure. Others are decent people, yet they too have worshiped the wrong god.

After a young farmer committed suicide, his wife said, "Farming wasn't just a job with Floyd. It was his identity, his nationality, his religion. Working with the ground gave us both a sense of connection with the Almighty. But it had gone sour by the time Floyd killed himself."

My heart goes out to people like Floyd. They have a deep appreciation of God's natural world and are willing to work hard. But whenever an occupation or anything temporal takes priority in life, it becomes our god. The apostle John admonished us, "Do not love the world or the things in the world. . . . For all that is in the world—the lust of the flesh, the lust of the eyes, and the pride of life—is not of the Father but is of the world" (1 John 2:15–16). This can apply to any earthly pursuit that becomes central in our lives.

When we love anything more than the true and living God revealed in the Bible, we are worshiping it. Whatever it is, it won't last. And it won't be able to help us when our plans shatter, our health fails, or death beckons. Only the true God can help us then. —H.V.L.

The "world" is whatever cools our affection for Christ.

Week 44

JESUS SERVES DISCIPLES

"If I then, your Lord and Teacher, have washed your feet, you also ought to wash one another's feet" (John 13:14).

THEME

SERVANTHOOD

Albert Einstein once remarked, "Setting an example is not the main means of influencing another, it is the *only* means."

In washing the disciples' feet, Jesus shocked His followers. This was not the beginning of the first valet school; Jesus was not some water-basin wonder. With a towel around His waist, Jesus washed soiled feet, but He was more interested in dirty people than dusty toes.

The disciples had been vying for leadership positions, and Jesus played chief footwasher to clean their hearts rather than their feet. Knowing that He would be going away, Jesus acted as a servant to combat the hotshot attitudes of the disciples. He hoped they would recall and imitate His humility.

The Old Testament writers described Abraham, Moses, Joshua, David, and Daniel as servants. Humble and caring leaders before God and others, they led without service charges.

In coming to this earth, Jesus became part of a long-running play, but He was not acting. He took the servant part for some thirty-three years to show people how to live (Philippians 2:7). Those who follow Him lead by example. They never make a grand entrance; they come in the service door, and others soon come after them.

Sunday

JOHN 13:1–17

**"I have given you an example, that you should do
as I have done to you" (John 13:15).**

Jesus Christ visibly demonstrated the love of God when He was on earth. In stooping to wash His disciples' feet, He mirrored the submissive step He had taken when He left heaven to become a man. He lived with the limitations of humanity, yet He healed the sick, reached out to the despised, and endured bitter hatred as His reward. He died like a criminal on a Roman cross. All of these things reflected God's love, for Jesus said, "He who has seen Me has seen the Father" (John 14:9). Jesus is no longer with us in His physical body—He now sits at God's right hand in heaven. Therefore, if God's love is to be embodied on earth today, it must be done through those of us who are Christians.

Not long ago, sixteen women from Evanston, Illinois, beautifully demonstrated God's love by rearranging their schedules to give round-the-clock nursing care to Martha, a 26-year-old woman with ALS (amyotrophic lateral sclerosis or Lou Gehrig's disease). They bathed her, fed her, talked with her, prayed for her, and witnessed to her. Martha, who had not accepted Christ as her Savior and couldn't understand how a loving God could let her get ALS, saw His love in these women and eventually became a Christian. Although feeble and unable to speak clearly, she gave a testimony of her faith and was baptized in a local church. A short time later, she died. She is with the Lord today because sixteen women, following Jesus' example, personified God's love. —H.V.L.

My life helps paint my neighbor's picture of God.

Monday

MATTHEW 20:20–28

"Whoever desires to become great among you,
let him be your servant" (Matthew 20:26).

When Pastor Howard Sugden preaches on the upper room, where Jesus washed the disciples' feet, he speaks of "God with a towel in His hand." That towel symbolizes One who "did not come to be served, but to serve" (Matt. 20:28). Yet how quickly we reverse the pattern and expect others to serve our needs. We may even go so far as to complain when other believers disappoint us and don't do as we expect. That's why we need to keep Jesus' example before us.

Vernon Grounds, then president of Denver Conservative Baptist Theological Seminary, challenged the graduating class of 1973 with the truth of John 13. Dr. Grounds gave the graduates a tangible symbol that he said would help them in their future ministries. As the classmates filed quietly to the front, they expected a special Scripture verse, a little book, or an inscribed medallion. To their surprise, he gave them a small square of white terry cloth. One graduate, who has served as an overseas missionary, says, "We were commissioned to go into the world as servants. That small piece of towel, frayed and grubby from years in my wallet, is a constant reminder of that moving moment and of our basic call to serve."

The example Christ gave in the upper room challenges us to ask ourselves if we have a servant's attitude. Perhaps it's time for us to realize that the "towel in our hand" is a servant's towel. —D.C.E.

The believer's talents are not to be laid up for self—
they are to be laid out in service.

Tuesday

**"But he who is greatest among you
shall be your servant" (Matthew 23:11).**

Music lovers, brace yourselves. Some of the greatest orchestral conductors of the past were sometimes podium tyrants. In an article in *The Indianapolis Star,* Robert Baxter wrote, "Their heyday came in the 1930s and '40s when Artur Rodzinski carried a loaded revolver to rehearsals, when Arturo Toscanini broke batons, . . . when Fritz Reiner pierced musicians with his laser-like eyes, and George Szell slashed them with his razor-sharp tongue." One player recalls, "Playing under them was like being in an open field during an electrical storm." Once an offended musician stormed out of rehearsal, shouting to Toscanini, "Nuts to you!" Toscanini bellowed back, "It's too late to apologize!" With such disharmony in relationships, it's a wonder these geniuses could get such beautiful music from their players.

Strong leaders don't need to instill fear and be autocratic to command respect. Jesus, the only perfect leader this world has ever known, showed us a better way. His podium was not the Mount of Transfiguration, where He revealed His deity. It was a Roman cross, where He served our deepest needs by paying the penalty for our sins. Now He draws beautiful music from sin-ruined lives—first by surrounding us with His love and forgiveness, then by serving through us as we joyously yield to His direction.

Those in positions of leadership can look to Jesus to learn the secret of leading by serving. —D.J.D.

**Leaders do not begin to serve until
they put serving into their leadership.**

Wednesday

MATTHEW 20:20–28

"And whoever desires to be first among you,
let him be your slave" (Matthew 20:27).

Sometimes I get the feeling that we are experiencing a leadership crisis among Christians. Although plenty of people are eager to assume the top positions, far too few are willing to accept the biblical pattern of authority. They assume that headship means dominance, so they ignore the basic teaching of passages like Matthew 20. The pattern established by Christ for leadership in the church can be summed up in one word: servanthood. Jesus Himself exemplified this when he washed the disciples' feet as "an example" (John 13:2–16).

In *The Mark of a Man,* Elisabeth Elliot told of a relative who was the dean of a Christian college in the Midwest. One night some boys in a dorm smeared the walls with shaving cream, peanut butter, and jelly. When the dean heard about it, he wondered what action to take. He could force the young men to clean it up or he could order the janitor to do it. Instead, he started to clean up the mess himself. Soon doors began to open, and before long the guilty ones were helping him wash the walls. Because he was willing to take the role of a servant, he solved the problem and taught the boys a valuable lesson at the same time.

Whenever we're in a position of leadership and seem to be failing, we should examine our attitude toward service in light of Matthew 20 and John 13. Perhaps we need more practice in the principle of leading by serving. —D.C.E.

Lead players are always improving their serve.

Thursday

LUKE 22:24–30

"Who is greater, he who sits at the table, or he who serves? . . .
I am among you as the One who serves" (Luke 22:27).

A young woman who lives with her parents on a small government allowance complains of continual depression and weariness. Yet when I suggested that she seek employment or engage in volunteer work, she resisted. She thinks that accepting a lowly task would be demeaning. But if she would swallow her pride and get busy, no matter how menial the task, she would not only feel better about herself but she would also bring honor to the Lord.

J. Gresham Machen, world-renowned theologian, accepted lowly work while serving as a YMCA volunteer during World War I. He was assigned the task of making hot chocolate at a canteen. Since it had to be ready at 7 A.M., Machen would get up before 5. He'd take bars of chocolate and shave them into slivers. Then he'd melt them, gradually adding condensed milk and water as the mixture heated. From 7 until 9 he kept busy serving the hot chocolate and often didn't get his own breakfast until the middle of the morning. Although Machen would have been an excellent counselor to the servicemen, he honored God by accepting a mundane task without complaining.

In Old Testament times, it was an honor for the Levites to do the manual labor associated with the tabernacle and temple. Likewise, the apostle Paul wasn't ashamed to make tents. The Lord Himself washed His disciples' feet. Any lowly task, done as unto the Lord, affords a unique opportunity to exalt Him and to demonstrate the reality of our faith. Christians can find joy no matter where they serve. —H.V.L.

Little is much when God is in it.

Friday

Jesus said to them, "Come and eat breakfast"
(John 21:12).

By the shores of the Sea of Tiberias with His disciples, Jesus served a breakfast of fish and bread. Just as He had done when He washed the disciples' feet, He was setting an example. And like Jesus, we are to serve one another, even our close friends and loved ones, for whom it is sometimes difficult to do humble tasks.

Professor Bill Brown of Bryan College told about a missionary who went to a tribe of Indians to present the gospel. At first the people received him with hesitation, referring to him as "the white man." As they got to know him better, they began to call him "the respectable white man." Later, when they saw the goodness of his heart and his desire for their well-being, they spoke of him as "the white Indian," indicating that they were accepting him as one of their own. When one of the Indians injured his foot in an accident, the missionary took the man into his home, washed his foot, and gave him medical attention. The people were amazed that he would do such a gracious thing. After this, they began to call him "the man from God."

That missionary displayed a Christlike attitude, for Jesus did not come to be served but to serve (Mark 10:45). If we humble ourselves and follow our Lord's example, we too will become known as the man or woman from God. —D.C.E.

**We can do great things for the Lord
if we are willing to do little things for others.**

Saturday

"But whoever loses his life for My sake . . .
will save it" (Mark 8:35).

Shortly after the Civil War ended, General William T. Sherman's victorious army was scheduled to march in a triumphal parade in a large city. On the night before, Sherman called General Oliver O. Howard to his room and said, "General, you were at the head of one of the divisions that marched with me through Georgia, and you ought rightfully to ride at the head of your division in the parade tomorrow. But I've been asked to let the general who preceded you in command represent the division. I don't know what to do." General Howard replied, "I think I am entitled to represent my division, since I led them to victory." "Yes, you are," said Sherman, "but I believe you are a Christian, and I was wondering if Christian considerations might lead you to yield your rights for the sake of peace." "In that case," said Howard, "of course I'll yield." "All right," said General Sherman, "I will go arrange it, and will you please report to me in the morning at 9? You will be riding with me at the head of the army." General Howard's willingness to submit to his commander and deny himself his rightful place led to the position of greatest honor.

Jesus said, "If anyone serves Me, let him follow Me" (John 12:26). When He was reviled and opposed, He did not insist on His rights but "committed Himself to Him who judges righteously" (1 Peter 2:23). That same spirit should characterize His followers. If we as Christians give our lives to serve others for Christ's sake, we will win His reward. Our "loss" will be our gain. —P.R.V.

Getting our own way serves only
to get in the way of our service.

Week 45

THE LORD'S SUPPER

"This is My body which is given for you; do this in remembrance of Me." Likewise He also took the cup after supper, saying, "This cup is the new covenant in My blood, which is shed for you" (Luke 22:19–20).

THEME

REMEMBRANCE

William Manchester in his memoir about the Pacific conflict of World War II wrote of how "abruptly the poker of memory stirs the ashes of recollection and uncovers a forgotten ember, still smoldering down there, still hot, still glowing, still red as red."

Remembering Israel's experience in Egypt, the disciples and Jesus celebrated the Passover, one of God's many memory devices. The Passover lamb reminded Jews of the animal blood spilled to protect their lives in Egypt. Because Jesus was the true Passover Lamb, He chose new symbols, bread and wine, for His broken body and shed blood.

God knows we have short memory spans; that's why He creates unforgettable memory aids. Yet sometimes we become indifferent to them or deliberately ignore them, allowing spiritual senility to set in.

Those concerned about forgetfulness fight it with attentive minds that meditate on who God is and what He has done. For ponderers and reflectors, the past is the road to a future of fresh experiences with God.

Most of all, graduates of God's memory school think about Jesus. He is always in their mind's eye. They see red as red.

Sunday

**Yet it pleased the LORD to bruise Him;
He has put Him to grief (Isaiah 53:10).**

When I saw my pastor's sermon title, "You Can't Drink Grapes," I wondered what his message was going to be about. His communion meditation centered on the two symbols Jesus used at the Lord's Supper: bread and wine. The bread symbolizes Christ's body; the wine His shed blood. The wine came from grapes, luscious and ripe, harvested from the vine. But before they became liquid, they had to be crushed so that all of the juice would flow out of them.

The same was true in the life of the Lord Jesus. To fulfill His purpose for coming to this earth, He too needed to be crushed. He came to pay the penalty for our sin. That price was death, a sacrifice He paid when He died on the cross. Even though Roman soldiers carried out the execution, the penalty was exacted by God the Father Himself. Isaiah wrote, "Yet it pleased the Lord to bruise [crush] Him."

It's true. We can't drink grapes. They must be crushed to give forth juice. And that is exactly what happened to Christ on our behalf on Calvary's cross. He poured out His physical life so that we might have spiritual life. When we drink the juice of communion, we are to remember the One who was wounded for our transgressions and bruised for our iniquities. —D.C.E.

**Natural life came by God's breath;
eternal life comes by Christ's death.**

Monday

LUKE 22:14–20

"Do this in remembrance of Me"
(Luke 22:19).

The Bible tells us to remember many things, but one of the most important is to remember Jesus as we partake of the Lord's Supper. Meditating on His suffering and death should always fill us with a deep sense of gratitude to God for providing our redemption.

When my friend Roger was a boy, he and his family lived on a farm alongside a dirt road. Only on rare occasions would an automobile pass by. But one day as Roger's young brother was crossing the road on his bicycle, a car came roaring down a nearby hill, struck the boy, and killed him. Roger said, "Later, when my father picked up the mangled, twisted bike, I heard him sob out loud for the first time in my life. He carried it to the barn and placed it in a spot we seldom used. Father's terrible sorrow eased with the passing of time, but for many years whenever he saw that bike, tears began streaming down his face." Roger continued, "Since then I have often prayed, 'Lord, keep the memory of Your death as fresh as that to me! Every time I partake of Your memorial supper, let my heart be stirred as though You died only yesterday. Never let the communion service become a mere formality, but always a tender and touching experience.'"

When we partake of the Lord's Supper, the thought of Christ dying on a cruel cross should move our heart and motivate us to holy living.
—H.G.B.

**Remembering Christ's *wounds*
should encourage us to obey His *words*.**

Tuesday

1 CORINTHIANS 11:17–26

"This do, as often as you drink it,
in remembrance of Me" (1 Corinthians 11:25).

Every year Americans observe a holiday called Memorial Day to remember those who gave their lives that others might live in freedom. Remembering their sacrifice should be the emphasis of the day, but many citizens forget, and think only of themselves.

In a *Detroit Free Press* article, Jack Kresnak wrote about a Memorial Day service near the Detroit River where 150 people were listening to a Naval Reserve captain lament the fact that the meaning of the day had been lost. A short distance away a young man in a safari hat and a three-piece suit rode a decorated bicycle dubbed "Spotlight." This "super-customized Schwinn" was covered with cardboard, gold spray paint, and pictures of girlfriends. It had two radios and twenty flashlights shining in all directions. Later, when asked about his escapade, the biker said, "I do this to get attention."

In 1 Corinthians 11 we read of a different kind of memorial day. It too lost its true meaning because people treated it casually. Instead of remembering Christ, who had died so that sinners could live, many Corinthian Christians thought only of themselves. The memorial meal became a time for eating, drinking, and making merry.

A similar thing can happen in churches today. When we partake of the Lord's Supper, we must examine ourselves to make sure we are not preoccupied with our own desires instead of thinking of Jesus' death. We must be sure to focus our attention on Christ. —M.R.D. II

The host at the Lord's supper is the Lord of hosts.

Wednesday

1 CORINTHIANS 11:27–34

For if we would judge ourselves,
we would not be judged (1 Corinthians 11:31).

In the 1960s, a respectable club in New York State refused membership to a young Jewish man. A minister who belonged to the club took a strong stand against this prejudice by denouncing it from the pulpit, even though many members of his congregation also belonged to that club. In his sermon, he said, "I must insist that the members of my congregation take a stand against a policy that is morally reprehensible." He ended by saying, "Anyone who has in any way—by thought, word, or deed—acquiesced with this position . . . is no longer welcome to receive holy communion . . . until he has worked out his own peace with God."

That clergyman had scriptural backing for citing unconfessed sin as a barrier to coming to the Lord's Supper. Some first-century Christians had made a mockery of the Lord's Supper by splitting into little groups and getting drunk on the wine (1 Cor. 11:21). The apostle Paul therefore made individual self-examination a part of the preparation for the communion celebration.

This requirement still holds true today. Although we all approach the bread and the cup as unworthy people, we must not harbor sinful thoughts, attitudes, and deeds. We dishonor our Savior's shed blood and broken body if we refuse to renounce and turn from what we know is wrong. The communion service is a blessed time—but first it is a judgment time. —D.J.D.

The Lord's table is first a *test*,
then a *testimony*.

Thursday

JOHN 14:25–31

The LORD will bless His people with peace (Psalm 29:11).

When Jesus was with His disciples in the upper room shortly before His crucifixion, He knew they would face turmoil and unrest in the days ahead. They would experience the distressing events of His betrayal, arrest, execution, and burial. Then, after His resurrection and ascension, they would face long periods of hard work, opposition, ridicule, and persecution. So in the quiet of those final moments together, He gave them words of comfort: "Peace I leave with you, My peace I give to you; not as the world gives do I give to you" (John 14:27).

Peace of mind and heart is still one of our most precious and needed commodities. In his book *A Time to Heal,* former President Gerald R. Ford repeated a story he had heard some years earlier. During the civil war in Greece in 1948, a villager was planning to emigrate to the United States. Before he left, he asked his weary, beleaguered, poverty-stricken neighbors, "What should I send when I get to America? Should I send money? Food? Clothing?" "No," one of his neighbors replied, "you should send us a ton of tranquillity."

When the burdens and pressures of life pile up on us, we, like those Greek patriots and Christ's disciples, need peace. We who know Jesus as Savior can trust Him to make good on His promise (John 14:27). When we stop to remember what He did for us on Calvary and rest in His loving arms, we will begin to experience the power of the Prince of Peace. —D.C.E.

Peace floods the soul when Christ rules the heart.

Friday

"Peace I leave with you, My peace I give to you;
not as the world gives do I give to you" (John 14:27).

A dear friend of many years, Ethel La Botz, sent me a letter in which she wrote: "As I was reading your devotional in *Our Daily Bread* called 'The Peace Corps,' I was reminded of what a missionary in Brazil told me when we were there. Reared in a godless home, she was unhappy and dissatisfied with life. Then one day she noticed an advertisement for the Peace Corps. The thought came to her, that's what's missing in my life—peace. So she joined and was sent to Irian Jaya, but she soon realized she couldn't find what she was lacking. Through her work, however, she came in contact with an old Indian. He was different from anyone she had ever met. She inquired as to what caused his peace, joy, and contentment, and he told her that Jesus was in his heart. So she started reading the Bible. Through the Word and the witness of the Indian friend, she found the peace that only Christ can give."

That same peace is available to all who by faith receive the Lord Jesus Christ as their Savior. "Therefore, having been justified by faith, we have peace with God through our Lord Jesus Christ," said Paul in Romans 5:1. Those who have peace *with* God can also experience the peace *of* God. This is what John 14 is all about. The Bible says, "Let your requests be made known to God; and the peace of God, which surpasses all understanding, will guard your hearts and minds through Christ Jesus" (Phil. 4:6–7).

Yes, in this troubled world we can find peace—the wonderful, satisfying peace of God! —R.W.D.

No God, *no* peace;
Know God, *know* peace.

Saturday

PSALM 103

Forget not all His benefits (Psalm 103:2).
Forgetting those things which are behind . . . (Philippians 3:13).

The spiritually healthy Christian knows what to remember and what to forget. A wise pastor told me that whenever he gets discouraged he brings to mind the awe and wonder he sensed when God saved him. But he said he deliberately avoids thinking about two men who did him a great wrong in his first pastorate and never made it right. When he recalled that, it aroused old feelings of resentment and hurt that destroyed his peace.

David wrote, "Forget not all His benefits." It's good to remember God's past mercies; how He forgave our sins, healed us, sustained us, and lavished His blessings upon us. Continually thinking about this will help us become more thankful and trusting.

The apostle Paul, on the other hand, spoke of "forgetting those things which are behind." Remembering his sin of persecuting Christians could have depressed him. Glorying in his successes as an honored member of the Jewish community and thinking of the special revelation he had received could have kindled feelings of pride. It is wrong to live in the sagging spirit of regret over past failures; but we can also make the mistake of resting on the laurels of yesterday to the point that we think we have arrived.

We must be selective in what we remember. We should cherish the memories that make Jesus and His salvation more precious, but we should forget those that hinder us as we run the race. —H.V.L.

We invite defeat by forgetting what we should remember
and remembering what we should forget.

Week 46

EVENT

GETHSEMANE

He knelt down and prayed, saying, "Father, if it is Your will, remove this cup from Me; nevertheless not My will, but Yours, be done." Then an angel appeared to Him from heaven, strengthening Him. And being in agony, He prayed more earnestly. And His sweat became like great drops of blood (Luke 22:41–44).

THEME

COMFORT

"He watch'd and wept; he pray'd and felt for all," wrote Oliver Goldsmith about one of his characters in *The Deserted Village*.

In great distress, Jesus went to an olive orchard to talk to the only One who really feels for all—the heavenly Father. Jesus wanted to forgo the humiliation of a criminal cross.

No Jew ever spoke to God as Jesus did in the garden; He called Him *Abba,* which is almost the same as *Daddy* or *Papa* in modern English. After His intimate conversation with His Father, He seemed ready to face His betrayer and judges, ready to begin His death march.

The disciples, particularly Peter, James, and John, could have comforted and supported Jesus, but they did not hear the death knell. While Jesus struggled with His coming agony, they slept.

God does not take naps. Always alert to our suffering, He comforts us in our troubles so that we can console others (2 Corinthians 1:3–4). In reaching out to others, we walk arm-in-arm with them—crying, praying, hoping—feeling all it means to be human.

Sunday

MATTHEW 26:36–46

"My soul is exceedingly sorrowful, even to death. Stay here and watch with Me" (Matthew 26:38).

Suffering comes to all of us, and no one can suffer for us. Even so, loved ones and friends can support us in many ways in those difficult times by their prayers and understanding. But when we are too proud to admit our need to others, we are in great danger.

The Sequoia trees of California tower as high as 300 feet above the ground, yet these giants have unusually shallow root systems, which reach out in all directions to capture the greatest amount of surface moisture. Seldom do redwoods stand alone, because high winds would quickly uproot them. They grow in clusters, their intertwining roots providing support for one another against the storms.

Support is what Jesus wanted from Peter, James, and John in Gethsemane as He faced Calvary. On the cross as the world's sin-bearer He would experience the Father's wrath and abandonment. That was the awful cup He prayed would be taken from Him. In that dark hour, He looked to His disciples for prayerful alertness and compassion. But they disappointed Him. The sight of His sleeping disciples must have made the isolation of Gethsemane even more painful.

If Jesus looked to human support in His crisis hour, how much more do Christians need one another when they suffer. We must be willing to ask someone to pray for us and with us. And we must be alert for opportunities to lend our support to others who are suffering. —D.J.D.

**Those who suffer need more than sympathy;
they need companionship.**

Monday

ROMANS 16:1–16

**Greet Priscilla and Aquila,
my fellow workers in Christ Jesus (Romans 16:3).**

The Bible tells us that God is the Helper of His children (Heb. 13:6). Most important, of course, He has delivered us from the condemnation of sin by providing salvation. But He also comes to our aid in many other ways every day. His example shows us that it is vital for us to do the same for other believers. Paul was especially concerned about encouraging Christians to help one another, and he commended those who had aided him in Rome. In his letter to the Christians there, he wrote, "Greet Mary, who labored much for us" (16:6). And of Phoebe he said, "She has been a helper of many" (16:2).

Edmund Hillary and his Sherpa guide, Tenzing Norgay, successfully completed their historic climb of Mt. Everest in 1953, a feat of remarkable courage and skill. Once during their descent Hillary lost his footing. Instinctively, Tenzing held the line taut and kept them both from falling by digging his ax firmly into the ice. Hillary recovered his balance, regained a foothold, and they continued their descent. When reporters later called Tenzing a hero, he refused to take any credit. Rather, he said, "Mountain climbers always help one another." He considered it a routine part of his job.

That's the way it should be with Christians. We are all pilgrims headed toward the same goal. When another's burden becomes heavy or someone stumbles along the way, we should give whatever assistance we can. Outsiders should say of us, "Christians always help one another." —D.C.E.

**When we share another's burdens,
both of us will walk straighter.**

Tuesday

LUKE 7:11–18

Jesus, when He came out, saw a great multitude and was moved with compassion for them (Mark 6:34).

At times, the world seems to be an uncaring, unsympathetic place. People are often cruel and indifferent, not giving a second thought to the plight of their suffering neighbors. Wrapped up in their own interests, they don't seem to notice the anguish and despair that is at their doorstep.

This could not be said of the Lord Jesus. Time after time He met the needs of suffering people. Luke 7 tells about Christ's compassion when He saw the widow stricken with grief over the death of her son. Jesus had compassion on her and healed the boy. Earlier, when He saw a man with leprosy—who was despised, ostracized, and no doubt terribly disfigured—He made him well (Luke 5:12–15). Still today, Jesus looks upon human need with compassion.

A little girl whose mother had been taken to the hospital was spending the night alone with her father for the first time. Soon after her father turned out the lights, the girl asked quietly, "Daddy, are you there?" "Yes," he assured her. A moment later she asked, "Daddy, are you looking at me?" When he said yes, she fell asleep.

Likewise, every child of God can depend on the Savior's look of love. No matter how painful the problem or how deep the sorrow, we know He has His eyes fixed on us. And knowing that our Savior's compassionate gaze always watches over us should make us loving, caring people. Although the world may turn its eyes from suffering, the Christian, following the example of our Savior, should be alert to sorrow and quick to respond. —D.C.E.

**God loves every one of us as if
there were but one of us to love.**

Wednesday

ACTS 20:16–31

**"I did not cease to warn everyone
night and day with tears" (Acts 20:31).**

Some people think crying is a sign of weakness. But our Savior wept. And the apostle Paul was not afraid to mention his own tears when he wrote to the Ephesian elders about his burden for the people he was trying to reach. Good servants or ministers of Jesus Christ will be like that—they will have tender, compassionate hearts. They will be so filled with concern and love that those feelings will often splash over as tears. If not tears on the cheek, certainly deep feeling in the soul.

One day D. L. Moody preached an especially moving sermon about the compassion of Christ. When a friend asked him how he had prepared such a message, he answered, "I got to thinking the other day about the compassion of Christ; so I took the Bible and began to read it over to find out what it said on the subject. I prayed over the texts as I went along until the thought of His infinite compassion overpowered me, and I could only lie on the floor of my study with my face in the open Bible and cry like a child."

As we stand in the shadow of the cross and let God's love in Christ flood our souls, our hard hearts will melt, and coldness will give way to warmth. If we allow the Holy Spirit to control us, He will produce in us a Christlike concern. Then His burden and His compassion for the unsaved will become ours. The love of Christ will cause us to reach out to others. And that caring attitude will be accompanied by timely tears. —P.R.V.

**Tears flow freely from the fountain
of a love-filled heart.**

Thursday

JOHN 11:17–37

**Rejoice with those who rejoice,
and weep with those who weep (Romans 12:15).**

Tears are stronger than words and more binding than treaties. In 1947, President Harry S. Truman visited Chapaltepec Castle, the West Point of Mexico. A hundred years earlier, when U.S. Troops captured the citadel, only six cadets survived, and they all committed suicide rather than surrender. As Truman placed a wreath on the monument to the heroes and bowed his head, the cadets in the color guard burst into tears. Someone said that nothing did more to help cement the two countries together than the emotion expressed on that occasion.

Christians, indwelt by the Holy Spirit, can express their deepest agonies and noblest desires through tears. When mingled with prayer, trust, or compassion, tears become a most beautiful and ennobling expression of the believer's faith.

I have no doubt that Jesus delighted in life's wholesome joys and pleasures, even though Scripture does not mention His smiles or laughter. Yet He was so in touch with the heartbreaks of sin all around Him that He wept unashamedly at a tomb, shed tears over the unbelief of Jerusalem, and entered fully into the sorrows of sin-laden humanity.

Our Savior's tears encourage us to be true to our emotions, letting the Holy Spirit use them to overcome barriers and heal relationships. Moistened eyes often convey faith, honesty, caring, love. We cry because hurting, hardened, unbelieving people need Jesus. And they just might meet Him through our tears. —D.J.D.

The soul could have no rainbow if the eyes had no tears.

Friday

MARK 14:32–38

"Take this cup away from Me; nevertheless,
not what I will, but what You will" (Mark 14:36).

To be healed or not to be healed—that is the question. Many sincere believers in the Lord Jesus claim that sickness is never within God's will for the Christian. Therefore we should pray for restoration with a tenacity that refuses to take no for an answer. According to them, the reason physical infirmity continues to linger in our lives is that we have become content with it. What we need, they say, is more faith and a rejection of the qualifier we usually add to our prayers, "If it be Thy will." They say that is nothing more than a copout.

But consider Jesus' plea in the Garden of Gethsemane. Although His prayer focused on the awful ordeal He faced, not sickness, God's response to it clearly shows that His glory is not always best served through instant, miraculous deliverance. In His humanity, the Lord Jesus drew back from the awful prospect of pain and suffering, just as we would from cancer or some other dreaded disease. And like Him, we have a right to ask that "this cup" be taken from us. Yet underlying our natural revulsion to disease and our longing for release, we must ask, what will glorify God the most? The Norwegian theologian Ole Hallesby said we should pray something like this: "Lord, if it will be Your glory, heal suddenly. If it will glorify You more, heal gradually; if it will glorify You even more, may your servant remain sick awhile; and if it will glorify Your name still more, take him to Yourself in heaven."

Anyone who prays "Thy will be done" from the heart, as Jesus did, will never say it's a copout. —D.J.D.

**When God denies us anything,
it's always to give us something better.**

Saturday

MARK 1:40–45

And Jesus, moved with compassion, put out His hand, and touched him (Mark 1:41).

People who enjoy good health sometimes neglect the less fortunate, and sometimes they even treat them cruelly. When I was very young, I saw a group of older boys teasing a retarded man unmercifully. I've also observed people deliberately avoid someone who looks "different" or who has a physical handicap. Perhaps they are embarrassed to be seen with such a person or are afraid of giving a little bit of themselves and getting nothing in return.

Jesus never responded that way. He was kind to afflicted people, and they thronged about Him. He took a blind man by the hand and led him away from the crowd before healing him. He touched the sick—even lepers. He stopped to expel demons from the possessed.

While visiting my brother and his family in Phoenix, my wife and I both observed my sister-in-law's kindness to people most others ignore. Every week she spends a large part of a day helping two aged shut-ins. She has also befriended a mentally impaired man who lives on her street. Almost every day he stops at her home for a brief visit. From the smile on his face, we sensed the joy she brings into his life.

How we treat the less fortunate among us is one measure of our likeness to Jesus. Because they often cannot give in return, we have a special opportunity to be truly unselfish. We should welcome every occasion to show Christlike compassion to those who receive so little but need so much. —H.V.L.

**A test of our Christian love is whether or not
we help those who cannot help us in return.**

Week 47

PETER'S DENIAL

One of the servants of the high priest . . . said, "Did I not see you in the garden with Him?" Peter then denied again; and immediately a rooster crowed (John 18:26–27).

THEME

DEFEAT

Thinking about the muddled mess of mankind, Gordon DePree lamented in his book *A Time to Grow,* "People sometimes disappoint me, and there are times when I disappoint others. This hurts. Ideals fall. Dreams fade. The concepts of life I was carefully constructing suddenly crumble into a rubble-heap at my feet . . . and I sit in the ruins, wondering if there is anything right about life, or if I even care."

After Peter had denied Jesus three times, He knew that nothing was right about life. He had become a blundermouth beyond belief. With a few foolish words he had wrecked his life, becoming a heap of twisted metal at the feet of his fellow disciples. He had failed Jesus.

How Jesus dealt with Peter afterward is an example straight from God's body shop. Following the resurrection, Jesus reaffirmed His love for Peter. He evidently met with Peter alone (1 Corinthians 15:5) and later reminded him that He had a job for him—caring for God's children (John 21:17). No wonder Peter would later write that we can cast our cares upon Him because He really cares for us (1 Peter 5:7).

Even though we may be abandoned at the junkyard, Jesus is calling for a wrecker. He will lovingly restore us to mint condition.

Sunday

LUKE 22:31–34

"I have prayed for you, that your
faith should not fail" (Luke 22:32).

With cranberries, it's the bounce that counts. According to *Science Digest,* processing cranberries involves pouring freshly picked berries down a series of steplike boards. At each level, only those berries that bounce over an eight- to ten-inch barrier pass the test. Each berry gets eleven chances. Those that fail are discarded. Some fruits are judged by firmness and color, but the cranberry is distinguished by its ability to "bounce like a golf ball."

The strength of our faith can also be judged by our ability to bounce back after defeat. Although setbacks hurt, they allow us to show our underlying confidence in Christ. Our Lord's words to Simon Peter suggest this. Jesus knew Peter was about to trip over his own self-confidence and zeal. He knew that Peter, who said he was willing to die for his Lord, would soon deny Him. The beauty of Christ's response to Peter's denial was that He saw beyond it to the disciple's repentance. He assured Peter that He had prayed that his faith would not fail. In essence, He was saying, "You will bounce back after your fall."

This experience in Peter's life can encourage us. We have the advantage of Christ's work and prayers on our behalf, and this gives us the confidence that He Himself sustains us. We too can be useful again to Him, even after a hard fall. A spiritual reversal should not cause us to give up. It's the "bounce" of our faith and His forgiveness that are all-important. —M.R.D.II

Defeat isn't bitter unless we swallow it.

Monday

JOHN 21:15–19

**And in those days Peter stood up
in the midst of the disciples (Acts 1:15).**

Remorse deprives many Christians of the joy that should be theirs. A man in his middle years has withdrawn from the people in his church because he feels so bad about his past infidelity—a sin that broke up his home. An elderly woman needs counseling from time to time because she can't forget an affair she had more than fifty years ago. A young woman sees a psychiatrist because she can't forgive herself for having had an abortion. Each of these people is now a Christian, but each is paralyzed at times by remorse over the past.

If anyone ever had good reason for allowing the memory of a grievous sin to put him on the shelf, it was Peter. He had been such a coward. He had fled Gethsemane at Christ's arrest, and then denied three times that he knew the Lord Jesus. Later, he felt so bad that he wept bitterly. Yet he did not allow his remorse over past failures to make him ineffective in his service for Christ. He accepted the Lord's forgiveness, and he received new hope from Jesus' commission, "Feed my sheep." In Acts 1:15 we find him back in his role as the leader of the disciples. By taking Jesus' words of forgiveness to heart and by forgiving himself, he put the past under the blood of Christ.

As believers, when we confess our sin, we can leave it with Christ and forget it. Then we can move on to find a new way to serve Him. We need never let remorse remove our joy. —H.V.L.

**Christians should seek to erase from their memory
the sins God has erased from their record.**

Tuesday

LUKE 22:54–62

Therefore let him who thinks he stands take heed lest he fall (1 Corinthians 10:12).

A frog placed in a pan of slowly heating water doesn't know he's being cooked. The body temperature of this little cold-blooded creature changes to correspond with the temperature of his surroundings, so he is unaware of his danger. Before he realizes that he's in boiling hot water, death overtakes him.

In much the same way, Peter's "spiritual crash" didn't just happen; it resulted from a gradual decline. The apostle yielded to circumstances that contributed to his downfall. In the upper room he was overconfident. Then, in the garden, he slept when he should have been praying. Failing to understand his Master's redemptive purpose, he resisted the idea that Jesus would have to suffer and die. As soldiers arrested Jesus, the apostle impulsively drew his sword and cut off the ear of the high priest's servant. Finally, gripped by fear when identified by a maid, he denied the Lord he loved.

We shouldn't regard Peter's dramatic denial of Christ as only a foreign, first-century failure. It reflects a trauma known all too well to those of us who have writhed in self-condemnation after being untrue to our Lord. And our failures, like Peter's, usually follow a gradual pattern of decline. That's why we must daily acknowledge our dependence on God and obey His Word. It's the only way to avoid the tragedy of a cold heart that gets us into hot water. —M.R.D.II

Collapse in the Christian life is seldom a blowout; it is usually a slow leak.

Wednesday

PHILIPPIANS 3:12–16

Forgetting those things which are behind and reaching forward . . . , I press toward the goal (Philippians 3:13–14).

I am a twice-a-week golfer at most, so I don't play enough to perfect my swing or to master all the shots. In every round, I make mistakes. A drive goes astray. An iron shot splashes beautifully into the creek. Or a putt breaks left when I was sure it would break right.

For this reason, I like these words from *The Tumult and the Shouting* by Grantland Rice: "Because golf expresses the flaws of the human swing—a basically simple maneuver—it causes more self-torture than any game short of Russian roulette. The quicker the average golfer can forget the shot he has dubbed or knocked off line—and concentrate on the next shot—the sooner he begins to improve and enjoy golf. Little good comes from brooding about the mistakes we've made." Rice then commented, "The next shot, in golf or in life, is the big one."

In Philippians 3, the apostle Paul gave essentially the same advice. He said that the key to forward movement in the Christian life is to set our eyes on the goal and keep looking ahead. When we look back to our past sins or shortcomings, we open the door to discouragement.

When past sin gets us down, when we find ourselves brooding about it, or when we get discouraged because of some failure, we can confess it to God, claim His forgiveness, and put it behind us for good. In the Christian life, as in golf, the next shot is the big one. —D.C.E.

We must never let defeat rob us of success.

Thursday

ROMANS 6:1–18

Shall we continue in sin that grace may abound? Certainly not! (Romans 6:1–2).

Some Christians seem to give up trying to grow in difficult areas of their lives. They have suffered so many defeats that they think they will never make any progress. They react much like a city government that stands idle while blighted areas deteriorate.

Some cities are showing remarkable success in bringing new life and radical improvement to decayed sections. They label these areas "enterprise zones," a name that carries with it the idea of potential for vast upgrading through much time and effort. By looking at the problem through new eyes, they see it as an opportunity for constructive restoration rather than ongoing deterioration. This new attitude is bringing results.

Christians need a similar outlook. We too should begin to see our own areas of perennial failure as "enterprise zones," where focused prayer and concentrated effort can produce improvement. We need not live in spiritual defeat. No sin has the power to conquer us. Christ's death on the cross broke the stranglehold of sin, and it no longer has dominion over us (Rom. 6:14).

When some sin has us in its destructive grasp, we should claim God's help, change our attitude about it, and turn our area of defeat into an "enterprise zone." —D.C.E.

Don't let yesterday's failures hamper tomorrow's efforts.

Friday

REVELATION 1:1–18

[Jesus] washed us from our sins in His own blood, and has made us kings (Revelation 1:5–6).

A picture of a gifted athlete sent to prison for using and selling illegal drugs made me sad. His friends said of him, "What a shame! Just think of the wealth and fame he could be enjoying if only he had kept himself clean!"

This man's failure to fulfill his potential pictures the whole human race. God made us in His image to obey Him, enjoy fellowship with Him, and rule over the earth for His glory. But because of our sinfulness, we don't obey Him as we should, enjoy Him as we ought, or rule over planet earth as we could. Immorality, crime, revolution, famine, international conflict, and potential nuclear holocaust continually remind us of our failure to live up to the potential the Lord built into us.

But thank God, that's not the whole story. He has provided a way to lift us individually from our moral failure and to elevate us to spiritual fulfillment. God became a member of the human family in the person of Jesus Christ, who lived a perfect life, died on the cross as our substitute, and rose from the grave. Now He forgives, accepts, and restores all who believe on Him. In fact, believers are now "kings," destined to rule with Christ (Rev. 1:5–6).

When we suffer a shattering defeat we don't have to stay down. The gospel is good news. Through faith in Jesus, God gives us new life and begins to lift us from our failure to the fulfillment of His purpose for us. —H.V.L.

Salvation makes useful saints out of useless sinners.

Saturday

**If a man is overtaken in any trespass,
you who are spiritual restore such a one (Galatians 6:1).**

A few years ago, an angry man rushed through the Rijks Museum in Amsterdam until he reached Rembrandt's famous painting "Nightwatch." Then he took out a knife and slashed it repeatedly before anyone could stop him. A short time later, a distraught, hostile man slipped into St. Peter's Cathedral in Rome with a hammer and began to smash Michelangelo's beautiful sculpture, The Pieta. Two cherished works of art were severely damaged. But what did officials do? Throw them out and forget about them? Absolutely not. Using the best experts, who worked with the utmost care and precision, they made every effort to restore the treasures.

Christians ought to have the same attitude toward believers whose testimony has been damaged by sin. When one of God's children falls into sin, our first and only thought should be to restore, not to condemn. Tenderly and compassionately we must pray and work to bring that one back to spiritual wholeness and fellowship within the body of Christ. The word *restore* in Galatians 6:1 is the same word translated *mend* in Matthew 4:21, where we read that James and John were mending their nets. It means "to make thoroughly fit." That should be the church's goal with any member overtaken in sin.

Condemning is easier than restoring. In disgust we may want to turn our backs on a sinning Christian. But the scriptural pattern is not for us to discard but to restore. —D.C.E.

**We can't expect others to see eye to eye
with us if we look down on them.**

Week 48

CRUCIFIXION

When they had come to the place called Calvary, there they crucified Him. . . . Then Jesus said, "Father, forgive them, for they do not know what they do" (Luke 23:33–34).

THEME

SALVATION

"Red never saw the bullet coming. Death was so quick that he probably never felt it. As the bullet penetrated the back of his head, Red's blood flowed out and began to blend with Wayne's. For a second the two men stood locked in an embrace of blood and death.

"Red stayed [alive] . . . just long enough to save a man's life and communicate the deepest and purest kind of love one man can have for another." Thus wrote R.C. Sproul of the March 16, 1945, rescue of point man Wayne Alderson by Red Preston during the invasion of Germany by the American Third Division.

In His death Jesus expressed a love deeper and purer than Red's. People have died for friends, relatives, and helpless strangers but rarely for enemies and evildoers. In dying for the latter, Jesus did the unexpected.

Spikes and rough-hewn T-beams hardly seemed the instruments of peace, but somehow the executioner's song became the victor's cry. As a carpenter, Jesus built with nails and wood; as a Savior, He framed a new world with the same.

One criminal understood this; the other could not comprehend how Jesus could save him by dying. God rescued Israel with His power, but crosses stood for shame and weakness. In this seeming weakness, God showed His strength—His true power to save.

On death hill outside Jerusalem, the blood of the three flowed together on the ground—if not literally, certainly symbolically. Although some reject Him, as one of the criminals did, Jesus offers to cross-link His life with ours, and that is the real point of salvation.

Sunday

MATTHEW 27:27–46

Then they crucified Him
(Matthew 27:35).

In 1968, Admiral Elmo Zumwalt, Jr., took command of the American naval forces in Vietnam. In an effort to reduce U.S. casualties, he ordered the waterways sprayed with the chemical defoliant Agent Orange. This would push back the jungle and make it harder for North Vietnamese to ambush Navy river patrol boats at pointblank range. One of those boats was commanded by 21-year-old Lt. Elmo Zumwalt III. The tragedy and irony of the story is that today he suffers from a usually fatal form of lymph cancer that both father and son believe was caused by his exposure to Agent Orange. Theirs is the heartbreaking story of a father who made a decision that unintentionally resulted in great suffering for his own son. Yet they both agree that it was the right one.

In conquering sin and death to provide salvation for us, God the Father intentionally made a decision that resulted in immeasurable agony for His only begotten Son. After deciding to save the human race through His Son, He watched Him suffer the mockery of the crowd, the lashes of the whip, the pain of the nails through His hands and feet, the inexpressible weight and humiliation of our sins, and the indescribable agony of isolation and abandonment.

Our lack of gratitude adds to God's pain. Certainly His amazing sacrifice deserves our unending thanksgiving. —M.R.D.II

The truest measure of God's love
is that He loves without measure.

Monday

ACTS 2:22–39

"Jesus of Nazareth . . . you have taken by lawless hands,
have crucified, and put to death" (Acts 2:22–23).

The question of who killed Jesus has fired controversy that has raged through the centuries. During the Middle Ages, the unruly Crusaders sometimes killed Jews on their way to free Jerusalem from the Turks. They considered them guilty of Christ's death and referred to them as "Christ-killers." Even today feelings run deep on this issue. A few years ago a Jewish professor objected to a brief reference in *Our Daily Bread* that the Jewish leaders of Jesus' day were partly to blame for the Savior's death.

According to Matthew's account, it appears that the Romans were responsible. The Roman governor Pilate delivered Jesus to death, even while declaring His innocence. And Roman soldiers led Him down the Via Dolorosa and publicly executed Him. Yet Peter, preaching several weeks later in Jerusalem, accused the Jews of crucifying Him (Acts 2:22–24).

People who receive Christ as their personal Savior do not argue about who killed Jesus. They know He died for every sinner (2 Cor. 5:15). On the cross, He paid the penalty for the sins of both Jews and Romans, as well as for ours (1 Peter 2:24). Ultimately, then, we are all responsible for His death.

Christ died for us. Our sins cost Him His life. By trusting Him, we receive forgiveness and eternal life. —D.C.E.

Jesus took our place that we might have His peace;
He took our sin that we might have His salvation.

Tuesday

COLOSSIANS 2:1–14

He made Him . . . to be sin for us, that we might become
the righteousness of God in Him (2 Corinthians 5:21).

More than four hundred years before Jesus' birth, the Greek poet
Agathon said, "Even God cannot change the past." Historically speak-
ing, he was right. What happens cannot be undone. Yet when God sent
His Son to die on the cross, He provided a way to erase our sinful past.

Here is how Donald Grey Barnhouse described what Jesus did for
us: "Just as a hole in the ocean floor would let sea water into the
volcanic fires, creating force that could blow the world apart, so the
Lord Jesus Christ by dying and rising again broke through the past
and allowed eternity to pour in, shattering, turning and overturning,
changing, and altering all things. He took the past of all believers and
cleansed it by His blood and transformed the life in such a way that the
time-rooted life gave way to life eternal."

The poet said, "I wish there were a land of beginning again." There
is. "The blood of Jesus Christ His Son cleanses us from all sin" (1 John
1:7). And the hymnwriter said, "Calvary covers it all, my past with its
sin and stain; my guilt and despair Jesus took on Him there, and
Calvary covers it all."

This is the wonder of the gospel. For those who have accepted
Christ's offer of forgiveness, He "wiped out the handwriting of requirements that was against us, . . . having nailed it to the cross" (Col.
2:14). God has completely cleansed our sin-stained past. —P.R.V.

**Salvation can change the worst sinners
into the most honored saints.**

Wednesday

For all have sinned and fall short
of the glory of God (Romans 3:23).

A preacher once asked a group of young people what they must do before obtaining forgiveness. After a few moment's thought, a young man replied, "Sin." That being the case, we are all candidates for forgiveness.

Dr. Karl Menninger related an incident about a man standing on a busy corner in the Chicago Loop. Said Menninger, "As people hurried by, he would point to one and then another and intone loudly the single word, 'Guilty!' Then, without a change of expression, he would assume a stiff stance for a few minutes and do the same thing again. One to whom he pointed turned to a companion and said, 'But how did he know?' That man could have pointed to any one of us" (*Fingertip Facts File*).

The Bible states clearly that "all have sinned." Everyone is guilty—by birth and by choice. All are therefore under condemnation of death, both physical (separation of the soul from the body) and spiritual (separation of the soul from God). The charge of "guilty" can be removed, however, by faith in the Lord Jesus. He died on the cross to pay the penalty our sin demanded; and because He was the perfect Son of God, God grants forgiveness on the basis of His atoning death.

Anyone who has not accepted Christ can do so today. His offer of free salvation still stands. Accepting Christ changes our verdict from "guilty" to "justified" (Rom. 5:1). —R.W.D.

There are none so good that they can save themselves—
and none so bad that God cannot save them.

Thursday

JOHN 12:27–36

"But for this purpose I came to this hour.
Father, glorify Your name" (John 12:27–28).

The Lord Jesus Christ was born into this world to die for our sin. In His youth and during His public ministry, the specter of the cross loomed before Him. He lived in its shadow, knowing that being about His Father's business (Luke 2:49) would lead Him eventually to drink the bitter cup of divine wrath (Luke 22:42).

Holman Hunt depicted the certainty of Christ's death in a painting titled "The Shadow of Death." It shows Jesus standing beside His workbench inside a carpenter's shop in Nazareth. He has laid down His saw and is lifting His eyes to heaven. His face is distorted, apparently with pain. He stretches, raising His arms to release the tension in His muscles. The evening sun, coming in through the open door, casts His shadow on the wall behind Him in the form of a cross. The tool rack runs parallel to the shadow of His outstretched arms. He looks as if He has been crucified. A woman, no doubt Mary, kneels on the floor, her hands positioned on a chest containing the precious gifts of the wisemen. She seems shocked by the shadow of her Son as if He were on a cross.

This painting expresses the central truth that Jesus Christ came to earth to take away "the sin of the world" (John 1:29). He could do that only through bearing our sin "in His own body on the tree" (1 Peter 2:24). We can rejoice because Jesus did not turn aside from living under the shadow of the cross. —D.C.E.

**The nail-pierced hands of Jesus
reveal the love-filled heart of God.**

Friday

Not by works of righteousness which we have done, but according to His mercy He saved us (Titus 3:5).

A headline in *The Grand Rapids Press* caught my attention: "Conversion to Hindu Faith Is Torturous." The article stated, "A West German businessman has completed his conversion to the Hindu faith by piercing himself through the cheeks with a one-quarter-inch thick, four-foot-long steel rod, and pulling a chariot for two miles by ropes attached to his back and chest by steel hooks. . . . Others walk through twenty-foot-long pits of fire, don shoes with soles made of nails, or hang in the air spread-eagle from hooks embedded in their backs."

What a contrast to the reality of Christianity. The teaching of salvation by grace, through faith, apart from human works, distinguishes Christianity from all other religions of the world. The conversion experience of a believer in the Lord Jesus Christ is not "completed" through acts of self-torture. We may have to suffer for the cause of Christ, and good works should always prove the genuineness of our faith, but neither suffering nor serving save us. Paul wrote, "For we are His workmanship, created in Christ Jesus for good works, which God prepared beforehand that we should walk in them" (Eph. 2:10). Self-inflicted torture is completely foreign to everything the Bible teaches about salvation.

We are not saved on the basis of what we can endure; rather, our hope is in what Christ has already endured for us on the cross. The Christian way is not conversion by torture—it's salvation by grace.

—R.W.D.

**We are saved by God's mercy, not by our merit—
by Christ's dying, not by our doing.**

Saturday

1 TIMOTHY 1:12–17

This is a faithful saying . . . that Christ Jesus
came into the world to save sinners (1 Timothy 1:15).

Thomas Bileny, an Englishman who died a martyr's death in 1531, described his salvation experience: "My soul was sick and I longed for peace, but nowhere could I find it. . . . But at last I heard of Jesus Christ. It was then, when first the New Testament was set forth by Erasmus, that the light came. I bought the book, being drawn by the Latin rather than by the Word of God, for at that time I knew not what 'the Word of God' meant. On my first reading I chanced upon these words, 'This is a faithful saying, and worthy of all acceptance, that Christ Jesus came into the world to save sinners, of whom I am chief.' This one sentence through God's inward working did so light up my poor bruised spirit that the very bones within me leaped for joy and gladness. It was as if, after a long dark night, day had suddenly broke."

When people recognize the awful reality of their sin before a holy God, they may be overwhelmed by a sense of hopelessness and despair. They cannot escape the fact that they are sinners, and they know they cannot save themselves. But the hope Thomas Bileny found is available to all. Jesus died for sinners, and He can replace hopelessness and despair with confidence and unbounded joy.

Pride makes it difficult to acknowledge the wickedness in our hearts. But admitting our sin is the first step to salvation. Then we must place our trust in Christ and accept His wonderful gift. —D.C.E.

We are dead *in* sin,
but Jesus can make us dead *to* sin.

Week 49

RESURRECTION

[The women] found the stone rolled away from the tomb. Then they went in and did not find the body of the Lord Jesus. . . . Two men stood by them in shining garments. . . . They said to them, . . . "He is not here, but is risen!" (Luke 24:2–6).

THEME

VICTORY OVER SIN

John Sobieski, the seventeenth-century king of Poland, defeated the invading Turks near Vienna in 1683. He described his victory by rewording Caesar: "I came, I saw, God conquered."

The resurrection shows God doing what human beings could never do. Like Caesar, many declare, "I conquered," thereby drawing their own winner's circle. But when it comes to raising the dead, human beings finish last.

When God ripped the death mask from Jesus' face, He not only revealed His triumphant Son, He also exposed and deposed Satan, sin, and death. In conquering death, He assured our future glory; in mastering Satan and sin, He secured the possibility of victorious living.

Knowing that humanity's death warrant would stand until time stopped, Paul sought here-and-now resurrection power (Philippians 3:10). He wanted to live God's good life despite sin's handicap. Paul did not expect perfection; but he believed that if God knew all about dying, surely He must know all about living. Real life had to be the life Jesus lived on earth, and the Holy Spirit could create that again in human beings (Romans 8:11).

We have won wars, lined the streets to watch victory parades, and celebrated our supposed invincibleness. Yet singing the winner's song does not fill the emptiness inside. Sometimes we turn from the heroes of the hour and see the true Conqueror making His way through the crowd, and we fall at His feet.

Sunday

**Now thanks be to God who always leads us
in triumph in Christ (2 Corinthians 2:14).**

As British writer Guy King stood on a railroad station platform waiting for a train from London, another train pulled into the station from the opposite direction. Members of a soccer team returning from a game in another city got off. News had not yet reached home as to the outcome of the game, so those awaiting the team didn't know if they had won or lost. A small boy wiggled his way through the crowd and asked one of the players the score. As soon as he heard it, he ran excitedly up and down the platform shouting, "We won! We won!" That youngster was brimming with joy because he identified himself with the players. In one sense, their victory was his victory.

We too can participate in a great celebration because Jesus won the victory over sin nearly two thousand years ago. He paid sin's penalty by dying on the cross, and He broke its power by rising from the dead. We share in His victory through faith because "as He is, so are we in this world" (1 John 4:17). He is the conquering Savior before whom no foe can stand. We can thank God "who always leads us in triumph in Christ" (2 Cor. 2:14).

Victory, not defeat, should be the norm in the Christian life. God sees every believer as being in Christ, whom He raised from the dead and seated "at His right hand . . . , far above all principality and power" (Eph. 1:20–21). Because He is the Victor and we are "in Him," we too can be victorious over sin. —P.R.V.

**We can be "more than conquerors" when we
yield ourselves to the all-conquering Christ.**

Monday

Peter therefore went out, ánd the other disciple. . . .
So they both ran together (John 20:3–4).

When the dark day of Jesus' crucifixion drew to a close, it seemed that the most wonderful of all lives had come to an end. For a few brief years, Christ had astounded the crowds and His followers with the wisdom of His teaching and the wonder of His miracles. But Jesus chose not to save Himself from the cross, and now His life was over. It seemed hopeless to expect more of Him now.

But hope returned that first resurrection morning. Shortly after dawn, Mary Magdalene told Peter and John that she and her friends had found the tomb empty. Artist Eugene Burnand painted Peter and John running to the tomb. In Burnand's painting the men's faces show contending emotions—anguish and relief, sorrow and surprise, despair and wonder—as they race toward the tomb. Their gaze is eagerly fixed forward, and their bending forms turn our attention to the sepulcher—an empty sepulcher—and to a living Savior.

Christ still lives. And He still works the wonders of salvation in the lives of His followers. But many of us go from day to day as if He were still in the grave. How much better to be filled with expectation, looking beyond the empty tomb to the One who is in heaven to fill our lives with the power of His resurrection. —D.C.E.

The Victim of Calvary became the Victor of Easter.

Tuesday

ROMANS 6:1–13

As Christ was raised up from the dead . . . ,
even so we also should walk in newness of life (Romans 6:4).

The day after Easter, the newspaper headline read: "Entire World Celebrates the Risen Christ." On the same page under smaller headings ran stories about war and death, racial clashes, and an ultimatum issued to the United States by a hostile nation. As I read the discouraging news, I thought, how contradictory. The headline declares that the entire world celebrates the risen Christ, but the balance of the page tells of people disregarding the blessing and grace Christ provided by His resurrection. Apparently the millions of people around the world who flock to churches on Easter don't all live as if they believe in the historical resurrection nor recognize its true spiritual significance.

Even Christians can err in this way. Sometimes we simply go through the motions of expressing our faith without acknowledging our identification with Christ. In Romans 6, Paul said that we have been crucified with Christ and have died to sin. But we have also been raised with Christ so we can "walk in newness of life." That's why the apostle said, "If then you were raised with Christ, . . . Set your mind on things above, not on things on the earth" (Col. 3:1–2).

Having been crucified with Christ, we are now privileged to live for Him. As we do, we show our gratitude for being "risen with Christ."
—R.W.D.

The power that opened Christ's tomb
opens the door to the fullness of life.

Wednesday

PSALM 138

The Lord will perfect that
which concerns me (Psalm 138:8).

Most of us will admit that we have personality flaws and character weaknesses. We see undesirable tendencies in ourselves such as selfishness, irritability, impatience, cruelty, vindictiveness, hot-headedness. They are with us because of our sinful condition. Yet many Christians testify that their defects and weaknesses have become a blessing, causing them to rely more heavily on Jesus. By acknowledging their weakness, these believers have experienced God's grace and strength.

We see this link between imperfection and improvement all around us in nature. For instance, scientists tell us that few things develop more orderly and predictably than crystals. Each kind of mineral and gem has its own special shape or appearance. In addition, every one is made up of a great number of atoms stacked in perfect alignment. Occasionally one of these basic particles gets out of line, but that is an essential step in the development of the crystal. Most gems owe their brilliant colors to these flaws.

We need not worry about faults or shortcomings in our lives, and we should not let them get us down. Instead, we should admit their presence, commit them to the Lord in prayer, and trust Him to give us victory. The psalmist said, "The Lord will perfect that which concerns me." —M.R.D.II

God's resources are greater than our need.

Thursday

1 CORINTHIANS 6:1–11

[Jesus] bore our sins . . . that we, having died to sins, might live for righteousness (1 Peter 2:24).

Counseling, mood-altering drugs, psychosurgery, and other forms of therapy are often needed to help and cure people with emotional disorders. But these treatments can't make them good. Charles Colson tells of a frustrated prison psychiatrist who exclaimed, "I can cure a person's madness, but not his badness." To do that calls for getting to the heart of the problem—sin.

The only way to make bad people good is to expose them to the gospel. Even Charles Darwin, the man who contributed so much to evolutionistic thinking, admitted this. He wrote to a minister: "Your services have done more for our village in a few months than all our efforts for many years. We have never been able to reclaim a single drunkard, but through your services I do not know that there is a drunkard left in the village!"

Later Darwin visited the island of Tierra del Fuego at the southern tip of South America. What he found among the people was horrifying—savagery and bestiality almost beyond description. But when he returned there after a missionary had worked among the people, he was amazed at the change in them. He acknowledged that the gospel does transform lives. In fact, he was so moved by what he saw that he contributed money to the mission until his death.

First Peter 2 reminds us that Christ's sacrifice on the cross not only paid sin's penalty but also broke its power. The apostle Paul, listing some terrible sins, wrote to the Christians in Corinth, "Such were some of you. But you were washed" (vv. 9–11). Praise God. Jesus does make bad people good. —H.V.L.

God formed us; sin deformed us;
Christ transforms us.

Friday

"Get behind Me, Satan!"
(Matthew 16:23).

When Peter objected to Jesus' statement about going to Jerusalem to die, he unwittingly spoke for the devil. A song portrays Satan as gleeful when he saw Christ on the cross, but I believe the devil was dismayed when he realized that Jesus was paying the price for mankind's sins and that His sacrifice would break forever the power of death.

From the time John the Baptist declared Christ to be "the Lamb of God, who takes away the sin of the world" (John 1:29), Satan tried to keep our Lord from going to the cross. In the wilderness temptation he suggested that Jesus take the kingdoms of the world without the ordeal of Calvary. He incited the Jewish leaders to hate Christ, hoping they might kill Him by stoning. When these attempts failed, he switched tactics. He induced Peter to speak against God's plan, and he "entered" Judas (John 13:27). He prompted Peter's denials of Jesus, the cowardice of the apostles, the brutality of the soldiers, and the heartlessness of the mob. Through all of this he hoped to convince Jesus that mankind wasn't worth dying for.

Satan lost that battle, but he continues to fight. He does all he can to hinder the spread of the gospel. He even uses religions that promote salvation by works and ritual. Despite his efforts, thousands are being saved through faith in Jesus' death, burial, and resurrection. They can joyfully sing, "Hallelujah for the Cross," because the cross and the empty tomb spelled Satan's ultimate defeat. —H.V.L.

Calvary stands for Satan's fall.

Saturday

REVELATION 6:12–17

Therefore, brethren, we are debtors—not to
the flesh, to live according to the flesh (Romans 8:12).

Following the terrible Mexico City earthquake of 1985, live satellite coverage carried the news of Mexico's anguish to a watching world. I sat in front of our television set stunned by the extent of the damage. Mountains of broken concrete filled the screen. Rescue workers dug frantically. Fires raged. Smoke and dust filled the air. Then suddenly in the lower left-hand corner of the screen appeared the words "Courtesy: SIN." The letters S-I-N actually stood for Spanish International Network, but for a moment it meant something different to me. It reminded me that in some way all trouble, pain, and suffering can be traced back to the problem of sin. That's not to say that God judged Mexico City with an earthquake. But if sin directly or indirectly causes such tragedy, or even the more disastrous quake described by John in Revelation 6:12, it deserves to be treated with contempt, not courtesy.

Since all human anguish can be traced back to the entrance of sin into this world, how can we take it so lightly? Why do we give it our attention? Why do we comply with an evil that causes a loving God to react with the judgment described in Revelation 6? We don't owe sin anything. Jesus paid sin's debt and broke its power when He died on the cross and rose from the grave. We can avoid the "courtesy" sin offers by living in the power of the resurrection. The wages of sin is death (Rom. 6:23), and that's a courtesy we don't need. —M.R.D.II

God will give us the victory
if we will go to the fight.

Week 50

ASCENSION

And He said to them, "Go into all the world and preach the gospel to every creature. . . ." After the Lord had spoken to them, He was received up into heaven, and sat down at the right hand of God (Mark 16:15, 19).

THEME

MISSIONS

"Is it true Dr. Grenfell that you are a missionary?" a woman asked Wilfred Grenfell, a medical missionary to Labrador. Grenfell replied, "Is it true, madam, that you are not?" With his question, Grenfell made sure the woman understood God's top assignment.

With "mission impossible" completed, Jesus left this earth, but not before giving an assignment to His agents. He had a job for them to do, but it was no secret mission. He spoke publicly about the task and never called His people private agents.

He told them to clearly report what they had seen and heard to everyone everywhere. This should have been no surprise to His Jewish operatives; God told Israel in the Old Testament to tell the surrounding nations of His mighty acts.

Judas, the double agent, defected early, but over five-hundred agency personnel got Christ's memo about a new mission. Peter, one of His top men, openly carried out his duties. Not fearing political intrigue, he even briefed a soldier named Cornelius about the mission (Acts 10:38–43).

Some have distorted the Director's words with secret codes and clandestine acts, but those who read the original document have no trouble understanding the mission. The only problem is the short supply of agents.

Sunday

ACTS 1:1–9

He said to them, "Go into all the world
and preach the gospel to every creature" (Mark 16:15).

While speaking to the Radio Bible Class staff at a chapel service, John De Vries of Bibles For India told what might have happened when Jesus entered heaven immediately following His ascension.

The angels, rejoicing that Christ's mission on earth had been completed, gathered to welcome Him home. They were eager to know who would have the privilege of proclaiming to the world the good news that Christ had been born, had lived, had died, and had risen from the dead to provide salvation from sin. In fact, the angels were hoping they themselves would be given the honor. So they were greatly disappointed and amazed when Jesus looked down to earth and pointed to the tiny group of followers He had just left behind. "Those are the ones I want to be My witnesses," Jesus announced. "I have given to them the commission to go into all the world and preach the gospel. They have experienced the thrill and reality of redemption from sin; they are to be My messengers!"

The torch of the gospel, handed to those early followers of Christ, has been passed down through the generations until today it is in our hands. The responsibility of proclaiming that Christ Jesus came into the world to save sinners is ours to fulfill.

Angels might long for the privilege of telling the world about Christ, but they have not experienced the joy of forgiveness and the hope of glory. That's why the task has been entrusted to us. —R.W.D.

Our only real excuse for living in this world
is to be witnesses for Jesus Christ. —Sweeting

Monday

MARK 5:1–20

"Go home to your friends, and tell them
what great things the Lord has done for you" (Mark 5:19).

Many Christians, enthusiastic about foreign missions, answer the call to service. By going to foreign countries, praying faithfully, or giving financial support they help reach the lost in faraway lands. Yet some who have a great burden for people in spiritual darkness across the sea seem oblivious to the same need in their neighbors across the street.

A young woman, excited about her salvation, wanted to share the gospel with others, so she asked her pastor where she might go to serve most effectively. He told her to come back the next day and he would have an answer ready for her. When she returned to his office at the specified time, the pastor handed her a folded slip of paper. "I'm suggesting someone who needs you right now more than anyone else in all the world," he said. The young woman quickly left the pastor's study, eager to read where her mission field might be. When she opened the note, she saw that the pastor had written two words: "Your father." She had been so enthusiastic about reaching the lost in distant lands that she had neglected someone close to home. Convicted of her negligence, she acted on the pastor's advice. She visited her dad regularly, ministered to his physical needs, showered her love upon him, and witnessed to him.

Serving the Lord on some remote mission field is challenging, and the tremendous sacrifices and hardships are praiseworthy. But, like charity, missions must always begin at home. —R.W.D.

There is no "home" or "foreign"
in God's missionary vocabulary.

Tuesday

1 CORINTHIANS 2:12–16

These things we also speak, . . . in words which . . . the Holy Spirit teaches (1 Corinthians 2:13).

Aphasia is a loss of the ability to speak, a condition that results when the message from the brain cannot get to the tongue because of an injury or illness.

A similar spiritual malady affects many Christians. They know Jesus Christ, but they never speak of Him. They are familiar with God's plan of salvation, but they never tell it to others. They do not demonstrate the impelling force of the early Christians who said, "For we cannot but speak the things which we have seen and heard" (Acts 4:20). This faulty connection between knowledge and testimony must be corrected. Often fear causes the breakdown, or sometimes sin blocks our freedom to speak about Christ. Only as believers rely on the power of the Holy Spirit and forsake their sin can they consistently share Christ with others.

Just before His ascension, the risen Christ assured His disciples of power to transmit His message to the world (Acts 1:8). That power is the indwelling presence of His Holy Spirit. Every believer has this source. But if we quench or grieve the Holy Spirit, our witness in words will be either ineffective or nonexistent.

We must keep the message of the gospel flowing to those around us who need to hear it. We can't let spiritual aphasia silence our witness.

—P.R.V.

**If we have God's Word in our minds,
He can put the right words in our mouths.**

Wednesday

**For the love of Christ constrains us
(2 Corinthians 5:14).**

When Hudson Taylor directed the China Inland Mission, he often interviewed candidates for the mission field. On one occasion, he met with a group of applicants to determine their motives for service. "And why do you wish to go as a foreign missionary?" he asked one. "I want to go because Christ has commanded us to go into all the world and preach the gospel to every creature," the candidate replied. Another said, "I want to go because millions are perishing without Christ." Others gave different answers. Then Hudson Taylor said, "All of these motives, however good, will fail you in times of testings, trials, tribulations, and possible death. There is but one motive that will sustain you in trial and testing; namely, the love of Christ."

A missionary in Africa, when asked if he really liked what he was doing, responded, "Do I like this work? No. My wife and I do not like dirt. We have reasonably refined sensibilities. We do not like crawling into vile huts through goat refuse. . . . But is a man to do nothing for Christ he does not like? God pity him, if not. Liking or disliking has nothing to do with it. We have orders to 'Go,' and we go. Love constrains us."

We may not be serving the Lord under dangerous or unpleasant conditions, but the work He has called us to do has its own unique difficulties. In times of trials and testing, only the love of Christ can strengthen us to go on. —R.W.D.

**Serving Christ under law is a duty;
under love it's a delight.**

Thursday

**"Go out into the highways and hedges,
and compel them to come in" (Luke 14:23).**

"Many churches today remind me of a laboring crew trying to gather a harvest while they sit in the toolshed. They go to the toolshed every Sunday and they study bigger and better methods of agriculture, sharpen their hoes, grease their tractors, and then get up and go home. Then they come back that night, study bigger and better methods of agriculture, sharpen their hoes, grease their tractors, and get up and go home. They do this week in and week out, year in and year out, and nobody ever goes out into the fields to gather in the harvest" (Paul W. Powell, *The Complete Disciple*).

The final command of Christ to His disciples was to tell everyone about His saving power. Just before He ascended to heaven, He said to His followers, "Go into all the world and preach the gospel to every creature" (Mark 16:15). Today, that great commission is still the responsibility of believers. But many church members, even though they have much Bible knowledge and have been Christians for years, never enter the harvest field.

I must confess my own guilt in this regard. I promote missions. I support missionary endeavors regularly. Some of my best friends are missionaries. But I haven't been out in the realm of the lost as I should be. It's time for all of us to confess our shortcomings and to get into the fields. —D.C.E.

**There is only one thing we can't do for missions—
get rid of our responsibility.**

Friday

"You shall be witnesses to Me in Jerusalem . . .
and to the end of the earth" (Acts 1:8).

Writing in *Outreach,* a publication of the Oriental Missionary Society, Richard D. Wood raised a thought-provoking question about our motives in supporting missions. He said tourists often came back from Haiti and said, "God broke my heart for missions in Haiti." But he wondered whether these people were moved more by the physical poverty of the Haitians than by their spiritual poverty. Was the lack of physical bread uppermost in the tourists' minds rather than the Haitians' need for the Bread of Life—the Word and Son of God? Mr. Wood recognized that God often has to wake us up, and showing us people's extreme physical need may be His way of doing so. But he wondered if those same people, if strolling through an average middle- or upper-class suburb in America, would cry, "God broke my heart in the suburbs." Would the sight of well-manicured lawns, expensive houses, and well-dressed people evoke that kind of response? Wood then pointed out that the gospel is for the suburbanite as well as the slumdweller. The character of God and the spiritual need of humanity—not our feelings and thoughts—provide the right motive for missions.

Everyone has sinned; and all, regardless of poverty or affluence, need the gospel. So each of us must reach out with the message of God's redeeming grace to men and women everywhere—in the jungles, but also in the suburbs. —R.W.D.

**Everyone outside of Christ is a mission field;
everyone in Christ should be a missionary.**

Saturday

MATTHEW 9:32–38

But when He saw the multitudes, He was moved with compassion for them (Matthew 9:36).

We who live in countries where the gospel is freely preached find it difficult to imagine the tremendous spiritual need in areas where people have never heard the gospel. When we think of the millions who do not know Christ, we need to be filled with compassion and moved to action, as our Savior was in Matthew 9.

While on furlough from missionary service in Africa, Robert Moffat (1795-1883) spoke in England about his work. A young medical student in the audience had hoped to serve on the mission field in China, but that land was closed. He listened as Moffat described a frequent sight in Africa. "There is a vast plain to the north, where I have sometimes seen, in the morning sun, the smoke of a thousand villages where no missionary has ever been."

"The smoke of a thousand villages." Those words painted a vivid picture and gripped the heart of the young student. This was the challenge he was looking for in his desire to reach the unreached. Filled with a new vision, the young man went to Moffat and asked, "Would I do for Africa?" That student was David Livingstone.

Christ said, "Lift up your eyes and look at the fields, for they are already white for harvest" (John 4:35). He still needs workers today. With Moffat and Livingstone, we can envision "the smoke of a thousand villages." Then we must ask God to show us what we can do to share the gospel with those who have never heard. —R.W.D.

We can reach out to a world in need with the Word it needs!

Week 51

PENTECOST

When the Day of Pentecost had fully come, they were all with one accord in one place. And suddenly there came a sound from heaven, as of a rushing mighty wind. . . . And they were all filled with the Holy Spirit (Acts 2:1–2, 4).

THEME

WORK OF THE HOLY SPIRIT

In his diary Jim Elliot wrote, "Am I ignitible? . . . Saturate me with the oil of the Spirit that I may be a flame."

The disciples went through emotional burnout. The trial, the crucifixion, and the burial nearly snuffed out their flame. The resurrection and forty days with Jesus served as a bellows, but the fire still flickered. Then the Holy Spirit came like a mighty wind, and they became human infernos.

The Holy Spirit participated in creation, empowered Old Testament people, revealed God's Word to the prophets, and played an important role in Jesus' birth; but He never came for a permanent stay until Pentecost. Since then He has made His home in every believer and makes God's firepower available to us all.

The greatest evidence of His work may seem to many the most mundane: He grows spiritual fruit. That does not seem as exciting as starting spiritual fires. But His fruit is characteristic of Christ's life, and so He works at reproducing the best life ever lived in each believer. Like the oil of the olive used in lamps, the juice of this fruit lights the Christian life.

Unlike Jim Elliot, most of us would prefer to hear the Holy Spirit yell, "Lights out!" so we could get some rest. Instead, as a battle commander, He cries, "Fire!"

Sunday

LUKE 24:44–49

**"Behold, I send the Promise
of My Father upon you" (Luke 24:49).**

One night the meeting place of a small and inactive group of Christians caught on fire. The blaze lit up the sky and attracted a crowd of people from far and near. A member of the church saw the town skeptic standing among the spectators and said, "I never saw *you* come near this church before." "No," replied the man, "but then I never saw this church on fire before either."

The church faces a challenge today, but the power to meet it is not found in fine buildings, modern equipment, large sums of money, or efficient programs. Only the Holy Spirit can enable believers to implement the Savior's command, but they must yield to His control. Otherwise the church will be powerless and will make little impact on the world.

The coming of the Holy Spirit on the Day of Pentecost marked the formation of the church. With its inception, the risen Christ also provided the power needed to propagate the gospel. Believers who formed the early church were to be witnesses of Christ in Jerusalem, Judea, Samaria, and to the end of the earth. The indwelling Spirit became the dynamic force to carry out the task of going into all the world.

Pentecost doesn't need to be repeated, because the indwelling Holy Spirit has never left. He is the Spirit of power, and He works through Christians who are yielded to Him. Luke records that the apostles witnessed "with great power" (Acts 4:33). This power is still present and available today. —P.R.V.

**The power that compels
comes from the Spirit that indwells.**

Monday

**Walk in the Spirit, and you shall not
fulfill the lust of the flesh (Galatians 5:16).**

Some beautiful oak trees stand behind our home. Every fall I notice that some of them retain their crisp dried leaves long after the basswood, maples, elms, and walnuts become bare. Even the strong winds of winter and the early spring rains do not completely strip their boughs. But as springtime progresses, the scene changes. Small buds appear at the tips of the twigs. Soon the dried remnants of the preceding season drop away because of the surging forces of new life from within.

The Holy Spirit graciously works like that in Christians. Old habits cling to our lives with tenacity. Even trial and adversity do not remove all the lifeless leftovers of our fallen human nature. But Christ continually seeks expression from within us. As we confess our sin, pray, meditate on the Word of God, obey, and fellowship with our blessed Lord, the dead works of the flesh gradually drop away.

When all our efforts to turn over a new leaf or pluck off the old ones meet defeat, we can take a lesson from the mighty oak. Then we can thank God for the wonder-working power of the Holy Spirit within us. As we yield to His gentle urgings to be kind, loving, honest, and faithful, the Holy Spirit will take care of those "old leaves." —D.J.D.

**If Christ is the center of our lives,
the circumference will take care of itself.**

Tuesday

JOHN 14:12–31

"I will pray the Father, and He will
give you another Helper" (John 14:16).

A theology student writing a term paper about confession meant to type, "When we confess our sins, He takes away our guilt." But the young man couldn't type too well, and when he came to the word *guilt*, he typed *quilt* by mistake. When the professor returned his paper, the student grinned as he read the marginal note: "Never fear, little one, you'll never freeze, because God gave us a Comforter."

Using his sense of humor, the professor had conveyed a marvelous truth. Jesus said that the Father would send the Comforter to abide with us forever. Pentecost fulfilled that promise (Acts 2:1-4). And ever since that historic day, the Holy Spirit has been faithfully carrying on His ministry in the lives of believers.

His comforting activities include: guiding us into truth (John 16:13), assuring us we are God's children (Rom. 8:16), helping us pray (Rom. 8:26), transforming us into Christ's image (2 Cor. 3:18), and strengthening us (Eph. 3:16).

Our response should be to learn all we can about Christ and by the Spirit put into action what we know. The Holy Spirit's purpose is always to glorify Christ, never to call attention to Himself.

Thank you, Father, for our Comforter. Help us not to grieve or quench Him. We face this day with confidence because of His blessed ministry in our lives.—D.J.D.

The Christian's heart is the Holy Spirit's home.

Wednesday

ISAIAH 44:1–5

"He who believes in Me, as the Scripture has said,
out of his heart will flow rivers of living water" (John 7:38).

A healthy tree consists of up to eighty percent moisture. It draws large quantities of water through its root system or absorbs it from dew and rain. In his book *As a Tree Grows,* W. Phillip Keller says, "the tree does not hoard this moisture for itself. The vast network of running roots beneath the soil often exceeds the outspread canopy of trunk, branches, and leaves spread to the sky. And vast quantities of water are lifted through the framework of the tree to be transpired into the surrounding air. This moisture, along with the discharge of oxygen, is what gives the forest atmosphere such a fresh fragrance."

Christians use the water of life in much the same way. In John 7:38, Jesus said that rivers of living water will flow from the heart of the one who believes in Him. He was referring to the ministry of the Holy Spirit in and through us. The Spirit, who we receive when we trust the Lord Jesus as our Savior, empowers and refreshes us, which enables us to help others. Our part is to read and study God's Word, to receive cleansing and renewal through confession, and to obey the Lord. Then, as we depend on the Holy Spirit, "living water" flows through us and provides refreshment and goodness to people around us. —D.C.E.

Only the Living Water can quench
the driving thirst of the soul.

Thursday

For we are His workmanship, created in
Christ Jesus for good works (Ephesians 2:10).

Several centuries ago, a Japanese emperor commissioned an artist to paint a bird. A number of months passed, then several years, and still the artist did not deliver the painting. Finally the emperor became so exasperated that he went to the artist's home to demand an explanation. Instead of making excuses, the artist placed a blank canvas on the easel. In less than an hour, he completed a painting that was to become a masterpiece. When the emperor asked the reason for the delay, the artist showed him armloads of drawings of feathers, wings, heads, and feet. Then he explained that he couldn't complete the painting until he had done exhaustive research and study.

In a sense, Christians are similar to that piece of art. We are "sealed with the Holy Spirit of promise" (Eph. 1:13), and predestined by God "to be conformed to the image of His Son" (Rom. 8:29). But the process takes time. The "artist" is the Holy Spirit—sent by the Lord Jesus at Pentecost to indwell believers. Slowly but surely He leads us to spiritual growth and maturity. Our transformation requires years of patience and will not be finished until we enter the presence of our King.

The day is coming when all Christians will be like Christ. But now we are growing and preparing. As we follow the Spirit's guidance through one experience after another, we become more and more like the masterpiece we will be someday in Glory. —D.C.E.

The work Christ accomplished for us on the cross,
His Spirit can now accomplish in us on earth.

Friday

**But the natural man does not receive
the things of the Spirit of God (1 Corinthians 2:14).**

A friend who is not a Christian told me, "I've read the Bible, but I don't understand it." His comment is not unusual. People of the world—even the highly educated and successful—cannot comprehend the truths of God's Word.

William Pitt, one of the finest statesmen in British history, became prime minister of England at age 24. William Wilberforce, a Christian, persuaded Pitt to attend a meeting in which a member of the House of Lords powerfully proclaimed the gospel. After the meeting, Wilberforce asked Pitt what he thought of the message. Pitt replied, "To tell you the truth, Wilberforce, I gave that man my most careful attention from start to finish, but I was totally unable to understand what he was talking about."

Education, culture, or great knowledge in matters of government and business are of no help in understanding God's Word. Only when people place their faith in Christ and become children of God does the spiritual darkness lift from their hearts and minds. The miracle of the new birth opens blinded eyes to the teachings of the Bible. At the moment of regeneration, the Holy Spirit comes to dwell in the believer, giving life and light. —P.R.V.

**When we open our hearts to the Savior,
God opens our minds to His Word.**

Saturday

COLOSSIANS 1:9–14

**"I will strengthen you, yes, I will
help you, I will uphold you" (Isaiah 41:10).**

When faced with adversity and temptation, wise Christians acknowledge two important facts: their own weakness and God's power to keep them from falling. If we dwell on our inadequacy, we cannot cope with the future. But if we draw our strength from a source other than ourselves, we'll be able to resist Satan's opposition and the world's pressure. That's why we need both the outer and inner support that comes only from God.

On my desk is a closed penknife, rounded and smooth on both ends. When I try to stand it on end, it topples over. If I were to explain to you how difficult it is to get the knife to stand, you probably would say, "No, it's impossible! You can't make that knife stand on end. You might as well give up and not waste your time." "But look, the penknife is standing!" I reply. "Sure," you say, "but you are holding it."

The standing penknife illustrates God's outer support. He strengthens us through the help of others. But we also need inner strength—the upholding power of the Holy Spirit.

Recently I watched a flour mill in operation. In the corner of the room lay empty sacks. If I had tried to make one stand by itself, it would have crumpled to the floor. But when the miller filled it with flour, it stood solid and unmoving, held up by the weight of the flour it contained. Likewise, the believer, filled with the indwelling Spirit, is able to stand.

Although we are weak, we are "kept by the power of God"—both from without and from within (1 Peter 1:5). —P.R.V.

God's resources equal our requirements.

Week 52

SECOND COMING

He who testifies to these things says, "Surely I am coming quickly."
Amen. Even so, come, Lord Jesus! (Revelation 22:20).

THEME

HOPE

On December 17, 1927, a submarine sank off Provincetown, Massachusetts, and forty crewmen died. In the failed rescue attempt, one diver heard a trapped sailor tap out a pathetic question in Morse code: "Is there any hope?"

The disciples must have been asking the same question at their last meal with Jesus. The One they loved the most was going away to a place where they could not immediately follow.

Although packing His bags to leave, He promised to return for them. When they least expected it, He would walk up the front path, climb the porch steps, and knock boldly on the door. Jesus told His disciples to feed on that hope because He was the hope for years to come.

This hope became a major theme of the New Testament. In essence, Paul pictured Christians skydiving in reverse, free falling upward through the clouds, reaching out their hands to His, and floating into eternity (1 Thessalonians 4:17). Peter proclaimed a sure hope because of Christ's resurrection (1 Peter 1:3) and challenged everyone to be ready to give a reason for that hope (3:15).

Until Jesus returns we have a message for those sleepwalking on trails that lead to a hopeless end. We on the other road—the one of endless hope—must awaken them with our shouts of joy, "He is the Christ. He is coming again. *He* is our hope!"

Sunday

1 THESSALONIANS 4:16–5:11

"Behold, I come quickly!
Hold fast what you have" (Revelation 3:11).

During the American Civil War, General William T. Sherman drove his troops on his decisive march to the sea. In a fort on Kennesaw Mountain, he left behind a small contingent of men to guard the rations. General John Bell Hood of the Confederate Army attacked the fort, and a fierce battle followed. One-third of Sherman's men were killed or wounded and J. M. Corse, the general in command, was severely injured. Just as he was about to hoist the white flag and surrender, a message came through the signal corps set up on a chain of mountains. General Sherman was within fifteen miles of the fort and sent the message: "Hold fast. We are coming." Those few words so encouraged the defenders that they held on and kept the fort from falling into the hands of their attackers.

Our heavenly Commander has also sent us the assurance that He is coming. The Lord Jesus said, "I go to prepare a place for you. And if I go and prepare a place for you, I will come again and receive you to Myself; that where I am, there you may be also" (John 14:2–3). The fact that our Savior is coming again gives us hope. It makes us want to stand our ground. It encourages us to continue fighting the good fight of faith. It assures us of victory. Fierce as the battle may rage and difficult as the conflict may be as we serve Him, we dare not give up. Christ is coming again—perhaps today. —R.W.D.

**When faithfulness is most difficult,
it is most rewarding.**

Monday

**"I have spoken it, I will also bring it to pass;
I have purposed it, I will also do it" (Isaiah 46:11).**

In 1854 the Russian poet and diplomat Fyodor Tiutchev described the frightening world conditions as he saw them then. In a letter to his wife he wrote, "What is bewildering is the conviction—and it is becoming more and more general—that in all the perils that confront us, the direction of affairs is given over to a way of thinking that has no longer any understanding of itself. It is like being in a carriage, descending an increasingly precipitous slope, and suddenly realizing that there is no coachman in the box."

The world does seem to be traveling in a runaway vehicle, hurtling wildly through the dark night toward terrible destruction. The racial tension in South Africa, the ongoing religious conflict in Northern Ireland, and continued death and fighting in the Mid-East could cause us to feel as if the world is reeling wildly out of control. But the Christian views this frightening scene differently. We believe that even though Satan is called the ruler of this age, God has a plan for this world and is in ultimate control. We have confidence in Isaiah's promise that what God has spoken will come to pass. We know that God "works all things according to the counsel of His will" (Eph. 1:11). God's hand "is stretched out over all the nations," wrote Isaiah, and "who will turn it back?" (Isa. 14:26–27).

In the midst of turmoil we have hope. God rules. —D.C.E.

**Earth changes, but thy soul and God stand sure.
—Browning**

Tuesday

HEBREWS 2:1–13

We do not yet see all things put under [man].
But we see Jesus (Hebrews 2:8–9).

The disasters, heartbreaks, and injustices all around us prove the truth of Hebrews 2:8. We live in an imperfect world in which many things are beyond our control. A thirty-year-old farmer, unable to make his mortgage payments, wishes something could be done to prevent drought. A young mother of three children, widowed by the crash of a commercial airplane, can't understand why modern technology can't prevent such tragedies. A well-educated, successful professional man, convinced that we are headed for a nuclear holocaust, talks about suicide.

It is obvious that we humans are not properly exercising dominion over the earth, as we were created to do. But knowing this does not fill Christians with dismay and hopelessness. We look up and "see" Jesus at God's right hand. We know that He possesses "all authority" in heaven and on earth because of what He did almost 2,000 years ago. He lived here as a man, overcame sin, paid the price for our transgressions on the cross, and broke death's power. He is in ultimate control of everything—even now. Someday He will return to earth and make everything right. Now, however, we see Him through the eye of faith, and we experience inner joy and peace no matter what happens.

—H.V.L.

When we can't see out, we can still look up.

Wednesday

You turned to God from idols . . . to wait for
His Son from heaven (1 Thessalonians 1:9–10).

Eugene Lang, a self-made millionaire, greatly changed the lives of fifty-nine students in East Harlem. Asked to speak to the sixth-grade class at a school with a high drop-out rate, he wondered what he could say to inspire these students to stay in school. He wondered how he could get them to even look at him. Scrapping his notes, he decided to speak to them from his heart. "Stay in school," he admonished, "and I'll help pay college tuition for every one of you." For the first time, those children had hope. Said one student, "I had something to look forward to, something waiting for me. It was a golden feeling." Nearly ninety percent of that class went on to graduate from high school.

People without hope are people without a future. But when hope is restored, so is life. Nowhere is this more true than with those who come to know Christ. He gives a sure basis for hope. He has promised to return to earth to receive His own (1 Thess. 1:10). Until then, we have help through the power of the Holy Spirit (1 Thess. 1:5). The believer anticipates a new kind of life that begins now and is fulfilled when Jesus returns.

Knowing Christ gives us a hope that makes life worth living.

—M.R.D.II

Hope is the anchor of the soul,
and the stimulus to action and achievement.

Thursday

[We] rejoice in hope of the glory of God
(Romans 5:2).

The glories that await the Christian defy our comprehension. What little we understand about them, however, fills us with anticipation. We look longingly to that day when we shall enjoy heaven in all its fullness.

In *Dare to Believe,* Dan Baumann told a story that illustrates the unique experience of knowing something is ours yet longing to enjoy it more fully. Every year at Christmastime, he would do a lot of snooping, trying to find the gift-wrapped presents and figure out what was in them. One year he discovered a package with his name on it that was easy to identify. His mother couldn't disguise the golf clubs inside. Baumann wrote: "When Mom wasn't around, I would go and feel the package, shake it, and pretend that I was on the golf course. The point is, I was already enjoying the pleasures of a future event; namely, the unveiling. It had my name on it. I knew what it was. But only Christmas would reveal it in its fullness."

That's the way it is for believers as we await what God has for us in heaven. Wrote Baumann, "We shall be glorified, but we are beginning to taste glorification now. . . . This quality of life begins the moment an individual places faith in Christ and thereby shares His life. We have eternal life—here and now—but it is only a foretaste of its fullness. God has whetted our appetites for the main course, which has to come later!"

Christians have good reason to rejoice in hope! —R.W.D.

Future prospects bring present joys.

Friday

LUKE 21:25–36

"Then they will see the Son of Man coming in a cloud with power and great glory" (Luke 21:27).

On Palm Sunday, 1981, millions of Americans shared a great sense of anticipation as they awaited the liftoff of the manned space shuttle Columbia. The media billed the event as "the dawn of a new age." More than 80,000 people crowded into Florida's Kennedy Space Center to witness the launching of the nation's first space plane. Hundreds of thousands drove to nearby roads for the best view they could get. And countless others watched the event on television. As the countdown reached the last ten seconds, the nation counted down in unison. Then at 7 A.M. Eastern time it happened. The great flying machine rose straight up. Orange flames and vapor engulfed the launch site as sound and shock waves thundered through the air and ground. The hopes of all future manned spaceflight seemed to focus on the success of that long-awaited mission.

As promising as that event was, it's nothing compared with another event—the return of the Lord Jesus to earth. He will usher in the dawn of a new age like we have never seen. When He comes in the clouds with power and glory, all other hopes will look empty and foolish.

The glory of what we put up into space is nothing compared with the glory that Christ will bring down when He returns. —M.R.D.II

The return of Jesus is sure, for what the Bible predicts and Christ promises, God will perform.

Saturday

He who testifies to these things says,
"Surely I am coming quickly" (Revelation 22:20).

The great preacher F. B. Meyer once asked D. L. Moody, "What is the secret of your success?" Moody replied, "For many years I have never given an address without the consciousness that the Lord may come before I have finished." This may well explain the intensity of his service and the zeal of his ministry for Christ.

One of the most encouraging teachings in the Bible is that of the Lord's return to earth. Three times Revelation 22 repeats this promise. As God was about to close the pages of divine revelation, He called attention to this grand theme, announcing in the words of Christ Himself, "Surely I am coming quickly." The last words of our Lord before leaving this earth twenty centuries ago remind us that He is coming back for us. With such a forceful assurance closing the canon of Scripture, we can have this hope continually in our hearts. The expectation of seeing our Savior, being like Him, and being with Him for eternity should prompt us, as it did Moody, to serve the Lord.

In this sinful world it's easy to lose our upward look. Yet we must keep the hope of Christ's return burning in our hearts. The apostle Paul talked about this when he said, "For our citizenship is in heaven, from which we also eagerly wait for the Savior, the Lord Jesus Christ" (Phil. 3:20).

The hope of His last words, "Surely I am coming quickly," should motivate us all to lives of sacrificial service. —P.R.V.

The hope of glorification keeps before us
the need of purification.

Note to the Reader